The Decline of Discourse

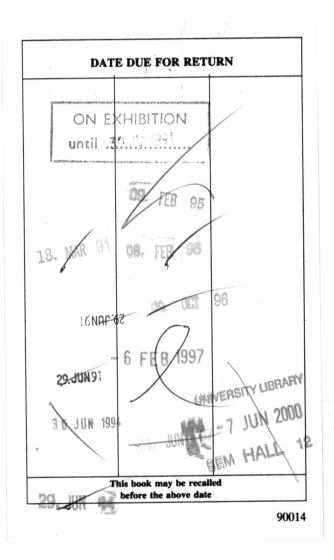

For Beth Anne
in loving partnership

The Decline of Discourse

Reading, Writing and Resistance in Postmodern Capitalism

Ben Agger

The Falmer Press

(A member of the Taylor & Francis Group)

New York • Philadelphia • London

USA The Falmer Press, Taylor & Francis Inc., 1900 Frost Road, Suite 101, Bristol, PA 19007

UK The Falmer Press, Rankine Road, Basingstoke, Hants RG24 0PR

First published 1990

British Library Cataloguing in Publication Data
Agger, Ben
The decline of discourse: reading, writing and resistance in postmodern capitalism.
1. Literature. History and criticism
I. Title
809

ISBN 1–85000–755–1
ISBN 1–85000–756–X (pbk.)

Library of Congress Cataloging in Publication Data is available on request

Printed and bound in Great Britain by
Redwood Press Limited, Melksham, Wiltshire

Contents

Acknowledgments

The following people offered very helpful comments about the manuscript: Paul Diesing, Ivor Goodson, Kate Hausbeck, Tim Luke, John O'Neill, Beth Anne Shelton and Philip Wexler. I am indebted to Philip Wexler and Ivor Goodson for their sponsorship of the manuscript at Falmer Press. They both provided astute editorial guidance. Malcolm Clarkson of Falmer Press afforded encouragement and support in every phase of this project. Christine Cox of Falmer Press skillfully coordinated the editorial and production side of things.

On the home front, Lionel S. Lewis, my chairperson in Sociology at SUNY-Buffalo, continues to extend his support and friendship, for which I am eternally grateful. His own work on higher education figures centrally in Chapter Six. He and Beth Anne Shelton are wonderful, humorous and humane colleagues in Sociology; they make collegiality much more than a slogan. Kate Hausbeck, a graduate student in Sociology at SUNY-Buffalo, did a masterful job of editing and checking the manuscript. My undergraduate work-study students helped me greatly with this and other projects. They are: Tasha Banks, Ivan Ramirez and Marcy Wong. Nancy Kamorowski and Laurie Lanning offered much-needed and timely clerical assistance with this and many other projects.

Thank you one and all!

Ben Agger
Buffalo, NY
December, 1989

Chapter 1

Theorizing the Decline
Of Discourse. . .

This is a book about the public world. It is also a book about a particular mode of writing called theory. I attempt to theorize about the
public world, keeping in mind the status of theory in that world. For
the most part, this book is written in straightforward descriptive and
analytic prose; I do not presuppose a deep grounding in recondite
European social theory, whether the critical theory of the Frankfurt
School or postmodernism and poststructuralism. In fact, as I argue in
this opening chapter, high theory is often so incomprehensible that
the very theory capturing the decline of discourse ironically ends up
facilitating it. Much of my own past work has risked this, although
one can defend dialectical complexity as appropriate to a dialectically
complex world.

In no way am I suggesting that world problems would be solved
if theory were clearer by the standards of British analytic philosophy
(Gellner, 1959). I am trying to theorize the decline of discourse
without allowing such theorising to contribute to it. This is a tall order
given the density of Barthes, Adorno, Derrida, Kristeva. It is tempting
to spend one's time simply explicating these important sources. But
that neglects empirical analysis and diagnosis, as well as political
recommendation, the tasks of this book. I want to understand how
what writers write is conditioned by large, often invisible forces and
then to help them – us – better protect ourselves against our own
commodification and stupefaction. In the process, I will examine
one of the central legitimating ideologies of cultural production and
reception today, postmodernism.

There is no single or simple "postmodernism" but only versions.
Indeed, I want to reclaim postmodernism for the project of radical social theory by carefully examining postmodernity (Habermas,

1981b), a civilizational stage in which we are supposed to believe that all fundamental social problems have been solved. This will involve me in a theoretical discussion of the meaning of terms like postmodernism and postmodernity; this opening chapter, where these terms are spelled out, frames the rest of the book, explicating my central empirical concept, *literary political economy*.

Theory declines in exact proportion to its academization. When theory becomes a body of knowledge to be carved up, dissected and then mummified by disciplinary museum keepers it loses its ability to sharpen insight. Unfortunately, this is the fate of much theory today, including oppositional theory. Indeed, the left perpetuates its own obscurantism by canonizing great books that once provoked radical opposition. Today books like *Capital* and *The Second Sex* inspire term papers or yawns, not political activism. Cells have become study groups. This is not to say that we should forego reading dense works of world-historical significance. One cannot understand the present without having grappled with Kant, Hegel, Marx, Freud, Wittgenstein, Husserl, Beauvoir, Sartre, Adorno, Marcuse – the list is virtually endless, as is the hermeneutic work required to master these difficult sources. But academization is the subtraction of Dionysian passion from thought; scholarship reduces thought to method, killing it.

I do not dispense with references to other writers; some of these aid archaeological investigation and extrapolation by curious readers. Referenceless writing pretends sheer originality and thus claims unchallengeable authority. But too often these citations burden one's argument so much that one ends up arguing nothing in particular; writing merely repeats the tried and true – the tired – albeit in a trivial revisionism deriving its license from the rearrangement of other people's footnotes and references. Ironically, the analysis of the decline of discourse presented here must pass through the very theories that hasten discourse's decline, often in spite of themselves. One of my main targets in this book is postmodernism – not the critical theory of modernity and postmodernity so abundant with insights into what is going wrong with the world, especially in the realm of culture, but the fashionable theory authorizing the fashionable literary lifestyle of cosmopolitanism. I want to use postmodernism against itself, rescuing it from its own sloganizing. People talk of postmodern this and postmodern that – art, architecture, advertising. But that only reduces the critical analysis of modernity to trendy cultural taxonomy.

One of the central valences of postmodernism is its fungibility.

Everyone claims it, but few have read in its sources. It is much harder to claim Marxism and feminism while ignoring their roots in radical opposition, although many academics try (see Jacoby, 1987). Postmodernism is postured by all sorts of establishment interests, who only deepen what Gramsci (1971) called hegemony. I want to unpack postmodernism by way of empirical categories like literary political economy, thus liberating its critical insights from their enslavement to the culture industry (Horkheimer and Adorno, 1972, pp. 120-167). My central claim is that postmodernism in its best sense is a radical theory of society, not a mindless vehicle of cultural production and consumption (see Wolin, 1984). Better, postmodernism must be written and rewritten as critical theory and not allowed to slip frictionlessly into the maw of cultural, political and economic co-optation.

We are in serious trouble when Jay McInerney and Tama Janowitz are lauded as postmodern writers, or Lyotard and Baudrillard elevated above Marx and Marcuse; or when a powerful editor sponsoring the so-called New Fiction takes on the moniker "Captain Fiction" and thus shapes literary taste and practice, or when advertising agencies and architects churn out "postmodern" copy, text, image, design, better to grease the wheels of capitalist culture, consumption and urban life. But my aim is not only to salvage the concept of postmodernity in terms of modernism's revolutionary ethos; that is precisely what is wrong with the academic project: footnotes fail to do our creative intellectual work for us. Intellectual pedigree is no substitute for intellectuality. Rather I want to deploy postmodernism as a mode of empirical description, analysis and diagnosis, allowing its dialectical comprehension of the inner tendencies of modernity – capitalism – to issue in rigorous social science that can guide reconstructive activities of all sorts, especially cultural ones.

Of course, few American social scientists would regard this book as an example of either rigor or social science. It will be dismissed impatiently as essayistic and carping, anathema to the number-crunchers and survey researchers ever in pursuit of better techniques, measures, hypotheses. So be it. Social science lost its mind long ago, at least in positivist America. It must be reinvented by writers unafraid to bridge the social sciences and humanities in order to plumb the social world for its deepest meanings and structures. I have already developed arguments for a literary social science, borrowing from the Frankfurt School's critical theory, feminist theory, poststructuralism and postmodernism (Agger, 1989a, 1989b, 1989c).

Those were largely programmatic arguments for an analytic discourse that neither embraced positivism nor renounced empirical social understanding, what Marcuse (1969), following Nietzsche, called "new science".

In this book, I write discourse, not merely theorize it; I analyze the *decline* of discourse using insights from discourse theory. This is ironic only because so much contemporary theory is incredibly obscure, doing little to rebuild the public sphere by its own example. Having said this, it is worth noting that the plain-language theorists who lambast Adorno and Derrida for their impenetrability fail to attend to the parallel obscurity of mainstream quantitative empiricism (which takes its own license from the British analytic philosophy laying waste to Teutonic thought and writing). Nevertheless, there is something regrettable about discourse theory that fails to be discourse itself – an ironic insensitivity to its own audience.

In this opening chapter I survey the contributions of critical theory and postmodernism to an understanding of the decline of public writing. This requires a certain suspension of disbelief in the sense that I am not going to describe the phenomena surrounding the decline of discourse until Chapter 2. Any theoretical overview that precedes empirical discussion risks its disconnection from it. One way to think about the logic of my argument is to view this opening chapter as a defense of postmodern critical theory that prepares the way for a later critique of postmodern *culture*, the shallow literary lifestyles pursued by those who write in order to live. I want to distinguish carefully between postmodernity and postmodernism. The former is a civilizational stage; the latter is a theory of culture and society. Obviously, the two are connected inasmuch as theory enters into the cultural discourses of the moment. But I want to situate postmodernism outside the cultural mainstream in order to utilize its critical distance from the so-called "postmodern" world it diagnoses. Postmodernism, properly understood, helps reverse the direction of postmodernity, notably what I call the decline of discourse.

Does Postmodernity Exist?

Let me offer some initial clarification of the ways in which I use the main theoretical categories employed throughout this book. Unfortunately, imposters threaten to usurp the legitimate meanings of these words, homogenizing them into safe, system-serving ideas. By *post-modernity* I am referring not to a concrete stage of civilization somehow set apart from "modernity", notably capitalism. Postmodernity ideologically postures as a post-modern stage of world history in order to suggest the end of class, race, gender and geographic inequalities; in this, it serves exactly the same purpose as Bell's earlier (1960) notion of the end of ideology. But just as ideology is still with us, now notably in the very concept of the postmodern or postmodernity, so history has not recently transcended itself into a friction-less, fractious-less, class-less, race-less, gender-less epoch. Postmodernity is myth. In its name people (e.g., Lyotard, 1984) justify their opposition to Marxism. Lyotard rejects "metanarratives" that would privilege one form of radicalism or another; but this privileging, in the name of putative postmodernity, is every bit as much a metanarrative as the ideological systems it opposes.

Partisans of postmodernity like Lyotard (1984) define the postmodern in terms highly reminiscent of Bell's earlier argument. Postmodernity is supposedly characterized by postindustrialism (Bell, 1973), the resulting end of class-conflict, a consumers' cornucopia of limitless goods and services, high technology as a panacea for solving all social problems, the end of ideology and universal global modernization. In this, Lyotard adds nothing to Bell. But postmodernity also suggests a kind of centerlessness to world history that serves as an axial moral and political principle of a new individualism. Where Bell (1976) decried the "adversary cultures" of narcissistic New Leftists, Lyotard and his ilk embrace an apparent eclecticism of personal, cultural and political styles. This New Individualism formulates itself partly in neoconservative economic and political theory (e.g., Nozick, 1974; Gilder, 1981). Postmodernism is its cultural expression, although, as I argue, this is not really postmodernism at all but only warmed-over end-of-ideology theory appropriate to post-1950s capitalism.

New Individualism is continuous with the "old" version: Mill, Locke, Coolidge, Frederick Taylor. It is different in that it is situated in a more affluent stage of capitalism – affluent at least for tenured intellectuals and Yuppies. Postmodernity enshrines individualism on the ground that what Lyotard calls the grand "metanarratives" are no longer relevant to middle-class individuals. C. Wright Mills' *White Collar* (1951) remains a cogent response to this overly optimistic perspective on universal *embourgeoisement*, just as it contains a pithy discussion of modern intellectuals in the section on "Brains, Inc." Mainstream sociology has always foretold the postindustrial future in which people would not lack for basic necessities but could spend their lives cultivating their own spiritual (and real) gardens; on this view, Marxism is not so much wrong as out of date. The notion of postmodernity approaches this sociological formulation of a post-Marxist future in largely cultural terms, making way for "postmodernist" strictures about literary lifestyles that I address in the balance of this book.

Postmodernity is a term used apologetically to describe and defend late capitalism (Mandel, 1975). There is absolutely nothing "post" about the current modernity, which is fundamentally continuous with capitalism from the mid-19th century in the sense that capitalism is characterized by private property, sexism, racism and the domination of nature. Saying that does not mean we should not theorize and retheorize late capitalism; there are some significant differences between capitalism then and now. But this rethinking should be done within Marxism and feminism, not outside of it. Postmodernity theory (see Kellner, 1988) is fundamentally opposed to the utopian prospect of a new world beyond class, gender and race oppression. It formulates the future in terms of New Individualism, as such leaving the capitalist, sexist and racist edifice intact. Freedom is characterized in terms of individual expression, taste, consumption, travel, leisure, clothing, lifestyle. Postmodernity theory is the latest alternative to radical social thought and action, not a successful undermining of it. Postmodernity theory is a more cosmopolitan version of the earlier, more puritanical postindustrialism (e.g., Bell, 1973); it is centered in New York City, the cultural center of the universe. Of course, its pretended cosmopolitanism is really parochial, as indicated by global Americanization.

Postmodernism as Ideology

Having essentially rejected the concept of postmodernity, let me discuss more fully the way it is theorized in the establishment version of postmodernism prevailing in the culture industry as well as in non-Marxist literary theory and cultural studies. To talk about a mainstream postmodernism seems ludicrous; Baudrillard, Barthes, Foucault are impossible to commodify and co-opt. Or are they? The local television critic in *The Buffalo News* occasionally writes of Foucault and Barthes, if only to show the local university community that he knows what is going on, as well as to elevate his chatter about network television into high cultural criticism. And postmodernism abounds on Madison Avenue as the latest signifier of cultural trendiness (e.g., Newman, 1985). It moves products, not minds.

This discussion of "bad" postmodernism, the kind that informs cultural production in capitalist countries today, suggests the possible development of a "good" postmodernism, what I call postmodernism as critical theory. I organize this comparison around six axial themes characterizing their different positions on issues of intellectual and social substance: values, history, politics, subjectivity, modernity and reason. I am going to simplify in order to make my point that postmodernism contains a powerful liberatory element largely suppressed by the culture industry's version of postmodernism, which is really only veiled capitalist modernism. My interest in this comparison is not scholastic for I maintain that postmodernism as critical theory issues in a politically relevant empirical sociology of culture for which the central concept is literary political economy, an issue I discuss in the last section of this chapter. I want these critical concepts to do empirical and political work; before they can, I must disentangle subversive from affirmative postmodernism.

The Rejection of Absolute Values

An ideological postmodernism, the kind dispensed in cosmopolitan magazines and taught in mainstream literary theory classes, maintains that there are no absolute values, in this drawing on a version of Nietzsche. Nietzsche centers both postmodernism and poststructuralism on the one hand and critical theory on the other. For Derrideans and Foucaultdians, Nietzsche is the author of anti-enlightenment, an emblem of the futility of (western) reason. For Adorno and his Frankfurt colleagues, Nietzsche is a profoundly dialectical critic of the Enlightenment, a harbinger of "playful science" – both new cognition and new society (Agger, 1976b). Of course, this second Nietzsche is the more difficult to exhume from his books. But no matter. Whatever/whomever the "real" Nietzsche, I believe that Adorno's attempt to ground a materialist concept of reason in Nietzsche's (1956) Dionysian attack on the Apollonian frigidity and rigidity of western rationality makes eminent sense. And it helps define the contours of a critical postmodernism with which to navigate through the rolling waters of the contemporary culture industry.

Returning to my theme, an ideological postmodernism uses Nietzsche among others as buttress for the notion that, because absolute values have disappeared, anything goes. Or, at least, the establishment of values in a "postmodern" period is not to draw on what Lyotard (1984) calls the grand "metanarratives" of Marxist and feminist reason. The rejection of absolute values (notably, for Nietzsche, Platonism) issues in nihilism – the rejection of all values (e.g., Rosen, 1969). This is the conventional reading of Nietzsche and one, it must be noted, amply plausible on the textual evidence. In any case, mainstream postmodernism (like poststructuralism, if one distinguishes between the two) rests heavily on the premise that one cannot locate an Archimedean point outside history from which to glimpse or postulate world-historical meanings, ethics, values, truth. Nietzsche's nihilism is converted into relativism by these postmodernists, thus casting doubt on the standard left-wing attempts to specify definitive values, whether a classless society or motherright.

The Eternal Present

Postmodernism also contains a conception of history that notably breaks with the eschatologies of classical western thought or, better, serves as their completion. Postmodernists collapse the future-orientation so typical of western eschatology into a kind of eternal present, a philosophical posture reminiscent of the sociological announcement of a postindustrial society (Bell, 1973). The future is now; technology has set us free; culture is so rich that we no longer have to search outside of time – in the future, a time that has not happened – for the riddle of history. Indeed, this establishment postmodernism obliterates history in a grandiose gesture of self-satisfaction. Of course, this bespeaks a thoroughgoing optimism about how far we have come. And it generalizes (I would say overgeneralizes) the good fortunes of western cultural, economic and political elites – call them Yuppies – to all of humanity. Support for this comes from what Baudrillard (1981) calls the political economy of the sign, notably the proliferation of western products and advertising in poor countries, "texts" that western postmods "read" to indicate global modernization – the veritable end of history prophesied by all eschatology.

This notion of an eternal present not only overestimates the glories of the present. It also forecloses the possibility of radical interventions. The end of history is also the end of hope, of utopian imagination. Postmodernism in its establishment version is at once blissfully cheerful about how good things are and world-weary, disdainful of the radical "metanarratives" that still seek a heaven on earth in the fashion of every utopia. The beats called this attitude "cool" or "hip", precisely the stance of postmods in the late 1980s and early 1990s. Indeed, fashionable men's magazines sell sneakers once popular in the 1950s under the sign of James Dean, the enfant terrible of 1950s avantgardism. Hip endures as the quintessential postmodern sensibility, expressing a combination of self-satisfaction and aversion to the passions and polemics of the political.

Antipolitics

The third dimension along which one can evaluate affirmative and critical postmodernism is politics. Whether postmoderns express their disdain for the political in terms of James Dean's nonchalance or the rock musician Steven Stills' 1960s notion that "politics is bullshit", it is clear that establishment postmodernism rejects politics as a venue of meaning. Of course, if history has ended, the telos of political activism – social change – is chimerical, archaic. One risks little generational oversimplification if one observes that members of the baby-boom generation, all now thirtysomething, were the exception, not the rule, in 20th century America in terms of their political engagement around issues like the Vietnam war, civil rights and the women's movement. The Ozzie-and-Harriet generation – their parents – shares with the post-1960s generation a quiescence about politics, indeed an antipolitics grounded in an aversion to eschatology. Young people curry cool, not the transformation of the world. This does not ignore a kind of social liberalism whereby people "care" about the environment, the rebellious students in China, animal rights etc. The thirtysomething generation helped mainstream a certain social liberalism fundamentally unthreatening to the dominant capitalist order, notably including the right of women to regulate their own reproductive systems as well as to work outside the home.

But this social liberalism, like all liberalism, is essentially privatized; it says little about how social structures should be changed. Postmodernism shuns politics as the site of venality, corruption, cynicism: images all the way from Watergate to Iranscam drum this lesson into our heads; politics is equivalent to a sick messianism. "Healthy" people seek careers, mortgages, perfect children, cultural status, spiritual plenitude. Thus, postmodernism contains powerful assumptions about the nature of politics fundamentally hostile to the left-wing "metanarratives", like Greek thought, seeking redemption in politics (e.g., Arendt, 1958). Politics today is widely viewed as an open sewer, not as the basis of a decent public life. Traditional conservatives join with radicals in lamenting the decline of the public sphere – here, the decline of discourse, one of its central aspects. Politics is shunned mainly by neoconservatives, who are disappointed liberals. The welfare state is viewed widely as the source of significant social problems, not their remediation, as originally it was for Keynes and FDR. This is a postmodern attitude par excellence: the best politics is antipolitics, an impugning of politics, politicians and all social movements seeking the truth in one or another concept of social justice.

New Individualism

Established postmodernism enshrines a revamped individualism, a post-liberalism, according to which the traditional democratic social contract (e.g., Rousseau, 1973) is reformulated so that individuals can "take" from the collectivity but need not "give" something in return, notably popular legitimation. Habermas (1975) already identified this "legitimation crisis" as one of the potential undoings of welfare capitalism. Possessive individualism (Macpherson, 1962) is nothing new; indeed, Macpherson shows that it is present in Locke from the beginning. But the New Individualism is even more possessive than ever, largely responding to the perceived failures of the welfare state to keep poor urban blacks and other minorities in check. New York liberals become neoconservative when Farrakhan embraces Hitler and when it is no longer safe to jog in Central Park at night. Bernhard Goetz, the subway desperado, epitomizes this postmodern New Individualism: when accosted by youthful black muggers, he drew his gun and blew them away. Interestingly, Goetz was not heroized only by working-class NRA red-necks; he was supported by all sorts of "sophisticated" liberals (i.e., neoconservatives) who were sick and tired of affirmative action, welfare safety nets, overall social permissiveness.

The sociology of race and racism is an interesting barometer of this New Individualism, as Feagin (1989) demonstrates. Gone are systematic appraisals of the structural roots of racism; in their place, we find various condemnations of the black family, black character structure, black language. The New Individualism in this regard can be traced back to Banfield's (1970) *The Unheavenly City* as well as to work by Moynihan (1969). What distinguishes it today, though, is its pervasiveness in the race relations literature. White racism (Kovel, 1970) is replaced by black sloth as an explanation of persistent and increasing economic inequalities between blacks and whites. Worse, there is a growing perception among commentators and social scientists that blacks are actually demonic, even wild animals (viz. the recent attacks of "wilding" where roving gangs of black youth terrorize random passers-by).

The New Individualism cowers before this savagery, ignoring its own responsibility for bringing it about. This is not to reduce character structure to social structure (Gerth and Mills, 1953) but to acknowledge the complex mediations between the two (e.g., Wexler, 1982). The brutalizing gang members are as much (or as little) products of their society as Bernhard Goetz. What is new about postmodern individualism is its defensive posture; earlier possessive individualism (Macpherson, 1962) attempted to better itself by striking out in wagon trains for the west coast, construing the future as a time ahead. The New Individualism protects its fiefs against the dispossessed, in the process theorizing its just desserts with various neoconservative defenses of property, family, state. Where original individualism was self-interested but optimistic, the New Individualism is both self-interested and cynical. It is precisely this cynicism that characterizes the mien of the mainstream postmodern; self becomes the central social agenda for late-twentieth century rationalists (Lasch, 1984).

Occidentalism/Modernization

I have already discussed aspects of the postmodernity thesis that closely resemble Bell's (1973) earlier notion of a postindustrial society. Postmodernism theorizes postmodernity, notably in terms of the six axial dimensions I am discussing here. In particular, mainstream postmodernism is a version of occidental modernization theory, in spite of its pretension to be pluralist or "decentered" (Luke, 1991). In fact, the occidentalism of postmodernism is concealed in the superficial valorization of "difference." Difference is but a slogan; deconstruction reveals it to be a myth, an ideologizing defense of the provinces, regions, languages, cultures and peoples colonized by America International. Where old-fashioned liberals construed American freedom as the freedom to dine out in ethnic restaurants, contemporary postmodernism pretends a global diversity just as it purports to borrow eclectically from different historical epochs, styles, value systems. What used to be called pluralism by old-guard liberals is now characterized by postmodernists as "difference". But there is no difference.

Postmodernism's conception of modernity is not eclectic but Eurocentric, indeed American. Economic imperialism is now matched by cultural imperialism, including an imperialism of the *Zeitgeist*. The Americanization of the planet proceeds apace, even in the Soviet Union and China. Few countries like Albania continue to hold out against Coca-Cola, blue jeans and superficial democratization. Of course, state-socialist countries democratize in order to modernize economically (Marcuse, 1958). Central planning does not work, as the Soviets and Chinese are now discovering. Hence they rush to loosen the constraints on personal expression in order to foster a character type suited to participation and productivity in the "new" socialist economies dominated by market production and frenzied consumption. The upheavals in the Soviet Union and China were virtually inevitable: People inculcated to be self-sacrificing "new men and women" are suddenly unleashed on a statist system that only bends gradually to the press of popular "participation", even if the participation is as fraudulent as it is in the capitalist west.

Where 1950s modernization theory (e.g., Parsons, 1951) recognized the colonizability of the "third" world, postmodernism recognizes that colonization is complete or nearly so. The Iron and Bamboo Curtains have largely come down; there is even talk of dismantling the Berlin Wall, symbolically and physically separating capitalist and communist worlds. This is not to say that east-west relations are entirely without vicissitudes; occasionally, internal crises spark when the Soviets shoot down an unarmed airliner or Americans become too aggressive in pursuit of oil and air bases. In the postmodern world, the more relevant structuring hierarchy is vertical rather than horizontal, north-and-south, rich-and-poor. Monopoly capitalism and monopoly socialism are instances of an overarching state capitalism, although many postmodernists and even some critical theorists characterize this emerging global monolith in deideologized terms (e.g., Sarup, 1989). Recall that postmodernity is a positive valorization among many mainstream postmodernist theorists like Lyotard.

Post-rationalism

Finally, postmodern theory suggests a concept of reason fundamentally different from that of Hegelian Marxism (Marcuse, 1960). Here the role of Nietzsche is central, especially the question of *which* Nietzsche is being used as authority, the irrationalist relativist of *Beyond Good and Evil* (1955) or the more dialectical critic of *The Genealogy of Morals* (1956). I do not want to labor over Nietzscheology but simply to note the centrality of Nietzsche's irrationalism and cynicism for postmodernism, notably for Foucault, Derrida and Lyotard. In attacking the Enlightenment as mythologizing, Nietzsche suggests an antirationalism or post-rationalism fundamentally at odds with the left projects of Marxists, feminists and opponents of racism. Indeed, the "other" left Nietzsche has already been rendered by Horkheimer and Adorno (1972) in their *Dialectic of Enlightenment*, where they explicate a dialectic of myth and enlightenment grounding their critical theory. In particular, the Frankfurt School has used Nietzsche as a linch-pin of its critique of positivism, indicating the extent to which positivism is the most recent and effective form of ideology in late capitalism as well as state socialism.

Now postmodernism in its affirmative formulation is anti-positivist, too. Derrida's critique of the metaphysics of presence is an unrelenting attack on positivism; indeed, in many ways it is an ingenious one, as is his "deconstruction" of western dualism. One can effectively radicalize deconstruction by using its interpretive methodology to show that apparent dualities are really hierarchies, thus buttressing the critique of ideology. But the efforts to radicalize deconstruction (e.g., Ryan, 1982; Eagleton, 1983) recognize that Derridean poststructuralism is not particularly radical at the outset, even though, as Jay has done, one can point out his filiation to Adorno's project in critical theory (Ryan, 1984). Radicalizing deconstruction threatens to deconstruct deconstruction, leaving little but the ashes of yet another failed critique of positivism.

The post-rationalism of postmodernism is not explicitly irrationalist or antirationalist in the fashion of earlier romantic critiques of enlightenment, science, reason. I use the term post-rationalism because it seems that when Lyotard (1984) argues against grand "metanarratives" of history he is not so much denying their rationality per se but simply their grandiose sweep, their Archimedeanism and Prometheanism. Or perhaps he is denying their attempt to impose reason's order on the recalcitrant, bitter world. Whatever the truth (and, after all, there are many contending postmodernisms available in the cultural marketplace), postmodernism does not choose against reason so much as locates a sufficient reason in the here and now – late capitalism. Instrumental rationality in Weberian terms is not recanted (after all, instrumental reason gives us high technology, a staple of postmodern cosmopolitanism's obsession with electronic media connections and entertainments); it is supplemented with expressive embellishments, whether spirituality or religion, that somehow extend reason into the region of the irrational, notably the extrasensory. Postmodernism equals modernity plus New Individualism (see, e.g., Kroker and Cook, 1986).

Derrida's (1976) critique of metaphysical dualism does not pose another way to view dualities and thus to create a non-dualist, non-hierarchical social order. Deconstruction in Nietzschean fashion becomes methodology, technique, obsession. The potentially ideology-critical program of deconstruction absolutizes itself, neglecting its own undecidability in Derrida's terms (see Fraser, 1984; Jameson, 1984a). Postmodernism and critical theory differ most markedly over Derrida's claim that "the text has no outside". As materialists, critical theorists recognize that the text is a world, an ensemble of substantive social relationships (here addressed in terms of literary political economy, particularly relations among writers, publishers and readers). But they also recognize that all the world is not text, especially where people break their backs and minds in waged and unwaged labor. Postmodernism is cultural-reductionist, ignoring the productive and reproductive infrastructure of capitalism and patriarchy, respectively. Of course, this "discourse" is rejected out of hand as emblematic of old-age Marxism, one of those *grand recits* so despised by the postmodernists.

But reason in Plato, Hegel and Marx's sense *is* a *grand recit*, a "metanarrative". It aims to produce a world in its image, notably in terms of various criteria of truth, beauty and justice. Abjuring reason as a metanarrative implicitly endorses unreason, the stance of all mythology. Derrideans reject absolutism absolutely, thus only reproducing the fatefully cyclical nature of enlightenment's reversion to myth (Lenhardt, 1976). This is not to say that anyone can simply posit a rational order and then attempt to bring it about, heedless of the consequences. As Habermas (1979) suggests, we must argue about reason until we achieve real consensus about it. Critics of Hegelian Marxism have never accurately understood that Marx's version of Hegel's reason was not simply speculative but firmly anchored in Marx's empirical reading of history's unfolding

(Lichtheim, 1971). This is not to assume that Marx is right about the vector of that unfolding, although I think he largely is. But the postmodernist aversion to world-historical narratives misses, and misunderstands, the historical-materialist effort to place such narratives on the firm footing of empirical social analysis. Marx annointed the proletariat as the world-historical agent of reason because he thought this was "necessary" historically, given the evolving internal contradictions of capitalism. Although his empirical version of history may have been mistaken in some respects, postmodernists cannot simply reject his attempt to reason history out of hand. To avoid grand narratives endorses the very ones playing out behind our backs, what Hegel called the "cunning of reason".

Postmodernism as Critical Theory

Having examined postmodernism's affirmative, apologetic version, I want to argue for a radical concept and practice of postmodernism that preserves the continuity between a rebellious modernism (e.g., Marx, Adorno, Kafka, Beckett) and a postmodernism that eschews the cultural conformity and self-inflation of the American culture industry (Horkheimer and Adorno, 1972, pp. 120-167). Huyssen (1986) leads the way in his dexterous treatment of postmodernism as radical cultural theory; others follow in his lead (e.g., Kellner, 1988, 1989a, 1989b, 1989c; Ryan, 1989). Huyssen suggests that one can use postmodernism both as a critique of the present and as a programmatizing sketch of utopia; in particular, postmodernism locates the liberatory potential of modernity – industrial capitalism – as well as of its modes of consciousness (e.g., democratic theory) while attacking the insufficiencies of modernity in a dialectical way. After all, Marx was a modernist; he valued capitalism as a prolegomenon to communism, nothing less. In this way, postmodernism functions as critical theory, thawing the social facts frozen by positivism into the dialectical pieces of history they really are.

In particular, this radicalized postmodernism opposes the conservative tendencies of modernism and modernity in much the way Marx did. The notion of the modern, like that of postmodernity, is fraught with difficulty. "Modern" in popular culture connotes positive social value – modern appliances, modern culture, modern consciousness. In this vein, modernity gives rise to modernization theory, the dominant mode of positivist social science since

Comte. Modernization theorists suggest that history is moving forward unilinearly toward a postindustrial outcome; this post-industrial order is depicted in the local terms of American sexist and racist capitalism (e.g., Parsons, 1951; Bell, 1973), confusing the particular and the general. As I said, postmodernity is just another term for postindustrialism; it adds a certain cosmopolitanism to the homelier, homier images of 1950s modernization theory: *Leave it to Beaver*, the epitome of suburban modernity in the 1950s and early 1960s, is replaced with the violence and high fashion of *Miami Vice*, the quintessential American postmodern television show (see Best and Kellner, 1988a, 1988b; Luke, 1989).

Now this shift from the modern to the postmodern seems truly wrenching from the perspective of narrow cultural focus. Some loathe it, especially neoconservatives wary of the New Individualism, where others applaud it as progressively avantgardist. Huyssen points out that postmodernism, in its authentic sense, draws heavily on the left avantgardism of forces like surrealism, Dadaism and situationism, giving the lie to the claim that cultural forms like *Miami Vice* or the Trump Tower are before-their-time – avantgarde. American Senators' wives crusade to rid the airwaves of the more demonic expressions of the avantgarde, fearing the corruption of children. More cosmopolitan postmoderns would probably view this as a silly excrescence of the Old Individualism; they celebrate the decentered orgy of postmodern significations as the latest in cultural enlightenment, gleaning this from *Vanity Fair, Rolling Stone*, even *The New Yorker* – all the places where the culture industry theorizes and elevates itself.

Having contrasted postmodernity, a myth invented by the ideologues of New Individualism to vanquish radical thought yet again, with a genuinely political postmodernism, let me briefly sketch the diverse resources of this postmodernism. Defining postmodernism is as difficult as dodging raindrops; nevertheless, it is an important task, especially given the co-opting way in which anyone and everyone claims postmodernism for one cultural fad or gadget after another. One can read in Hassan (1987), Jameson (1981), Eagleton (1985), Spivak (1988) or Huyssen (1986) for different perspectives on postmodernism; indeed, postmodernism has become a veritable cottage industry, spawning primers purporting to simplify an incredibly ingrown subject (Klinkowitz, 1988; Sarup, 1989). In trying to "define" postmodernism I am not simply summing others' usage of the term for there is too little commonality of usage to make that effort worthwhile. My definition of postmodernism helps it do useful critical and political work. Let others add to a trendy cultural glossary (e.g., Gitlin, 1988a) indispensable for Sunday *New York Times Book Review* readers and others who aim to be in the know about the latest twists and turns of the *Zeitgeist*.

The Absolute Within Relation

In comparing postmodernism as critical theory to its affirmative mainstream version I will move along the six axial dimensions on which I located the first version of the postmodern. To some extent, this is an artificial exercise in that the different varieties of post-modernism are complexly entwined with each other. Where some call Foucault a neoconservative (Sarup, 1989), others regard him as a first cousin of the Frankfurt School (Smart, 1983; Dews, 1984, 1987; Agger, 1989c). There is continuity as well as rupture between my two senses of postmodernism here, just as there was continuity as well as contradiction between capitalism and socialism for Marx. Even a fanatical exercise in "scholarship" would not resolve the issue for, above all, commentators on postmodernism have not yet discovered a key with which to code one author, writing or theory as genuinely postmodern whereas others are merely pretenders.

First, a critical postmodernism differs from its affirmative compan-ion version on the issue of the absolutism of values. Where Lyotard rejects the axiological absolutism and Archimedeanism involved in the *grand recits* of world history, a critical postmodernism would not simply reject the notion of stable values with which to orient both theory and practice. This is very much the Nietzsche question raised earlier: can one read or write a Nietzsche who not only railed against the pretensions of the Enlightenment but who also implied a new order of value free of mythic residues? Of course, no amount of interpretive casuistry will make Nietzsche into a Marxist and feminist, even if one takes seriously Adorno's sympathy for him. Yet it seems to me that a postmodern critical theory can suggest a concept of the normative that neither succumbs to unreflected absolutism (e.g., Platonism) nor embraces relativism willy-nilly as a counterposition, especially inasmuch as relativism is absolute in its own right.

Many on the left (e.g., Kamenka, 1962; Heller, 1976) have specu-lated about appropriate standards of value with which to guide the construction of socialism. Feminists have been debating this issue vigorously (Gilligan, 1982). A left and feminist version of postmodernism might well propose a notion of values that appear absolute (i.e., non-negotiable, fundamental to the creation of a new order) but are in fact situational (Weedon, 1987). One might well disqualify the death penalty as barbaric but recognize that the very discourse of "death penalty" is an artifact of a society legitimizing certain kinds of death (e.g., from starvation or war). This is very much how I read the Foucault (1977) of *Discipline and Punish*, where he argues convincingly that criminality is an historical product of criminologists and of the state.

In fact, Foucault's writings about the relation among knowledge, discipline and power strike me as eminently a contribution to an empirical and political critical theory. One might read Foucault as a Marxist who borrows from what sociologists would call labeling theory. In any case, a relational view of absolute values could serve critical theory well, suggesting the discursive and epistemic grounds of values and thus helping us deconstruct them. Postmodernism offers Marxism and feminism an internal method of self-interrogation with which to examine fossilized assumptions about the nature of oppression and freedom. Call this deconstruction; call it immanent critique; or call it self-criticism. Names do not matter. The point is that critical theory must be equipped to posit a rational society without losing sight of its own investment in particular modes of rationality that are not treated simply as incommensurable language games (Wittgenstein, 1953) but can be argued for, defended reasonably. As I understand it, this is the sense of Habermas' recent (1984, 1987b) contributions to the reconstruction of historical materialism as communication theory.

An Unfulfilled Present

Where mainstream postmodernism views the present as eternal, the end-of-ideology and of industrialization having been reached, a more critical postmodernism regards the present as somehow connected dialectically both to past and present. This is the sense in which I understand Marx to have written a theory of modernity; he favored modernity – the technological and civil infrastructure of industrial capitalism – but he wanted to push one more stage beyond modernity toward socialism. This is a crucial source of confusion for postmodernists that I address concretely in the chapters that follow: On the one hand, the depiction of postmodernity is not always sanguine, especially where postmodernity connotes cynicism, pessimism, the New Individualism, red-baiting. On the other hand, the diagnosis of postmodern*ity* often tends to become postmodern*ism*, negation fatefully turning into its opposite, even unconsciously. Indeed, mainstream postmodernism endorses the postmodern scene (Kroker and Cook, 1986), reveling in the erosion of meaning, hope, utopia. But even left postmodernisms risk conflating themselves with the sorry social condition they explore and reject. Thus, Marxist postmodernists forget that Marx would have reserved the term "postmodernity" only for the end of prehistory – socialism. Late capitalism is precisely not postmodern but modern, as Habermas (1987a) and Kellner (1988, 1989a, 1989b, 1989c) have pointed out.

Redefining the Political

Where poststructuralists and postmodernists like Derrida and Lyotard seem to endorse an antipolitics, rejecting both dominant institutions and oppositional social movements (or at least those that theorize themselves in terms of metanarratives like Marxism and feminism), left postmodernists (e.g., Aronowitz, 1981; Agger, 1989a, 1989c, 1990) attempt to redefine the political. My (1989a) argument about a "fast capitalism" in which image and thing blur, thus reducing the critical distance of thought and writing, suggests that we can find politics today everywhere but in the political arena, traditionally defined. Left postmodernism does not abandon political praxis. Chic postmodernism endorses postmodernity, where left postmodernism regards postmodernism as yet another ideology cloaking the real in sheer appearance (although I (1989a) argue that it is harder than ever to disentangle reality and appearance, the special nature of fast capitalism).

Postmodernists like Foucault (1977, 1980) who rethink the nature of power in a disciplinary society (O'Neill, 1986) also seem to shun large-scale social movements that seek to shift power. Again, this reflects the political ambivalence of the postmodernity/postmodernism problematic: that power takes new forms not imagined by prior radical critics like Marx does not mean it is impregnable. Here, postmodernism (Foucault, Lyotard) borrows heavily from poststructuralism (Derrida, Barthes, French feminism, Lacan). Derrida and Barthes posit the death of the subject, suggesting an antisubjectivism that permeates all poststructural and postmodern thought. However valid this may be on the evidence (after all, the Frankfurt School theorists also suggested the "decline of the individual" (Horkheimer, 1974) as a tendency in late capitalism), poststructuralists and postmodernists *ontologize* the death of the subject, thus fatefully depoliticizing their own critique of dominant culture and society. Habermas' own (1984, 1987b) reconstruction of critical theory as communication theory indefatigably defends the notion of personal and interpersonal agency (notably through his "universal pragmatics" of communicative competence) as an indispensable condition of any critical theory and hence critical social practice. It is one thing to note that people are less and less in control of their discourses, lifeworlds and productive/reproductive activities; it is altogether another thing to chill this disempowering into a veritable social metaphysic in the fashion of both poststructuralism and postmodernism.

Laclau and Mouffe (1985), among others, seek alternative "subject positions" from which alienated but constitutive individuals can launch oppositional projects. Although they abandon Marxism, they also resist the fatalizing assumptions of poststructuralists and postmodernists who reject any talk of constitutive subjectivity as metaphysical treason. They try to redefine the political, although not in a way that is ultimately successful given that they jettison so much of the materialist apparatus. But that is precisely what left postmodernism must do – reconceive of politics in a way that we can formulate and enact new modes of opposition and reconstruction. The death of the subject is only temporary. Once we historicize subjectivity, we can rethink the modalities of personal and public life in an energizing way.

Objective Subjectivity

This rethinking of the political gives rise to, and is reflected in, a left postmodernist conception of subjectivity. For the most part, I find this concept of an objective subjectivity already available in the Freudian Marxism of the Frankfurt School (e.g., Jacoby, 1975), although a left feminism has important things to say about the matter, too (Jaggar, 1983; Fraser, 1990). The New Individualism of neoconservative postmodernism is contrasted with an objective concept of subjectivity grounded in one or another depth psychology connecting psychological and social-structural dynamics, whether Freudian, Freudian-Marxist or feminist-Marxist. The American women's movement says it best: the personal is political (and vice versa). The psyche and family are legitimate political agenda items. The Frankfurt theorists (Marcuse, 1955), with their heterodox version of psychoanalysis, suggested some private-public links quite unconventional by orthodox Marxist standards. Marcuse (1969) recognized that revolutionary product must be borne of revolutionary process lest the "revolution" turn out to be what Korsch called a dictatorship *over* the proletariat, as horrifying as the capitalism it replaces.

Western Marxism (Agger, 1979a) (including phenomenological Marxism (Piccone, 1971; Paci, 1972)) joins left feminism in making the personal-political link thematic, both for theory and practice. Together they help fertilize a critical postmodernism that refuses to dispense with a concept of the subject; instead, together, these theoretical currents suggest a notion of objective subjectivity, of historical subjectivity, as well as a concrete notion of intersubjectivity (Piccone, 1971) that provides a semblance of radical energy in an overstructured, overdetermined world. The left has never been able to relinquish an active concept of subjectivity without descending either into fatalism or authoritarianism. State socialism is all state and no socialism, just as democratic centralism, Lenin's euphemism, was very short on democracy. A critical postmodernism rebuts left determinism yet again, whether it is structuralism (Althusser, 1969) or garden-variety economism (Mandel, 1968). One might imagine that poststructuralism in its very nature would reject the structuralism of Levi-Strauss (1963, 1966). But it also turns its back on subjectivity and thus political activism. Derrida's claim that he is a Marxist, and the promise of a book by him called *The Political Derrida*, are not convincing. Either political transformation is present in theoretical concepts from the beginning or it is not; it cannot be imported from the outside.

The Non-modern

Luddism is antimodern; modernism ambivalently values capitalist progress but, in its avantgarde formulation, rages against it (e.g., Dadaism, situationism (Debord, 1983), surrealism); an establishment postmodernism endorses the present as a plenitude of postmodernity – the eclipse of the old "isms" (like Bell in his "end of ideology" thesis). What, then, of a critical postmodernism? How does it conceive of a post-postmodern future? I return to this question concretely in Chapter 8, when I discuss the autonomous and transformative lives that writers might lead. Theoretically, we can

say this: a left and feminist postmodernism rejects the whole continuum of modernity, modernization and postmodernity as a fatefully
teleological discourse. Instead, left postmodernism poses the possibility of a future stage of social history characterized neither by
anti-modernism nor pro-modernism (given the ambivalent status of
modernism – both capitalism and Adorno) but by *non-modernism*.

I reject the notion that we are now in a stage of postmodernity fundamentally discontinuous with earlier capitalist modernity. Jameson
(1984b) and Kellner (1988) are among the left theorists who support
my contention. Aronowitz (1981, 1990), too, suggests that postmodernism and poststructuralism are often faddish and betray the
historical-materialist project, although he takes the lead in showing
how we can learn from them in deepening our own version of the
totality. Indeed, his 1988 book on science converges very much with
the sense of my argument here for a renewed form of public reason
within a materialist framework. Ryan (1982) and Eagleton (1983)
join this discussion about how to salvage the critical and dialectical
insights of French social theory, notably deconstruction. In many
ways, Huyssen (1986) has gone the furthest toward embracing postmodernism as critical theory, although he may well have passed the
point of no return beyond which postmodernism's neoconservatism
swallows its avantgardist radicalism. This largely depends on how
we define postmodernism and then what we take from it in the way
of ideology-critical resources. Kellner (1988) is absolutely correct to
note that there is no systematic postmodern social theory but only
various people who claim postmodernism in the feeding frenzy of
intellectual trendiness, particularly in France.

For my part (Agger, 1989a, 1989c) I have tried to formulate a
postmodern Marxism in terms of what I call disciplinary reading.
What I call a critical theory of significance broadens disciplinary
reading from sociology per se to what Foucault (1977) called the
disciplinary society in general. Fast capitalism is my term for our
present social formation; in it I attempt to preserve the sense of
continuity between modernity and postmodernity as well as to
suggest its distinctive features: "Fast" capitalism speeds up the
rate at which concepts and images blur with the reality to which
they bear a representational relationship, a twist of Adorno (1973b),
Baudrillard (1983) and others who have theorized the relationship
between ideas/ideology and reality. In Jacoby's (1976) terms, fast
capitalism causes the "rate of intelligence" to decline, thus checking
the tendency of the rate of profit to fall.

But words cannot do our thinking for us, let alone our political work. Jameson (1981) struggles to elaborate a total theory of political unconsciousness; Aronowitz (1990) attempts to restore radical democracy to a Marxism nearly overtaken by the secret vanguardism of French social theory, particularly postmodernism. All of us struggle to hold onto a notion of totality, resisting the decenterings of our grand narratives by those (e.g., Lyotard, 1984) who may well have neoconservative motives (as Habermas (1981b) has cogently argued in his original piece on modernity and postmodernity). Adorno (1973b, 1974a) suggested the inversion of positive totality into the negations of post-fascist capitalism: "The whole is the untruth". Although at a certain level it is difficult to deny the absolute nature of world horrors, especially in the nuclear age, Adorno himself (e.g., 1973b) attempted to render negation and negativism dialectical. I think of my own effort to redevelop left-feminist postmodern critical theory as an example of "negative dialectics", combining a totalizing Hegelian-Marxist foundationalism with methodical circumspection about the pitfalls of totality. Sartre (1963, 1976) also offers a theory of totalization largely ignored by the postmodern left, an irony given how his version of political existentialism energized a variety of currents of political dissent in France (e.g., the 1968 May Movement) that both directly and indirectly issued in more recent theoretical developments around postmodernism and poststructuralism.

Dionysian Reason

The antirationalism of establishment postmodernism can be countered by a new formulation of reason that in significant respects makes good the search for a non-Archimedean, non-authoritarian concept of totality. Reason in Hegelian-Marxist terms is both a way of conceiving and of working toward a good society; it has both subjective and objective components. Habermas' continuing effort to think through the communicative as well as institutional requirements of the "rational society" (e.g., 1970b, 1971, 1984, 1987b) reflects the double character of reason in the Frankfurt tradition, as does Marcuse's (1960) book on Hegel. There appear to be three choices of a concept and practice of rationality available to postmodern theory: we could decide to embrace the dualism of technical/instrumental and self-reflective/communicative rationalities, in the fashion of Habermas' essentially Kantian Marxism (Agger, 1979b) – or we could dispense with the notion of reason and its metanarrativeness altogether, as Nietzschean postmodernists like Lyotard do. Finally, as I propose, following the Freudian Marxism of the Frankfurt School (Agger, 1982), as well as the Frankfurt reading of Nietzsche, left existential-phenomenology (Merleau-Ponty, 1964a, 1964b) and left feminism (Jaggar, 1983; Donovan, 1985), we can heal the reason/desire split in a new concept of rationality that is both libidinal and cognitive/communicative. Although Habermas (1971, pp. 32-33) rejects this tendency in the original Frankfurt School as "mysticism", I embrace Marcuse, Adorno and Horkheimer's attempts to formulate a non-dualist rationality that preserves the concept of a redeemed totality and helps provide bridging principles between the levels of personality and social structure.

Whether or not one invests doctrinally in a left psychoanalysis (e.g., Jacoby's discussion of "negative psychoanalysis", 1975), or for that matter in left existential-phenomenology and socialist feminism, I believe it is possible and necessary for critical theory to develop a notion of rationality that staunchly defends itself against the post-rationalism of Lyotard's postmodernism. In Nietzsche's terms, this rationality combines Dionysian passion and Apollonian intellection, precisely the non-dualist rationality of Marx (1961) in the 1844 manuscripts. Without conceptualizing reason in these terms, critical theory is defenseless against the rising tide of antisubjectivism, anti-rationalism, neoconservatism and New Individualism virtually endorsing postmodernity as the world-historical solution to capitalism, sexism, racism and the domination of nature.

This is precisely the issue in the rest of this book, which addresses concretely how large institutional forces press down on writers who write to make a difference, to initiate social change as well as answer to their own creative muses. Writers who refuse to concede to the commodifying forces of popular culture and academia need some concrete notion of *how to think and live* in order to survive the corporate and profit impulses of the culture industry. They need a Dionysian rationality alert to the irrepressible requirements of its own desire to think, write and live free of the commodifying, hegemonizing forces of postmodern textual politics. There must be hope, as well as a concept of the hoped-for, in addition to the hard materialist analysis of how to make a living, start bookstores and journals, create community. As much as anything, critical writers need a source and focus of *dialectical imagination* (Jay, 1973) with which to fan the embers of their own lonely dissent. The decline of discourse *can* be countered by articulate, activist writers who engage in the creation of what Sartre (1965) called committed literature. But the first issue is how to generate commitment; from that follows a practical conception of what-is-to-be-done in the way of dehegemonizing the literary, hence public, world.

Literary Political Economy:
Toward a Dialectical Sociology of Culture

In this book I derive categories of an empirical sociology of culture from my general postmodernist framework, albeit the postmodernism of critical theory and not Lyotard's affirmative postmodernism denying the *grand recits* of Marxism and feminism. I characterize this sociology of culture as *literary political economy*, building on the Frankfurt analysis of the culture industry (Horkheimer and Adorno, 1972, pp. 120-167) as well as Jameson's (1984b) discussion of postmodernism as the "cultural logic of late capitalism". This is in aid of a concrete discussion and diagnosis of the falling fortunes of literary and hence public intelligence, framed in terms of the phenomenological experiences of writers struggling both to survive and to make a difference. As for all Marxism, the central analytical category of literary political economy is *commodification*, capturing the idea that writing, like all commodities today, increasingly trades only through its "exchange value", as Marx called it (e.g., see Best, 1989). This is obviously true of writing in the realm of popular culture, including advertising, television, journalism, film and trade fiction. It is also indirectly true of academic writing where we understand that journal and monograph space is a scarce resource and thus becomes necessary real estate for those who would rather publish and prosper than perish (Brodkey, 1987).

Commodified discourse is *displaced* from the realm of authentic writing proper, whatever that might mean, into the regions of popular culture and academia (Ross, 1988). The displacement of discourse definitely lowers the rate of public intelligence in that writers write not for expressive and political reasons but to please editors and publishers concerned both to maximize profit and enforce social control. Discourse's displacement is a structural tendency in a commodified literary world; I examine this tendency, as I examine commodification, in terms of its real impact on writers' lives. The commodification of discourse exacts grievous costs from writers who come to their craft in order to ventilate a certain aesthetic and political desire.

My version of literary political economy derives from what I have characterized as a left and feminist version of postmodernism or simply critical theory. One of the tensions in the balance of this book is the alternation between the trendy, glitzy postmodernism of the culture industry and an academic world that *endorses* the commodification and displacement of literary craft and an alternative, fugitive postmodernism that criticizes literary postmodernism as both faddish and ideologizing. Although this issue turns on how one defines postmodernism, I am convinced that a discussion of literary political economy cannot address only the political economy of trade publishing, television, advertising, movies, journalism and academia without also examining the legitimating ideologies, *increasingly self-styled "postmodern"*, attending on the economic ramifications of the commodification and corporate control of discourse. In other words, I want to "deconstruct" the stories publishers, producers, editors and even authors tell themselves and others about the nature of postmodern literary lifestyles as a way of piercing the haze surrounding what is really happening in literary political economy on a structural level. As Horkheimer (1972b) and his Frankfurt colleagues (Horkheimer and Adorno, 1972, pp. 120-167) knew from the beginning, an adequate analysis of the culture industry cannot neatly separate infrastructural from superstructural phenomena, even less in "postmodern" or "fast" (Agger, 1989a) capitalism.

Postmodernism as a legitimating ideology in contemporary literary political economy justifies all manner of authorial self-sacrifice and conformism. Its peculiar nature is that it does this behind the facade of literary desublimation which, as ever, proves to be *repressive* (Marcuse, 1955). The postmodern auteur is portrayed as cosmopolitan, networked and networking, brazen, supremely self-confident. In fact, this conceals a hollowness and insecurity only exacerbated by life in the literary fast lane. This holds true for academia as well as popular culture – perhaps more for academia where "points" are tallied entirely in reputation and citations if not also sales and dollars. Everybody is running scared, although by the look of things people seem to be enjoying these halcyon days of limitless literary opportunities and upward mobility. Postmodernity is the best and worst of times: writers wear a brave front but inside they feel empty. Bravado is both a survival strategy, part of the repertoire of coping and people-handling skills of the late 20th century rationalist, and ideology, an index of one's belief in the world's fundamental goodness. Unfortunately, few on the inside see this for what it is: as the Frankfurt School knew, the culture industry proceeds *through* people's obliviousness to it, the nature of contemporary ideology.

In this sense, my empirical and political aim in this book is to formulate a mode of counterhegemony, of literary resistance, to the culture industry and its postmodern patina. I ask what writers can do to avoid being crushed by the logos of the postmodern; I then inquire into what writers can write in order to change the world. Of course, these are portentous questions and I have few definitive answers. I am not unduly hopeful. But neither am I hopeless a priori. Articulating the problem of the decline of discourse this way helps slow it, if infinitesimally. At least, we writers, by framing our own complicity in literary political economy in terms of our susceptibility to its postmodernist ideologization, can avoid the worst aspects of false consciousness, what Nietzsche called the love of fate. Whether capitalism is destined to survive attempts to revolt it is an empirical question; but we know with certainty that fate is redoubled by fatalism, the stance of the postmodern who rejects subjectivity, reason, totality – optimism.

Saying this suggests a self-help book – one for writers. There is nothing wrong with self-help except its institutional housing alongside the other deceptive mechanisms of third-force and new-age affirmation and acquiescence. We have to help ourselves and others. Community begins at home, in neighborhoods and classrooms, between couples and among small handfuls of souls struggling to overcome their mortal and political isolation. And social change movements in their full-blown nature are nothing more than communities arrayed together strategically. If this is a self-help book for radical writers, it wants to extend that help into a larger framework of literary and political community in which people can cluster together for shelter and perhaps even the first halting steps of social change. There is nothing wrong with a radical concept of subjectivity as long as we realize that subjectivity is already objective (Adorno, 1978b) and intersubjective (Husserl, 1965). In fact, we cannot do without a notion of struggling, imaginative subjects – writers and readers. Absent such a notion, we on the left fail to take existential responsibility for changing our own worlds. The powers will not do it for us.

Writers must write through it all, neither heroizing themselves nor reveling in their isolation. Literary work can be political especially where politics is found everywhere but in the political arena, traditionally defined. And where politics is increasingly textual politics, we simply cannot afford to ignore literary political economy and its accompanying postmodernist ideology out of economistic prejudices. By now, the analysis of the culture industry has become an integral part of western Marxism and left feminism, whether as critical theory, Birmingham cultural studies, left deconstruction, feminist literary criticism, Marxist aesthetic theory or the radical sociology of culture. This book contributes to that tradition, reformulating some of the categories of culture-critical analysis in the direction of recent postmodern critical theorists like Jameson (1984a, 1984b), Huyssen (1986) and Kellner (1988), among others. The decline of discourse is a factor, a moment, in overall domination. It can be slowed, perhaps even reversed, as long as literary workers, both popular and academic, recognize and reorder their own roles in the textual politics enmeshing us in the overall political fabric.

The culture industry is a vehicle of mass unconsciousness today. But it is not a *deus ex machina*. The logic of cultural capital does not transpire above the heads of men and women, readers and writers. As such, it can be transformed, if not heroically through singular expressions of outrage or optimism. At issue here are writing and reading, publishers and producers, the literary labor market, the role of the intellectual, the nature and future of ideology – public culture. These are the topics I will consider in the rest of this book.

Chapter 2

The Absent Public

The demise of the public sphere has been a refrain of much social criticism at least since the 1950s (O'Neill, 1972; Habermas, 1975; Sennett, 1978; Agger, 1985). Plato started it all when he idealized the Greek polis as the site of human sociability as well as governance. Most recently, critics have blamed the demise of publicity on television, the women's movement, the New Left, technocratic education and academia (Bloom, 1987; but also see Wolfe, 1989). Although diagnoses vary, it is assumed that the standard of public reason needs no defense; the "public sphere" speaks for itself as an important social and political value. While much of this recent social criticism hits near the mark – after all, who does not value the notion of the intimate polis in this age of gigantism? – the discussion has by and large failed to explicate the notion of the public sufficiently. As a result, social critics propose simple-minded solutions that do not get to the heart of the issue. The notion of an authentic public life is confusingly held up by both the right and left as a standard against which to orient social and political analysis.

Although I do not discard the left-right polarity, I want to outflank it in a way that breathes new life into social criticism and thus our political imagination. I, too, lament the absence of the public (Agger, 1989a), yet I do not want to understand its absence in terms of a certain aristocratic notion of the intellectual life essentially derived from Plato. Instead, I want to consider what some people call the postmodern condition (Lyotard, 1984; Hansen, 1987), Nietzsche's meaninglessness, in light of the decline of discourse – the absence of readers and writers able to connect with each other in the community-building work of public speech. Although it is convenient to blame the lack of shared cultural values, or the wrong values, for public anomie, one can better understand the decline of discourse in terms of specific institutional changes in the social relations of discourse, notably how people write and read about their worlds.

In itself this is nothing new. Since the early twentieth century philosophers affiliated with the project of logical positivism have decried the Teutonic complexification of language as a civil plague (see Gellner, 1959). They have prescribed so-called ordinary language as a solution of sorts, ridiculing obscurantism as a tool of political oppression. Although jargon is part of the problem in a technical civilization, it is not the whole problem. The positivist condemnation of abstract language pins the blame on writers so ethereal – elitist – that they simply cannot talk to members of the general public. I do not deny that the problem of cultural stupefaction is compounded by writers who refuse to write publicly on grounds that to do so is only to write down. Yet this standard of public writing assumes that a public exists for whom writers could write if only they were not jargonizing academics.

Where both left and right critics of the demise of the public sphere lament the absence of general discourse, most of them blame writers for ignoring the public. True, academization has contributed to the increasing obscurantism of narrowly differentiated disciplinary writing. Writers are not blameless, especially tenured academics who could perhaps teach themselves and thus their readers a more accessible style with which to broach the big issues of the day. Yet readers share the blame, too. Authorial obscurantism is matched by readerly intransigence; few are patient with the dense and important tomes of classical thought or recent European theory, demanding an "easy read" and instant comprehension. Publishers shape writing to fit this standard of prosaic accessibility and comprehensibility.

Blame could be apportioned everywhere; the decline of discourse is a general condition that must be traced to a variety of institutional and personal circumstances. But this book is not about blame. I want to describe and diagnose the shifting forces of textual politics in what some call our postmodern age (Habermas, 1981b; Benhabib, 1984; Foster, 1984; Huyssen, 1984; Silverman and Welton, 1988). As I discussed in Chapter 1, to some postmodernism means the end of ideology, the cessation of political contention, while to others it connotes a world that is decentered, devalued, degraded (Newman, 1985; Kroker and Cook, 1986). For me, as I will elaborate, postmodernism is a version of critical theory, suggesting the possibility of fulfilling the ambitions of the Enlightenment – reason, freedom, justice. I am especially interested in postmodernism's two faces, either justifying the present helter-skelter literary world dominated by corporate giants and bureaucratic universities and peopled by powerless, purposeless writers or, alternatively, suggesting a new standard of public reason that fundamentally democratizes literary, and hence political, relationships. In my concluding chapter, I characterize this latter version of postmodern writing as the public voice.

I begin this study by addressing the thesis of the declining public sphere in terms that interrogate taken-for-granted assumptions about authorial responsibility for the decline of disourse. Although obviously writers could write differently (as I try to do here and as others do), they are enmeshed in political-economic relations of presentation and production largely conditioning the styles with which they compose themselves. Of course, to be "largely conditioned" is not the same thing as to be caused willy-nilly; people make choices they could have made differently. But that is beside the point. My first concern is basically a structural one. I want to ask what it could possibly mean to write intelligibly at a time when inquisitive general readers, members of the public, have virtually disappeared (Jacoby, 1987).

This is not simply to invert the argument for authorial guilt: stupid readers incorrigibly make writers' lives impossible by watching network television and reading *People* magazine. Although true, writer-reader relations are dialectical; they condition each other. People write incomprehensibly because readers cannot comprehend difficulty, allusion, irony and indirection. And the public is largely absent in this sense because it has been pandered to for so long. I want to examine the modalities of this dialectic without pretending an easy solution – better writing, new journals, more liberal-arts requirements in college. All of these are symptomatic; the real problem is the political and economic totality, irreducible to the single gestures occupying individuals when they sit down to write, read or teach. Although these small gestures matter, they have largely been swallowed into the social relations of presentation and production governing literary practice as they govern social, economic and political practice. Culture is not a world apart (Marcuse, 1964; Horkheimer and Adorno, 1972, pp. 120-167).

There are no simple explanations to be found. It is facile to say that people write obscurely "because" the educated reading public is absent. It is equally facile to excuse stupidity on grounds that writers have lost the ability to communicate. Both are true; neither is true alone. To understand the decline of discourse we must investigate what I call textual politics, the ensemble of relations enmeshing writers, readers, schools, publishers, bookstores, academic disciplines, journals, even the visual media (Brodkey, 1987).

None of us is immune to the enormous pressures exerted on us to become thoughtless ciphers, merely conduits of conventional wisdom conveyed conventionally. Although there was no original conspiracy that fashioned our eventual complicity in the literary politics of the postmodern, we cannot begin to fathom the predicament of the absent public without understanding the eclipse of textuality in structural terms. Too frequently critics pin the decline of publicity simply on temperamental factors – authors "unwilling" to write clearly, readers "unwilling" to tolerate difficulty. Although these things undoubtedly operate, they are more effects than causes. The real issue is the way we have organized textuality in late capitalism (Coser, Kadushin and Powell, 1982; Shatzkin, 1982; Agger, 1989a).

I analyze the capitalist organization of textuality in terms of *literary political economy*, a dialectical sociology of culture that I derived from my discussion of postmodernism in Chapter 1. The central concepts of this literary political economy, explaining the decline of discourse today, are literary *commodification, displacement* and *hegemony*. Literary commodification describes the way in which writing enters either the economic or academic marketplace, to be exchanged for money and/or status. Literary displacement describes the way in which writers no longer write thoughtful public prose accessible to inquisitive general readers but, as employees of publishers, producers, television studios, advertising agencies, newspapers, magazines and universities, write under administrative imperative. Of course, this assumes that writers who write for a living in the corporate and academic setting lose a crucial measure of autonomy: as wage workers, their creativity is subordinated to the profit and discipline requirements of their pay masters. Literary hegemony refers to the way that the dominance of prevailing cultural standards is reproduced by individual writers and readers in their own literary practices. These three concepts together help explain and oppose the culture industry, the textual politics of late capitalism (Jameson, 1984b).

Literary political economy is structural. That is, I am not particularly concerned with the quality of the individual products of commodified literary endeavor; indeed, there are isolated works of art and artifice that are genuinely creative, in spite of their commodified nature. After all, the individual creator has little control of the disposition of her or his work. "Discovered" artists are not necessarily responsible for their sensationalization. My argument here is about the tendencies of literary commodification to cause public speech – discourse – to decline: This transpires above the heads of individual writers, editors, readers, publishers. It is part of the "cultural logic of late capitalism", as Jameson (1984b) has called it. Although individuals "matter" in the tableau of world history, they scarcely matter at a time when gargantuan structures overdetermine our quotidian existences, enslaving us to their logics of accumulation, expansion, colonization, discipline.

To say this invites an ideologically poisoned reading; I may be heard to offer yet another Marxist account of culture, here of writing and reading. While I am a Marxist, to be Marxist today is up for grabs. Here my account is Marxist to the extent to which I insist that we must comprehend large structural forces like the displacement, commodification and hegemony of discourse. In Chapters 3 and 4 I discuss the displacement of discourse into popular culture and the university. In Chapters 5 and 6 I suggest the larger socio-cultural and political implications of discourse's commodification and hegemony; in particular, I suggest that discourse is found everywhere *but* in traditional books. In my final three chapters, I evaluate some alternative formulations and practices of textuality.

These things all fit together; none is reducible to another. We cannot comprehend, and thus remedy, the decline of discourse without considering the dominance of the university over intellectual life. Similarly, any story is incomplete without considering carefully the role of the marketplace in determining authorial choices and chances. Where in the following chapters I enter directly into diagnosis, I begin by describing the problem confronting critics of public life today. I choose to emphasize the sheer absence of a reading public. At once this invites the accusation of elitism; who am I to insult the reading public? But intelligence is a situational outcome of particular epistemic organizations of knowledge. I focus here on the way cultural production is differentially controlled by powerful interests. We are trained to be smart or stupid depending on our proximity and utility to power. No Marxist would dispute the fact that knowledge is a powerful form of social control today, facilitating and enhancing the legitimacy of private wealth. People from Basil Bernstein (1971) to Ivan Illich (1977, 1978, 1981) remind us of how dominance is defined in the knowledge relations between people and institutions. Keeping people ignorant about high science and technology assures control of the scientific-technical apparatus by elites. This much is unmysterious by now (Marcuse, 1969; Habermas, 1970a; Agger, 1976b; Aronowitz, 1988). Thus, in suggesting the absence of a reading and writing public I am not engaging in simple moral condemnation nor recommending the Greek great books as a sufficient solution. *I am pointing to an absence that is effectively a product of particular social and economic arrangements of knowledge.*

The reading and writing public is declining largely because readers and writers have gone elsewhere; their discourse has been displaced. It is not only that intelligence has diminished – e.g., the ability to consider and formulate complex arguments about the nature of the world – but that intelligence has been removed from a traditional literary culture into other realms, notably popular culture and academia. Intelligent, inquisitive people still exist, but they are not found reading and writing public books of the old-fashioned kind. Rather, they serve other masters, working in television, journalism, the university and the professions. Although I do not deny that people can do interesting and even socially important work in some of these pursuits, it is patent that the displacement of discourse into these literary venues basically upholds the status quo; instead of standing at one remove from power in considering its authority and legitimacy, intellectuals are sucked into institutions either supporting power directly (academia and the professions) or diverting and anesthetizing people (popular culture).

Thus, the modalities of public ignorance have everything to do with the institutional forms intelligence is allowed to take. I do not glorify the intellectual life per se but rather argue for a concept of intellectuality bearing heavily on the value of our overarching social, political and economic institutions. One of our problems when we consider intellectual life is that we almost invariably idealize a concept of intellectuality detached from other social institutions (Arendt, 1958; Lobkowicz, 1967). This book is not about whether intellectuals should be plugged in or out – either located squarely in dominant institutions or living and working strictly on the margin. I am more concerned with the ways in which intellectuality is channeled to serve dominant institutions, thus losing the vitality of public life taken up with lively debate about larger social purposes. I am concerned not with intellectuals per se but with discourse – the life and times of public vernacular.

This sort of public talk is nearly absent today; people do not read or write generally but are increasingly subordinated to the economic and ideological requirements of popular culture and academia. We on the margins of the literary mainstream do what we can to survive. Those of us who want to write have few alternatives to working in Hollywood, writing for *The New York Times* or teaching and publishing in an ivy-covered world. This is not simply to disqualify popular culture and academic life as inferior worlds. "One" can do good work in journalism, film, music and the university. Yet there is little evidence to suggest much good work going on in these domains. Instead, popular culture is often moronizing and academic life crabbed and irrelevant (Grossberg, 1986). Either writing is dominated by Nielson ratings or adjudicated through the domestication processes of disciplinary scholarship. In both cases, public life is not enriched by prose sufficiently general to bring people together around the debates first captured in our image of the Greek city-state. Citizens of the polis in effect ran their own society through vigorous public participation in discourse, the conversations of public life.

I realize that these are sweeping generalizations. Jacoby, who (1987) makes this argument with respect to academia, has been targeted by academics, left, right and center, who reject his sweeping criticism. Typically, people who mount this argument with respect to popular culture are conservatives of one kind or another. At root, these arguments about the content (or lack of it) of academic and popular cultures rest on empirical examination. Notably, one would have to read academic journals and read and view popular culture to arrive at one's own conclusion in this regard. I do not assume the depravity of academic and popular cultures; these are empirical generalizations, nothing more. As such, I hope we can change popular and academic writing by resisting the hegemony of literary commodification and corporate control – by writing and living differently. I do not exhaustively make my case here by citing numerous examples of declining discourse. I am saying. . ."Assume for the sake of argument that I am correct. *Then* let us try to unravel the implications of all this for what writers write and thus how they could write differently".

Discourse: The Main Players

I formulate the thesis of the eroding public sphere in terms of the decline of discourse. I understand this decline as a function of the displacement, commodification and hegemony of literary activity in postmodern capitalism. Readers approach textuality in terms of the knowledge units or entertainment it provides. And writers are geared narrowly to the political-economic and ideological requirements of popular culture and the university. In the case of popular culture, discourse merely repeats conventional wisdom conventionally; television and movies are so appalling because they are repetitive. In the case of academic writing, virtually none of it matters except to narrow specialists trained tellingly in discipline. One might say that popular culture is "too" relevant, academic writing not relevant enough. In both cases, people write for television or academic journals because they have no other outlets: they write for profit or for tenure, not for public edification.

This is an immediately practical problem for people who value public intellectuality and teach in universities. I am continually confronted by students who want to make a difference by contributing their own voices to public life. Whether in politics, science or art, these students inhabit a world in which the standards of intelligence have fallen and discourse has become merely a career – advertising, screenwriting, academia. Smart people are led to eschew public discourse in favor of the highly differentiated and largely market-driven venues of popular culture and academia. After all, how else can writers survive? Freelancing is a precarious profession at best; as Irving Howe (1982) said in his autobiography, in some ways the stability afforded by academic employment liberates one from the vagaries of the literary marketplace.

From a societal point of view, the absence of a general literary culture vitiates democracy. The Greek city-state and New England town meeting suggest an imagery of small-scale self-governance inherently at odds with the gigantism of the corporation and political state. Without public discourse, there is little in the way of buffering between the individual and huge megainstitutions of politics and economics (Habermas, 1984, 1987b). When people who want to speak publicly lower their sights and enter the hurlyburly of popular culture and academia, we all lose. Public discourse declines further, only entrenching those who hold power. The less genuine discourse there is, the more confident power can be about its own invincibility.

This is not to say that having writers write accessible books will change the world. Intellectual democracy does not spell the real thing if productive and reproductive relations go unchanged; yet the decline of discourse is a factor in overall domination and the falling rate of public intelligence (Jacoby, 1976) only further diminishes transformative opportunities. Reversing the decline of discourse would help restore the public sphere (O'Neill, 1972; Keane, 1984; Offe, 1984, 1985) and, with it, active public discussion of social and economic purposes. Discourse, generalized across all social and economic strata, conveys the critique of ideology and thus helps reverse false consciousness (Lukacs, 1971).

Of course, this is already to degrade a notion of genuine discourse into a slogan itself – as such, anathema to discourse preserving, even provoking, the possibility of its own reformulation. Left jargon is jargon nonetheless. Yet one can understand discourse in terms of a number of concrete literary and social manifestations, thus preventing its degeneration into another simple-minded word with which to condemn thought thoughtlessly. Discourse must embody public comprehensibility; that is, it eschews narrow subservience to disciplines, with their highly differentiated argot. Saying this does not solve our problem, however, because comprehensibility itself is very much contingent on the overall level of public intelligence (Jacoby, 1976). That people can comprehend sit-coms and mass-market news magazines does not make these examples of authentic discourse. The criterion of comprehensibility primarily distinguishes real discourse from its academic imposter, whose abstruseness is virtually a literary requirement.

Genuine discourse admits of, even promotes, its own reformulation (Agger, 1989c). To be discourse, writing must solicit its own response by readers empowered to understand it and then engage with it. Most popular culture cannot meet this standard of discursive writing. Much academic writing, too, fails to invite dialogue, instead reporting itself as an objective account purged of authorial intentionality, perspective, passion. I will discuss popular culture and academic writing more extensively below in light of these public requirements of discourse. Indeed, I defeat my ideals of textual publicity and openness to the extent to which I render them formulaic: "Discourse is. . .this or that". One knows when one is in the presence of discourse; one knows this best where one is invited into the sense and sentience of texts that do not stand over against one as deadening cultural objects. I am less interested in hard-and-fast definitions and conceptual refinements than in making sense empirically of the problem at hand, the decline of public intelligence (Horkheimer, 1974).

One might define discourse somewhat differently as writing that refuses its absorption into the maw of the culture industry (Horkheimer and Adorno, 1972: pp. 120-167), as such becoming merely a cultural commodity. But this definition is too broad: it would include obscure, obscurantist cultural expressions that do not meet the aforementioned criterion of dialogical public speech. One of the problems with postmodernism as it extends earlier avantgardism and subversive modernism (e.g., surrealism, Dadaism, expressionism) is that it tends to valorize the *unpopular* as a sufficient alternative to commodified, banalized mass culture. In spite of Adorno's fondness for Schoenberg and Beckett, these figures in their rarefied voices do not help constitute a genuine public sphere in the late twentieth century. By the same token, they are not to be disregarded simply because they demand a great deal from the listener and reader. Yet in resisting their own absorption, they court incomprehensibility, as does much theory itself, the topic of my concluding chapter. Aesthetic and expressive distance – difficulty – does not willy-nilly constitute public speech. Comprehensibility is an invalid criterion of truth only in a world in which comprehension stands for deception.

This is not to imply that "the public" is always right. It is no more right than it is wrong where textual politics are concerned. The problem with conventionalist accounts of truth is that they trade circularly on standards of comprehensibility currently abroad today. College textbook publishers in requiring manuscripts to read at the junior-high school level only reproduce a junior-high school college student body. Yet, in their defense, they are constrained by the current level of literary competence. Ill-prepared college students are defeated by more demanding textbooks, let alone by Plato's *Republic* or Marx's *Capital*. How can those of us who have been educated in sophisticated literary worlds deny our students basic sustenance – the pedestrian textbooks that we ourselves, as academics, often write?

Then again, my "defense" of college text publishers is only intended facetiously (Fein, 1979; Kuklick, 1979; Wells, 1979; Herrick, 1980; Perrucci, 1980; Villemez, 1980; Maslow, 1981; Papp, 1981; Porter, 1981-1982; Gomme, 1985; McCarthy and Das, 1985). Textbook publishers do not care about public discourse but that books written too hard or too high fail to capture a market share. Comprehensibility is simply an issue of supply-and-demand, guaranteeing that epistemological problems will be solved strictly in economic terms. Having said this, though, the "solution" is neither to abolish college textbooks nor to exhort acquisitions editors to commit themselves morally to "better" books. These are just slogans in their own right. Nothing changes unless everything changes; yet for everything to change, particular things must change simultaneously. In Chapters 7, 8 and 9 I give the lie to a summary agenda of reforms to be visited on popular culture and academia. Piecemeal changes are only that. Heroic individuals cannot wriggle free of the logic of commodification, thus degradation, for very long (Marx, 1961; Marx and Engels, 1964; Braverman, 1974; Marx, n.d.). Eventually we all tend to return to the enveloping institutions sustaining us as writers.

This will sound cynical to struggling young writers trying not to compromise their integrity, whatever that might mean (Gardner, 1983; Becker, 1986). Although I am in favor of integrity, one must be unsentimental about the material world especially when it crushes down on us with a vengeance. It is easy to tell young academics turned down for tenure that they still have their books, intellectual identities and integrity. That will neither pay the rent nor give one bonds to a larger intellectual community necessary to fertilize discourse. To the extent to which one's writing is governed by market criteria, one is enslaved to the exigencies of conventional wisdom. After all, "new" products are merely iterations of old ones that are packaged, composed, slightly differently. Baudrillard's (1981) political economy of the sign expresses this well, as I have tried to do in a somewhat more materialist way (Agger, 1989a). The name "new" passes for real innovation. That is why popular culture and academic writing both endure virtually as canons – bodies of knowledge with little room for innovation, let alone subversion.

Too much of the prevailing discussion about the demise of public life implies moral and cultural solutions, better values, more great books, less individual timidity. Authors like Allan Bloom (1987) prescribe the classics as castor oil, while Russell Jacoby (1987) from the left exhorts academics to shed the skin of disciplinary specialization and the circumscribed prose this requires. In a sense, both accounts are correct as symptomatic descriptions; few would disagree that our present generation of college students is woefully ill-prepared in matters of cultural literacy and that academia causes the rate of intelligence to fall still further. Bloom's diatribes against the New Left, women's movement and rock-and-roll notwithstanding, few of my political ilk really disagree that academia has failed to inculcate central cultural and intellectual values, if not the ones cherished by Bloom.

Laments like Bloom's and Jacoby's suggest themselves as exceptions to the rule, and in some sense they are. Although I disagree with virtually every word of Bloom's diatribe about the left, his book is unusually written for intelligent readers without specific background in philosophy or sociology. Similarly, Jacoby's (1987) book makes few claims on readers unfamiliar with Jacoby's own prior work in social and psychoanalytic theory (Jacoby, 1975, 1983) and intellectual history (Jacoby, 1981). These books are as rare as four-leafed clovers: they are the vaunted public books whose absence is widely lamented today. Yet they are decidedly the exceptions. Indeed, Bloom's book is widely criticized (by academics) for lacking the supporting apparatus of scholarship – notes. And while Jacoby's book sports endnotes, left critics have hammered him for offering an overly simple thesis, refusing to couch his argument in the nuance typically characterizing academic prose.

Although Bloom's and Jacoby's books are unusual in that they penetrate a nonacademic "trade" market of book buyers (as does Todd Gitlin's (1987) book on the American New Left), they are "phenomena" not likely to be repeated. It is not even clear that many people read and digest them. Although Bloom has sold millions (Jacoby much less), the books are institutions in their own right; everybody talks about them but few have actually engaged with their arguments. If they have "read" them at all, it is cursorily, just as one scans the Sunday paper's movie and book reviews in gaining a certain amount of cultural capital (Bourdieu, 1977, 1984; Lamont and Larreau, 1988) with which to navigate professional and personal life as an educated person. And Bloom almost did not get his book published at all (personal connections helped); for his part, Jacoby was published by an editor who "acquired" him first while working at a university press. For every Bloom and Jacoby, there are probably scores of authors who have written similar manuscripts never to see the light of day.

Book publishers figure centrally in my account, as do the academics who run the leading journals and advise the major academic publishing houses. In anticipating market, they help constitute it. Many studies have been done about the book world (Coser, Kadushin and Powell, 1982; Mohanty, 1986). They generally suggest the remarkable extent to which editors operate intuitively when they project probable markets for their books. Although publishers increasingly seek to make marketing a science, following the fashion of the capitalist marketplace generally, the personal judgments of editors count for a lot in the evaluation of manuscripts. Of course, these decisions are not entirely untutored by commercial experience. Yet it is facile to suggest that publishers reproduce a backward public simply by giving it what it wants. This quickly becomes a self-fulfilling prophecy: publishers publish ever-the-same books for an ever-the-same readership characterized by pedestrian tastes in literature. This is circular: market research reproduces the market it mirrors.

The main players in my argument are writers, readers, commercial and academic publishers, academics, booksellers, entertainment mavens – virtually everyone involved in the literary production, distribution and consumption processes. The main logic in my analysis is the commodification, displacement and hegemony of discourse, a force transpiring virtually above the heads of men and women involved in the local contexts of cultural production and reception (Horowitz, 1986). The main players are largely out of control of the main logic; their intelligence is degraded virtually without their awareness of it. Public life (Jameson, 1981, 1988) has taken on a certain character and texture by now; discursive opportunities within it are largely decided for us. I neither exonerate particular individuals nor place the blame entirely on invisible forces we cannot control. By writing about discourse I hope to promote it, and thus to prepare the way for a revivified public sphere. People for whom I usually write would characterize this public as democratic and socialist; I hold with that. Yet language devilishly makes trouble for itself where the usage of conventional terms destines a conventional reception – democracy as America, socialism as Siberia. What matters is less the word "discourse" than the concept nonidentical to it. Already in this short chapter the word has promised too much in the way of social analysis and reconstruction. Yet we are captive of words, especially today in a sloganeering era. Cliches dominate thought where we refuse to think the dialectical ironies contained in every account of the world. Language intends to change the world it only pretends to copy.

My Literary and Political Aims

Having suggested a rough outline of a critique of public culture as a way of framing my argument, let me clarify my aims here. Although I want a whole new world, saying that only strains credulity in a time when utopia stands for tyranny or lunacy. It is nearly impossible to avoid concretizing one's critique and thus agenda. I want to open up a concept of discourse allowing me to criticize the commodification and degradation of what passes for discourse today. Although that is not much in the way of critical understanding (let alone transformation), perhaps it reverses the momentum of public stupefaction ever so slightly, an especially important issue where the future of young writers is concerned. Autobiography plays a central role here: I seek to give advice to my students who want to change the world yet threaten to be swallowed by the entertainment industry, on the one hand, or academia, on the other. Pedagogy and politics converge where teachers must dole out advice to their students, the best hope for the future. It is inadequate to tell writers "just to write" without cautioning them about the dismal prospects of surviving in a world dominated by corporations making the news, owning the news and dispensing entertainment in one fell swoop. By the same token, the privileged academic life is hardly insulated where the university is dominated by a state and corporate agenda requiring research to be practical and by a logic of production discouraging intellectual risk-taking. These are hard truths in an era where more and more people want to write; just about everyone "has a book in them", from political veterans and baseball players to evangelists and movie stars. Indeed, a chapter title in Ueland's (1987) self-help guide for aspiring writers is "Everybody is Talented, Original and Has Something Important to Say". It seems that everyone writes and no one reads; of course, this is an exaggeration. Few people write and even fewer seem to read writing as the discursive, hence political, practice it is.

That is precisely my problem, then. The status of *text* has changed; books are no longer found in the bookstore. They are "read" off television, movies, newspapers, dense scientific prose. Narrative declines in an era when the world narrates itself subtextually (Mueller, 1973; Wellmer, 1976; Eagleton, 1983). This already sounds mystical. Surely, books are books, things things. But the background of my argument about the decline of discourse involves understanding the displacement of textuality into discourses that do not read or write discursively, notably popular culture and academic journal prose. I want to focus this discussion in addressing its implications for writers and readers themselves. At issue in a discussion of discourse is the status of *what it means to write a text*.

The temptation simply to recall a golden age of busy publicists is nearly irresistible. One can easily revel in an earlier time when everyone knew what a book was and could engage with great texts interrogatively (if only because there were few texts around at the time). Yet this temptation must be avoided. There has never been a golden age of any sort from which one can gauge the present as a kind of decline. Although one can still use the word "decline", as I do in my title, it might be heard to suggest a prehistorical utopia. That courts the glorification of all sorts of class, race and gender inequalities. The Greek city-state, seemingly a paradise for discourse and textuality, rested on the labor of slaves and women. Intellectual life for most of world history has been the life of a privileged few. By the same token, there is nothing inherently wrong with television or academia. I address them only in terms of the implications they hold for reason and thus social justice.

In that sense, then, my political aim is not to restore a fallen order of being but to rethink what it means to be literary in terms that resist the equally overwhelming temptation to view the present as a chapter in the story of progress. To this extent, the textfulness of past orders usefully counterposes to the textlessness of the present world in which texts are things and things texts (Agger, 1989a). I am not blindly in favor of the past – slavery, war, elite privilege. The past is not a feasible utopian destination; it is already behind us. I want to resist the tendency to idealize the "communications revolution" (McLuhan, 1964) in times when there is precious little communicating going on. This study is critique of ideology, not utopian planmaking. Although there is a time for blueprints, it is hardly now. The transformative imagination is under siege by the hegemonizing forces turning most of us into conduits of the factual, frivolous, everyday. The word "discourse" is less a plan of a better society than a way of evaluating the discourselessness of the day in surprising terms. At the present, that is a suitable radical aim given the paucity of other political possibilities.

In turn, my literary and political aims are contextualized in a larger discussion of methodology and strategy. The decline of discourse matters not because I want everyone to read and write about Chaucer but because textual politics are closely entwined with the "other" politics – the disposition of power. The less the overtly political world is an important site of public disputation and consensus formation, the more extrapolitical worlds take on significance as the venues of struggle and hope (Arac, 1986). People refuse to vote "because" they watch electoral politics as a spectator sport. I put the word *because* in quotations because I realize it is not as simple as that. Yet I am talking about tendencies, not fixed realities. The passions of the public and political fade where politics is displaced into other arenas. It is widely believed in western "democracies" that "politics does not matter". I would say that politics still matters but that politics is now found in places other than the voting booth. For people of my theoretical and political persuasion, this is not hard to swallow. Marxism suggests that depoliticization is a crucial topic for political theory.

Textual politics matter precisely because public concern is displaced into popular culture. Writers act politically where they eschew the political as their ostensible topic. By avoiding traditional politics, writers and readers politicize realms heretofore believed to be "beyond" politics, notably culture and science. Today there is much more activity in popular bookstores than in traditional electoral politics. The culture industry is industry itself. As well, credentialled intellectuals send more correspondence to academic journals and publishers than to political candidates or the popular press. These are telling displacements of the political into realms

The Decline of Discourse

heretofore regarded as extrapolitical. Although I would maintain emphatically that Marx never meant political-economic analysis to ignore culture (e.g., Horkheimer, 1972b), dogmatic tendencies in Marxism (e.g., Slater, 1977; see Agger, 1983) have gotten the better of his dialectical understanding of textual politics.

As I discussed in Chapter 1, the decline of the public sphere is increasingly summarized in the term *postmodern*. As I said, this is the newfangled word for what Daniel Bell (1960) earlier called the "end of ideology" – an era beyond heated political contention. Postmodernists aver that the old passions of right and left have been eclipsed; politics, like cultural life generally, is best characterized by a healthy eclecticism. "Difference" is the new political metaphysic, uniting mainstream liberals and the postmodern left. Everything and anything goes in the postmodern period, especially when God and Marxism are dead. It is a cliche to dismiss this attitude as nihilism, suggesting solid – perhaps "traditional" – values in counterpoint to the valueless (Trachtenberg, 1985). But the Enlightenment critique of nihilism is correct. The decentering of values does not make values bad (Arendt, 1958; Habermas, 1981b). By the same token, postmodernism settles no epistemological or political argument in rejecting argumentation as antediluvian. Its postured pluralism, as ever, conceals deep divisions in worldview.

Many endorse postmodernism profoundly for that seems to quiet political passions. People affiliated to various literary theories (see Eagleton, 1983) are fond of decentering and deconstructing – any- thing and everything. That is as wrong as a Marxism reducing the world to surplus value. The logic of capital is only "tendential", as Marx (n.d.) called it. History is not a one-way street: understanding it *changes* it, vitiating the notion of social laws. Deconstruction as methodology makes relativity and self-contradiction absolutes, thus losing the specificity of its critique (Ryan, 1982). In attacking an unthinking modernism, postmodernists imply their own logic of unbroken development, albeit with the aid of antiquity. Marxism and capitalism alike are jettisoned for their totalizing nature. Thus postmodernists hope to correct ideological blindness with a pastiche of ideologies (Jameson, 1984b). Postmodern stands for a certain sophistication and world-weariness, exactly the sort of American who values New York City as the center of the cultural universe. Where Marxism falsely promised basic sustenance for stomachs the world over, the postmodern sensibility dines at 9 o'clock in trendy restaurants touted by *New York* magazine.

I am tempted to dismiss postmodernism as an invention of

publishers and writers wanting to sell books under yet another simplifying brand-name. It is that, too. But it is also an escape from the political – from perspective, generally – as unwarranted today as ever. A friend of a friend "loves" New York but "hates" having to see the homeless. Her frenetic career-building shields her from what she denies is a natural outcome of her own privilege. The media and publishing doyens centered in New York add fuel to this fire by reproducing the writers and readers whose taste they claim only to measure through market research. Although this book is not a diatribe against New York cultural mandarins, we in the United States cannot comprehend the decline of discourse without understanding cultural and political-economic hegemony in terms of the literary practices of cosmopolitanism.

Already this risks a pastoral reading. I am not saying that Kansas is any better, or any different. Yet trends start somewhere and they are redoubled through careful cultivation. It is no wonder that people want to move from Topeka to Manhattan, to work in theater, publishing, even academia. The postmodern takes shape in the blitzed-out posturban; one knows one lives in utopia when one pays a fortune for a dismal studio apartment. The cosmopolitan invents itself as metaphysic – the postmodern – in a gesture of self-aggrandizement (Jencks, 1987). Decenteredness claims itself as a new center. Although there are still people out there capable of reading, writing and living critically, they are not necessarily the ones who inflate their autonomy pretentiously. Frequently, lifestyle substitutes for real achievement; even at that, lifestyle is constructed by Madison Avenue to move products, even – especially – books. One is what one claims to have read.

The postmodern is simply another trend; it is a dangerous one where it announces the end of ideology yet again. But, as I argued in Chapter 1 and will argue again in Chapter 9, postmodernism can be reformulated as a critical theory of the culture industry, a project to which this book is a contribution. Luckily for the left, ideology does not end, even if renamed postmodernism. The horrors of the present are not art; politics is not eclipsed by culture; books must still be read and written by circumspect readers and writers who resist the gravitational pull of their thoughtlessness. Postmodernity is a time when writing is governed by the ability of authors to name their own reception, thus destining it. One gains access to print if one can give editors a handle with which to understand the market potential of one's work. One promises to be another Bloom, another Lasch, even another Marx. These claims translate themselves into reality where slogans substitute for things themselves. Books are purchased for their self-advertisements and for the publishers' inflated claims for them. It is suicide to publish books without a hook, a self-referencing, self-differentiating mark of the difference-within-sameness of one's work. Smart editors allow, even encourage, writers to name themselves; such an editor once asked me to describe my potential market and then believed me, marketing my book as such. Other editors pretend to know it all, refusing the claims authors make on behalf of the market location of their work. Sometimes they are right; usually they want to arrogate all the textual-political power for themselves. One cannot understand publishing unless one unpacks the deep-seated envy of writers and academics by editors who ironically hold power by controlling access to print. This envy corrodes writer-editor relations. Self-righteous male academics believe themselves inherently superior to the cadre of women editors who have come to dominate aspects of book publishing, notably as front-end, low-pay "acquisitions" editors.

Of course, no Marxist would suppose that publishing is a world apart – or media, journalism, entertainment. Everything is tainted by the logic of capital – commodification. Critiques of the decline of the public sphere typically suppose that words can somehow evade the general tendency of the rate of intelligence to fall in a capitalist society (Jacoby, 1976). This is an illusion entertained mainly by proud writers. In Bloom's success we see not only largesse but a victory for the purity of the word; the person making grandiose claims can still be heard in a cacophonous world. But the social category of the intellectual is bankrupt today (Gouldner, 1979). We who write are only employees – of CBS, *Newsweek*, the *Times*, Harvard, Wisconsin, SUNY-Buffalo. Our work is commodified and thus reduced to the denominator of the marketplace that we reproduce in our own duplicative work. It is folly to suppose that the thinker can inhabit a world apart for there are no such worlds. There never were. Intellectuality has always been a privilege subsisting on the backs of most everyone else.

Certain critics take this as an occasion for smashing all intellectuality; I oppose that not in the name of aristocratic values but simply because it solves nothing. People must be encouraged to write and read, thus to understand and oppose. Indeed, in my final chapter, I sketch a role for postmodern intellectuals. Marx is profoundly right to insist that people must work through their false consciousness; how this happens varies with time and place. The decline of discourse is not the only social problem, simply one that makes it very hard to see the others for what they are. If people could write and read across the commodification of culture and the academization of knowledge, then we could begin to touch each others' solitude in a political way. The powers defend their own privilege by keeping us apart (Portoghesi, 1983), we watch television and movies and prowling popular bookstores in which we acquire imageries disqualifying political imagination out of hand. Writing, which has become simply a diversion, plays a directly political role. And it is governed by its own political economy – what I call the textual politics of the postmodern. This book is my way of understanding it.

Literary Hegemony: Understanding Declining Discourse Phenomenologically

In order to summarize my opening chapters and prepare the way for what is to follow, let me resort to phenomenological description – the depiction of the world in terms of lived experience. I am a writer, obviously. Most of my readers are writers, too, even though some may be occasional ones, or unpublished ones, or eventual ones; perhaps they are students in the process of deciding on their future trade. In any case, for all of us the problem of declining discourse is most of all an authorial problem: for some reason, people are not writing broadly accessible books and publishers are not publishing them. Whether we are Marxists and blame this squarely on publishers (as I tend to do), the answer is never that simple. Yes, publishers, editors and reviewers are obviously entwined in the circuitries of literary production. But authors are also involved in those processes and, as such, they can change them. Or can they?

From the point of view of our lived experience as writers, virtually all of us believe that the only things preventing us from going to our desks each morning to write great thoughts are lack of caffeine, inspiration or a friendly editor. Or perhaps we would believe that our economic responsibilities prevent us from devoting ourselves fully enough to our craft. All of these things could be, and probably are, true for many of us. Only the lucky few manage to avoid drowsiness, lethargy or editorial rejection completely; and virtually no one who writes has a nest egg sustaining one forever. But, beyond these understandable impediments, virtually all of us believe that *we can make a difference* – that the absence of a viable public culture is as much as anything an authorial responsibility. After all, there seems to be nothing standing in the way of creative genius; we can always point to unlikely examples of people locked up in prison, or locked into poverty, who nevertheless manage to add their brilliance to public culture. And, for those of us who live more pampered lives, taking graduate degrees and living comfortably off the various occupational sinecures of the modern world, it is hard to imagine that writers do not control their own fate at some ultimate level.

But whether we call my analysis Marxist, neoMarxist or something else, this is the wrong way to view the problem. Indeed, very few are sufficiently liberated from daily exigency and throttled imagination to be able to compose themselves creatively. It is a postmodern myth, deriving from erstwhile liberalism and individualism, that we can "be all we can be", in the case of writers that we can write ourselves out of Kansas and thereby change the literary world. Granted, accidents do happen. Yet sheer compositional skills are not enough to guarantee success. But I am saying more than that, too. Even if we could find especially nurturant and emboldened editors, most writers today live under, and thus unconsciously reproduce, *literary hegemony*, a notion taken from the Italian neoMarxist Antonio Gramsci to describe the way in which (in Marx and Engels' (1947) terms) the ruling ideas remain the ideas of the ruling class.

Although Gramsci (1971) agreed with Marx on this, he was more interested in explaining how, exactly, the disempowered contribute to their own disempowering by buying into mistaken, self-defeating worldviews. Although Marx (n.d.) sketched the outlines of such an analysis in his discussion of the labor contract between worker and capitalist (that ends up being a legal fiction, the capitalist structurally exploiting the worker's labor power), Gramsci and other western Marxists after him have devoted their attentions to the suffocating, invisible and self-reproducing nature of what Gramsci termed "hegemony". It is not enough to notice that publishers are corporations controlling access to print. It is also important to recognize that writers themselves have the stuffing knocked out of them in a world of literary gigantism and corporate control.

Literary hegemony helps explain the fact that there are not many would-be literary heroes out there, whether in SoHo or San Diego, who have squirreled away path-breaking manuscripts in their desks, simply awaiting a good turn of editorial fortune. Literary hegemony helps explain why writers cannot just go to their typewriters or keyboards and *change the world* by adding their words to it, the populist myth of the Great American Novel notwithstanding. Of course, all writers would believe differently: We love to imagine that we are the next Updike, Sagan, Socrates. But – my ultimate point – the world has no room for these savants anymore; popular culture keeps people down and dumb. It is composed to be sold as well as to divert people from the ordinariness and unhappiness of their lives. If there are literary heroes abroad, they are probably only cunning creations of the advertising agencies which dominate the commodified literary world. With all due respect to Updike (the person), it is clear that "Updike" the literary symbol is a quite arbitrary outcome of fortuity – lucky reviews, editors willing to gamble on him, advantageous movie treatments, good placement in literary networks and a chunk of hard work and indefatigable self-promotion.

This is not a judgment on his particular fiction; that is another story better told by literary critics. But we must be clear that writers do not just become Updike anymore than Meryl Streep becomes a movie star simply because she is "good", whatever that is supposed to mean. I tend to think that Updike and Streep – the names that move books and pack theaters – function simply as placeholders, holding public attention in the absence of "better" writers and actresses. Literary hegemony results in stupidity and stupefaction not least among those who annoint themselves cultural creators (Freire, 1970; O'Neill, 1976, 1985). Having nothing to say is not an individual failure of intellect, craft or energy as much as a structural outcome of literary political economy – what I am here calling literary hegemony, the dominance of authorial activity by standards merely duplicating what is currently "hot" or "warm".

Many writers will turn this page and snicker, recognizing that I am trying to have my cake and eat it, too – writing a book about how books do not matter. Both are true; neither is true: Books have been eclipsed; books ought to be written precisely to reverse the momentum of their degradation. I do not succumb to self-inflation by pretending to be an exception to the general rule. I simply want to raise questions about whether writers, in their scribbling, can make a significant difference. We writers automatically assume that we matter; I agree that we do, but not in the heroic ways usually imagined by lonely auteurs awaiting their own discovery. More often than not, the world reproduces itself *through* us, imprinting our work with the subtle codes of acquiescence littering the public landscape today. For the most part, supposed literary difference (". . .best first novel since. . ."; ". . .pathbreaking treatise. . .") is nothing more than advertising copy. Literary hegemony happens when writers believe this about themselves.

Chapter 3

What Writers Write

The Exigencies of Writing for a Living

If the reading and writing public is absent, it is important to know where it has gone. The decline of discourse does not silence writers; they merely write things other than discourse – accessible, intelligent books standing at one remove from the reality they address while provoking dialogue. Today, writers contribute to popular culture and academic journals, the twin outlets for suppressed discourse at a time when one cannot simply live by one's wits alone. One needs security, a niche, even tenure. This is not to condemn people who write for television or academic journals; I am one of them, too. It is to understand the social implications of this shift of authorial activity from the public sphere to specialized institutions not particularly friendly to discourse as I have construed it. Most of the rest of this book will be about the impact of institutions on individuals; this does not deny that individuals bear some responsibility for what happens to them or that, over time, institutions can change. Thus, although I am pessimistic about the fate of public discourse today, optimism accompanies every literary act, this book included.

In recent years the life of the mind has become a business. To survive, writers must not only write well and often. They must also bend their work to the demands of the marketplace if they compose television and movie scripts, journalism, trade books or academic research. Although these markets are quite different in certain respects, writing for them shares common features. In particular, the writer who hopes to survive by writing popularly or academically must anticipate one's reception and then adjust one's work to suit the audience, mediated by editors accountable to publishers, producers and academic professional associations. On some level, every writer must do this; after all, the point of writing is to be read (Iser, 1978). Yet the exigencies of the popular and academic marketplaces exert special pressures on writers who write to live. In effect, one is hostage to those for whom one is writing, losing vital creative autonomy.

The exigencies of writing for a living are unmysterious in the late twentieth century. Almost everyone works for somebody else; virtually no one is self-employed anymore, the American mythology of entrepreneurialism notwithstanding (Bendix, 1974). Yet we must consider carefully the effect this has on writers who live to write. Although every writer must anticipate a certain reception, thus helping bringing it about, only writers constrained by market forces formulate their work in response to supply and demand. I am not simply suggesting that writers in a better world ought to be uniquely exempt from the capitalist market; I think everyone should be. I am only trying to consider some of the implications this holds for the struggling writer. In particular, the writer who seeks financial solvency must displace his or her work from the realm of general discourse into either popular culture, from scriptwriting and journalism to novels and biographies, or academic argot.

This chapter discusses that process of displacement; I describe it largely in terms of the literary opportunities it opens up and closes off for writers. I suggest some of the negative implications this holds for public reason – what I am calling discourse. My main thesis is that market forces compel writers to forego the composition of challenging public books addressing a non-specialist audience; instead they must write for the popular and academic markets (Madison, 1966). Although authors have made choices to write bestselling trade books or academic monographs for tiny audiences, these "choices" are largely dictated by the vocational opportunities available at the time (Reuter, 1980). There are few opportunities for writers outside of popular culture and academia.

Although I do not want to hedge my argument with too many qualifications at the outset, let me anticipate a likely response. It might be said that people who write popularly and academically can compose the large public work addressing an intelligent audience. Indeed, popularization might make way for the kind of broad-gauged "discourse" I am advocating here. It does happen. But it happens so rarely that much ink is spilled when a Bloom, Jacoby or Lasch makes it on the bestseller list. It is so unusual for a public thinker to be read that when it happens journalists and reviewers take notice. Such books surprise editors and publishers. Few would have guessed that a major house like Simon and Schuster could sell over a million hardback copies of a serious book without notes by a scholar best known for his translation of Plato's *Republic*. It utterly defied the market research on the book, or on any book like that. Although I reject entirely Bloom's ideological premises, at least he had the temerity to write the sort of book so glaringly absent from the American intellectual scene.

This already raises some methodological and theoretical questions, notably about how I can dismiss so much of popular culture while valorizing "public" books written in a public voice, as I call it. One might argue alternatively that popularity serves the purpose of authentic publicity – discourse and hence democracy. Yes, this might be true. After all, I reject obscurantism as inherently self-defeating, left no less than right. But popular culture today is structurally dominated by commercialization and commodification, the profit motive. In and of itself, this profit impulse depresses the level of authorial craft and intelligence, catering to the pedestrian level of taste today. This argument often draws the charge of elitism. But it is nothing more than a sociological observation about the institutional and intellectual dynamics of the culture industry. As Marcuse (1964) once remarked, one can learn a great deal about American culture by watching an hour of commercial television.

I could spend many pages demonstrating the symptoms of the decline of discourse, driven by the commercialization of literary production. This is less a matter of grammar, spelling and syntax than of diminished authorial imagination. A stroll through Waldenbooks, an hour spent watching television, a perusal of the front page and op-ed page of the newspaper, and an examination of academic journals will clinch my argument: writers write repetitively, prosaically, dully. Writers who cling to the illusion of their own heroic autonomy are in fact mostly conformists, but less because their nerve failed them than because literary political economy makes us all conform: we conform to the order of things (Foucault, 1970) spelled out by our editors, producers, chairpeople, colleagues, readers (who are themselves products of the prevailing culture industry). Writers' prose does not sparkle with insight or imagination. It is not electric with argument carefully framed and passionately delivered. Grammatical and cultural authoritarians (e.g., Hirsch, 1987) can always find examples of busted syntax and cultural illiteracy. I do not disagree with their account of the symptoms of dwindling public intelligence. However, I think the decline of discourse is most clearly manifested in the uninspired, quiescent writing dominating the literary scene today. Magazines, books, movies, television, newspapers, advertisements, academic work seem unrelievedly *all the same*. This months's *Esquire* is equivalent to next month's *Vanity Fair*; movies iterate themselves with roman numerals; Ludlum is LeCarre; ABC NBC CBS. Writers are *not* writing public writing, although many of them write popularly and productively. What is missing is *difference*, as well as discerning intelligence.

The reception of Bloom's best-selling *The Closing of the American Mind* (1987) has been fascinating and instructive from this point of view. Many liberals and radicals simply cannot get beyond his bitter attack on the New Left and his bizarre assault on 1960s youth culture, particularly rock music. It is clear that Bloom sells because his political conservatism strikes a sympathetic chord in Reagan's America. For their part, academics of all political stripes who decry Bloom because he wrote a serious book without the usual apparatus of scholarship characterize his omission of this apparatus as "authoritarian" – readers cannot check his sources. Although that is true, it is hardly the most important instance of authoritarianism in Bloom's argument. And jealous academics vent their rage against Bloom on grounds of shoddy – no, nonexistent – scholarship. That is why I love the Bloom book, if not Bloom himself.

The phenomenal success of his book can be explained only partly with reference to its conservative coda. Bloom sells partly because he is both readable and provocative; he can be grasped by people who have not studied Heidegger or the Frankfurt School. Obviously, some readers value a serious book not larded with scholastic argumentation. There is hardly anything else worth reading in the local commercial bookstore, perhaps even at the campus bookstore chains. In large measure, writers and publishers have been astonished by Bloom because they never imagined that one could successfully write his kind of book – a speculative essay unashamed of its personal and polemical nature.

The recent book by Russell Jacoby, *The Last Intellectuals: American Culture in the Age of Academe* (1987), is a study in contrasts as well as similarities. The books are often compared because they seem to be coming at the demise of intellectual culture from opposite political viewpoints. Where Bloom churlishly blames the New Left for corrupting the university and its classical liberal-arts curriculum, Jacoby takes members of the erstwhile New Left to task for joining the establishment university, thus losing their ability to engage publicly with large issues in nonobscurantist language. Indeed, my study here derives from Jacoby's observation about the academization of political criticism since the 1960s. His publisher, Basic Books, is not the same sort of commercial house as Simon and Schuster.

It publishes academic books with some popular appeal, yet it is restrained in its marketing campaigns. Thus, bookstores do not sport cardboard displays of Jacoby's book, as they do with the paperback version of Bloom. Jacoby is selling on the strength of his wide critical notice (much of which has been unfavorable).

Now Jacoby is doing much less well commercially partly because he is left where Bloom is right. The average well-heeled Sunday *New York Times Book Review* readers are not likely to care about the self-neutralization of the New Left. Indeed, they may laud it. These readers are more likely to worry about the closing American mind, especially where the hairy left is demonized. But there is another reason, too, why Jacoby has become prominent, if not well rewarded, for his intellectual labor. His book is a scholarly study in the fashion of the usual books published by commercial academic houses like Basic. He unravels his argument carefully through chapters packed with digressions, citations, notes; his endnotes are as important as his main text. There is no doubt that Jacoby's book makes more difficult reading in this sense alone. In addition, apart from some personal allusions in his brief introductory chapter, his book is much less auto-biographical than Bloom's, except for those of us who understand Jacoby's anger about the academization of American culture in terms of his own stalled academic career. Although Jacoby writes forcefully, he does not dazzle with the pyrotechnics employed by Bloom. Jacoby self-consciously avoids rhetorical flourishes, preferring indirection to a sledgehammer. This is not to deny that Bloom's book is well-written, whatever that might mean. Both books can be read by nearly anyone with a college education; the sentences make sense and follow from each other. Yet Jacoby's is the denser, more academic text.

Although I applaud Bloom's book but not Bloom, I greatly admire Jacoby but wonder whether his book is really an example of the kind of "public" book he advocates. Let me be clear. I think the *The Last Intellectuals* is an urgent, important book; I wish I had written it. Yet it is not the sort of large public book written by Bloom if only in the sense that it relies so heavily on the scholarly apparatus; it is not the sort of book recommended by Jacoby as an antidote to the decline of discourse. This might seem puzzling, even downright wrong, given his book's wide critical notice. People who have never heard of Jacoby, let alone read his other important scholarly books, talk about him now as if he were just discovered. Yet where millions buy Bloom even if they do not really read him, only thousands purchase Jacoby (and yet perhaps more of them work their way through his text because it is more difficult to reduce his argument to a slogan). Jacoby's book is phenomenal in part because it inserts itself into a dialogue with Bloom; at least, both writers talk about the crisis of American culture in terms of university life. This is not to say that Jacoby is responding to Bloom or the other way around but simply that people who run publishing and commission and write book reviews consider the two books together. Although Jacoby is benefiting little from the remarkable sales of Bloom, he gains from Bloom the patina of having written a broadly public book.

I am not laying any indictment at Jacoby's door. He takes pains in his book not to exempt himself from his condemnation of his New Left comrades who have tortuously jargonized themselves. And I do not believe that *The Last Intellectuals* in a better world could not qualify as a public book; it is elegantly straightforward and should be comprehensible to any reasonably well-prepared person. But Jacoby's academic presentation destines his book to have a different readership from that of Bloom. When all is said and done, *The Last Intellectuals* is an academic work by and for academics, editors and book-reviewers.

Bloom and Jacoby are exceptional figures. Until Bloom, publishers never believed that they could get rich publishing "difficult", erudite books on portentous themes. I have talked with many editors since Bloom and, to a person, they believe that Bloom (or another Bloom) will not repeat himself. Editors talk about this by saying that "the wave has crested" with respect to the broad-gauged cultural criticism of Bloom, Jacoby and Lasch. Again, market planners are in the saddle. In fact, Bloom's book will not make it easier for the rest of us to get published; it may only mean that his next book will find an aggressive commercial publisher. Already the publishing industry is writing off his success as unusual; they fail to learn from Bloom the possibility of public discourse. I am unconvinced that the Bloom book was anything more than accident owed largely to a retrenching political and moral climate. Bloom's success reflects high-brow taste in Reagan's America. I do not read too much into his unlikely example. But it is telling that publishers can be so certain that we will not see another Bloom, that his wave has crested. Of course, in thinking that, they ensure it for they are the gatekeepers who matter (Bystryn, 1978). People can scribble away at their manuscripts aimed at a broad, intelligent readership without finding a publisher willing to gamble. Publishers are no more willing after Bloom than they were before Bloom.

I have asked a number of editors at major commercial houses whether they would have published Bloom had his manuscript come across their desks. More than a few responded in the negative.

The publishing world does not like the Bloom book, and not only because they did not think of it first or oppose his politics. It defies their conventional wisdom about what will sell. Recondite political philosophers who read Greek are supposed to stick to the academic journals and university presses; they have no business publishing big books with commercial houses. Although I cannot trade on insider gossip, I would love to know more about the difficulties Bloom had in convincing Simon and Schuster to publish his book. Is it really true that Saul Bellow, his friend from Chicago, had to intervene? This makes for more than salacious gossip; it tells us about the exigencies of writing for a living. While Bloom is securely employed at the University of Chicago, the aspiring writer who wants to duplicate Bloom's good fortune ought not hold out much hope for it. So far, Bloom is the only Bloom.

In my discussion of Bloom I have neglected the issue of talent or merit (Lewis, 1975). Many people (especially Platonists like Bloom himself) would argue that Bloom profited because Bloom deserved to profit. His clarity of vision, not the vagaries of the book market or the impact of his publisher's advertising campaign, has put his name in lights. I do not deny that Bloom can turn a phrase. Yet that is somehow beside the point. What makes books move is the publisher's investment in advertising coupled with the extent to which the book can garner critical notice – not necessarily good reviews, just attention. In Bloom's case, Simon and Schuster realized that Bloom was "speaking" to all sorts of nonacademic readers and thus they put significant money behind the book in their marketing campaign. In my campus bookstore, the cardboard display of Bloom in paperback could as well contain books by Robert Ludlum. No one would accuse Ludlum of being a savant, simply a savvy fiction writer.

And critical notice largely depends on the prestige of the publisher, the topical nature of the book's theme and the energy devoted by the publisher to seeing that reviewers review it. That some books are reviewed but others are not does not reflect their superior merit; that some books receive favorable reviews does not mean they are better. Merit is quite beside the point; all sorts of junk gets published and quality writing rejected. There are no Archimedean standards for evaluating literary work. And, in any case, market success is dictated by market forces. In a certain sense, Bloom is the least responsible for the phenomenal success of his book. Advertising makes the book; he only writes it.

The issue here is not quality. The exigencies of making a living bear down heavily on the writer; although one might hope that good writing will be noticed and rewarded, that is not an iron law. What matters to a writer's livelihood is what matters to the market – the demands of the reading public as mediated, both reflected and reproduced, by editors and publishers (e.g., Reynolds, 1980). Although we say that the consumer is sovereign, that is a sociological question; by now, we realize that taste is shaped (Ewen, 1976). In any case, merit is a nonissue where we are talking about earning a living from one's writing. Indeed, I would go further and dispute any essentialist notion of merit as a discernible thing in itself possessed by some people but not others; that is one of the unfortunate legacies of the Platonism dearly loved by Bloom and his mentor Leo Strauss. Although I retain the distinctions between good and bad, just and unjust, beautiful and ugly, such distinctions must be argued, constructed; they do not simply present themselves to the discerning eye.

This is where literary political economy does its best work. It helps us relate the economic exigencies of earning a literary living to the commercialization of both taste and aesthetic judgment (Compaine, 1978; Horowitz, 1986). We do not studiously consider the worth of cultural artifacts but derive our judgments of them from their market and status locations. In fast capitalism (Agger, 1989a), all things are texts narrating their own value, from Guess jeans to Porsche cars. People do not just wear or drive these cultural objects but read and write them. Their exchange value is equivalent to their semiotic value (what Baudrillard (1981) calls their sign value), determined by the busy advertising scribes who turn things into texts. The Platonist response to the semiotization of exchange value, translating price into taste, is inadequate simply because it substitutes one arbitrary set of standards – Plato's timeless Ideas – for another, market worth. Why should a capitalized Truth disclose itself to philosophical view but not to the rabble? Elitism is no antidote to literary commodification, although it is a suggestive one at a time when cultural standards appear to have slipped. That is precisely the reading given to Bloom's book. He is read (correctly) to blame our civic malaise on relaxed academic standards, which he traces to the alleged Nietzscheanization of the New Left. Cultural elites jump on the Platonist bandwagon where the marketplace itself is widely perceived to have failed us as an arbiter of aesthetic judgment.

This is all the more reason for the left to develop an approach to culture that is neither relativist nor Platonist. As Breines (1985) indicated, the left's right is wrong. My discussion of postmodernity suggests a retrieval of Enlightenment rationalism within a materialist framework. Cultural evaluation turns on the issue of whether expression serves the purpose of building community, soliciting dialogue, dissent, correction – discourse. But I am getting ahead of myself. Let me return to a discussion of the writer's life today especially as it is conditioned by literary political economy.

It is harder than ever to earn a living from one's writing (Hardin, 1975; Holt, 1979; Powell, 1979; Brady and Fredette, 1981; Kingston and Cole, 1981). Although freelancing was never a route to riches, the freelancer today writes for a highly competitive market in which innovation is discouraged by publishers and editors. The most telling blow to freelancing is the oversupply of writers who, rationally or not, set out to earn a living simply through their freelance work. The abundance of writers allows publishers to be highly selective, enforcing whatever standards they choose. And it produces vocational discontinuity for writers uncertain about where their next assignment, hence paycheck, is coming from. Of course, why the glut of writers willing to risk poverty and lunacy in the open marketplace of institutionally unprotected artisans does not dry up is an interesting question in its own right. One answer, to be explored in my next chapter, is that writing is an outlet for intelligent people in unintelligent times. Another answer has to do generally with the rise of mass media and particularly with the glamorization of writers as celebrities in this post-Watergate era. Although Woodward and Bernstein were regularly employed journalists, not freelancers, the example of their success suggests to young writers that they, too, can hit it big by following the right lead at the right time. It matters little that Woodward and Bernstein were journalists, not freelancers, especially now that Woodward has made a fortune writing trade books on the Supreme Court, John Belushi's death and the CIA. They epitomize gung-ho entrepreneurial writing tantalizing to the Yuppie literary generation.

In the 1940s and 1950s members of the New York social-democratic intellectual circle like Irving Howe (1982) sought to cushion themselves by taking jobs in colleges and universities. They exchanged economic insecurity for the bureaucratized routine of the academic office, a reasonable thing to do given the falling fortunes of freelancers. The academization of intellectual life is now matched in the 1980s by the popularization of certain cultural vocations in media and entertainment as avenues for literary accomplishment. While certain talented screenwriters manage to convey some of their political message even in Hollywoodized form, and a few intrepid journalists do important muckraking, the exigencies of making a living have domesticated rebellious literary spirits; working for Harvard, the *Times* or Hollywood tames the sensibility of the person of letters, politics, social action. This is virtually unavoidable.

Whether or not intellectuals "deserve" a living is not the main question here. I would say that they are no more or less deserving than anyone else. At issue is the way in which intellectual life is displaced into spheres of cultural expression governed by the economic and academic marketplaces. Discourse seems to erode precisely to the extent to which literary expression is displaced into popular culture and academia, sublimated into writing for money and for tenure. Discourse is not necessarily beyond the cash nexus; one can imagine a world in which writers, no less than carpenters and lawyers, are waged because they do valued and socially necessary work. But as our world is structured today, the wage nexus erodes autonomy, creativity, critical insight (Kostelanetz, 1974). The more writing is subject to the marketplaces of entertainment and academia, the less it is able to think. After all, discourse is good because it helps form a community of competent, convivial speakers, ever a useful archetype of a free society from Plato through Marx to Habermas. At the very least, a discursive society helps counter the hegemony of expertise propping corporations and the state. A discursively competent citizenry threatens the status quo.

In my last chapter I return to a discussion of the future postmodern intellectual. In a sense, that is a discussion not of specialized mental workers but of citizens (Wexler, 1991), people who speak and write in a public voice. Intellectuality ought to be democratized and hence imploded as a distinctive social category. Any discussion of intellectual life nearly always assumes the elite status of intellectuals, people paid to do "nothing" but think and write. Yet Gramsci's (1971) notion of the "organic intellectual" suggests a standard of publicity, and hence of a reconstructed polity, open to all. The key that opens intellectual life to everyone is discourse, the speech and text of reason.

Popular Culture I: Trade Books

Let me turn descriptively to the families of cultural commodities produced by intellectuals' displaced labor. In the next chapter, I will evaluate the ways these displaced literary activities inauthentically gratify writers content to live from paycheck to paycheck. As with everything in a commodifying society, alienation seems to be a matter of degree (even if it is not, at root); for many of us acculturated in genteel circumstances like the university to be writers and thinkers, it seems better to work for the local newspaper than in an automobile showroom or corporate law firm. This is largely a deception for capitalism alienates everyone equally, if in superficially different ways.

Popular culture is a term coined by sociologists to contrast with the "high" culture of privileged social strata – network television rather than live symphony performances, for example (Grossberg, 1986). As such, the term paints with a very broad brush. Here, I want to narrow the term sufficiently to talk about displaced literary activities in which writers engage, from writing trade books to working in the electronic media. I will then consider the literary practices of workaday academics as authorial displacements. I do not believe that these displaced literary activities are inherently degrading. Simply because something is "popular" does not make it bad; people who sleep in water beds, watch television and douse their salads with Thousand Island dressing while devouring *People* magazine are no less worthy than people who read *The New Yorker* after dining out in a chic Manhattan bistro. The issue is not simply taste but how our activities are effectively dictated by the compulsive logic of commodification governing everything in this society, including reading and writing.

Indeed, one of my aims is to suggest a version of intellectuality that does not displace its busy literariness into commodified popular culture or the deadening academic world. Popularity is only a sign of disrepute where the popular is synonymous with unconsciousness. What many social critics do not recognize today is that academic writing is equally unconscious, and a good deal less significant (Agger, 1989b). In fact, most people watch television, go to movies and read the national magazines. A new concept and practice of the popular would not only preserve what little genuine intellectuality exists but would generalize it across the public sphere. The popular can be rescued from its own enslavement to commodification and stupefaction in a world in which people, including writers, own and control the primary products of their production.

This is not to say simply that writers should expropriate the apparatuses of cultural production, although some immediate problems of intellectual eclipse would surely be resolved that way. Although I as a Marxist envisage economic solutions to a host of glaring social problems including the decline of discourse, it is not enough to wrap my diagnosis in the usual formulaic terms – work-ers' control, here. Slogans are just that: their provocative vitality is betrayed by their unthinking repetition. The rate of discourse's decline is accelerated today by the extent to which writers and read-ers repeat the tried-and-true. This is virtually inescapable where the popular marketplace is governed by a commercial logic of repetition and where the academic marketplace is ruled by an intellectual norm of replication, concretized in the notorious referee system.

Thus, it is not enough simply to repeat Marxist solutions to the commercialization, commodification and corporate control of trade and academic publishing, even though those solutions are exactly correct. Nothing can change the distortion of discourse without liberating it from the logics of capital and discipline; authorial self-management is necessary but insufficient. Yet I want to understand a socialist and feminist version of the intellectual life in terms that combine economic and literary concerns; agendas are worth only as much as the paper on which they are written. We must deeply understand what is happening to writers like ourselves as a way of moving toward a fuller theory of the totality within which we can locate a large variety of oppressions, occlusions, distortions. After all, the decline of discourse is not only important to the privileged few who write and read books in leisure, a tiny fraction of the world's many. It is a general problem where discourse is a circuit of power and thus a possible medium of liberation. The decline of discourse is matched by its concentration. That is the symptomatic problem from which this book begins (Bureau of Competition, 1978; Powell, 1980).

In a sense, then, I want to broaden the notion of writing, even of cultural production. I am not talking only about valorized bourgeois cultural products like books and movies but about the whole host of ways in which people express themselves, extending themselves beyond their own isolation. A discursive polity would be char-acterized by a thoroughgoing transvaluation of the cultural and the textual: these would no longer be elite notions designating a restricted set of artifacts (e.g., books) but generic categories of public speech, including dance, music, poetry, conversation, speech-making and pedagogy as well as more traditional textual activities. The Eurocentrism of cultural production, restricting culture to high culture, would be undercut in a discursive society in which everyone had access to, and competence in, the public voice. By writing, then, I refer not only to the word and image production preva-lent today in the commodified literary world but also, potentially, to nontraditional literary venues either beyond exchange value or denigrated as marginal. Indeed, the redefinition of public speech in a discursive polity is a crucial feature of radical social change, both initiating and reflecting progress toward a new polity.

I begin with a discussion of earning a living as a writer. Larger, more portentous discussions employing the theoretical abstractions of Marxism and postmodernism must be reserved for later. Although we cannot understand the plight of writers without also understanding the structure of discourse's inherence in political economy, it is important to begin with lived experience. I am talking to and about readers and writers, members of the somewhat educated public – the people who write for and read *Time* and *Atlantic Monthly*. The decline of discourse diminishes the opportunities for writers to make a living simply writing. For the market to drive writing is especially troubling where market standards replace qualitative judgments on the part of editors and even writers themselves. When I talk about the displacement of discourse I suggest, at least by implication, a standard of nondisplaced, authentic writing somehow autonomously conducted beyond the constraints of the market and the academy. I do not suggest a golden age of wordsmiths, when the public forum was open to all sorts of self-employed, self-directing auteurs. Such an age never existed; writing at best was an elite activity. And, where today the market and academy constrain literary endeavor, yesterday authorial autonomy was reduced by the church. If one wrote errantly, one could lose much more than one's job.

Writers who write books for the marketplace compose what are called trade books (Reuter, 1980; Coser, Kadushin and Powell, 1982, pp. 59-61; Ueland, 1987). I am especially, but not entirely, interested in nonfiction work here. Trade books are published by commercial houses and sold in the big bookstore chains. They are reviewed and ranked in weekly newspaper review sections as well as in popular magazines. Trade publishing is entirely governed by a market logic; publishers publish books they expect will sell enough copies for them to make a profit. For the most part, authors of trade books are not academics, although occasionally a person like Todd Gitlin, employed as a sociologist at Berkeley, will break across the invisible line separating trade and academic books (Gitlin, 1987). In Gitlin's case, it is fascinating what his publisher, Bantam, has done to turn a book with the apparatus of academic scholarship – notes – into a genuine trade book. Instead of removing his notes altogether, they expunge the superscript numbers signifying notes from the body of the text and instead allow his endnotes to stand at the back of the book. Instead of providing numbers indicating the notes in the body of the text, the publisher and author signify the pieces of prose to which the notes in the back are to be connected. Although it is almost impossible to read the notes this way, this choice was made to make the book appear to be a trade, not an academic, book – even though the compulsively inquisitive reader still has access to notes of a sort.

The precise definition of a trade book is unclear: In general, one could say it is a book that trades popularly (Whiteside, 1981; Crider, 1982). The category itself serves to alert publishers, editors and marketing managers to a book's location in the literary marketplace. A trade book might best be defined by what it is not: specialized, academic, difficult. "Trade" is a signifier connoting a work's profit potential and thus provoking a certain editorial and advertising posture by the publishing house (including those university presses that increasingly publish trade books in order to make money). Designating a book a "trade" book makes dollar signs flash in publishers' eyes (e.g., Jensen, 1984).

Trade books belong to popular culture simply because they are meant to be popular; their value lies in their appeal to a book-buying public. Although occasionally an author, like Gitlin, can write intelligent books for a mass public, trade publishing is a degraded form of literary work. Trade authors have devilishly difficult relations with acquiring editors. They must convince editors that their work has broad market appeal – that it will sell. Similarly, editors must make judgments about marketability before the book has been published. Although this process of market estimation is relatively unambiguous in the business world, it is nonetheless fraught with difficulties. Sometimes it is simply impossible to ensure a market for one's product especially if the product radically departs from the standard form. Market research joins forces with advertising and sales where it attempts to predict consumer preferences in order to shape them (e.g., Maryles, 1978). Advertising can largely, if not entirely, determine sales, especially where advertising campaigns are heavily informed by the expertise of market research and demographic analysis.

Only those living in the never-never land of the ivory tower would suppose that literature is less susceptible to marketing than soap or cars. Discourse displaced from the public sphere into the marketplace is no different from other commodified products of human artifice. Yet the commercialization of discourse in trade books is different from the commercialization of other consumer durables in the single sense that the mimetic logic of the marketplace cannot be applied as directly to books as to soap. We all know that "new and improved" soap is still the same old soap. Markets are made on the basis of advertising promising innovation only at the margin. But books inherently differ from one another. A biography of Lincoln is not Gore Vidal's latest novel; nor is Vidal's latest novel equivalent to that of Graham Greene. Although people like Vidal and Greene move books simply on the basis of their names, which have become institutions by now, lesser writers who write what are called "midlist" books compete for market share on the basis of quite unpredictable criteria of judgment.

Although experienced editors may make good guesses about market, based on ample experience in the book world, there is no substitute for empirical evidence. The surprise bestseller comes out of nowhere; Allan Bloom's recent book is a good example. It is important to notice here that the trade market is governed by a logic of duplication effectively constraining the authorial choices available to writers when they compose their works. Publishers and editors suspect that books must emulate the successful ones before them; as with soap, innovation is more a matter of words than substance. As a result, they make publishing decisions largely out of obeisance to a marketplace that has already rewarded certain publishing decisions in the past and disappointed others. An inherent conservatism – that of literary duplication – takes over.

One of the main problems of an affirmative postmodernism is that it utterly ignores literary political economy, here the way literary market determines literary product. Instead, postmodern cultural theories trace cultural shifts to various ideational and intellectual shifts in the *Zeitgeist*, themselves influenced by the conscious choices of individual writers, editors, publishers. Postmodernism on this level is idealism, ignoring the role of the market in literary outcomes. The postmodern theory of culture vests constitutive authority in intellectuals, media mavens, collective consciousness. Although individuals can matter, literary political economy addresses the large structures that play out over the heads of individuals, conditioning the literary "choices" available to them. A genuinely dialectical approach to cultural studies would address both the shifting forces and forms of literary political economy and the transformative opportunities open to individual writers and editors.

Although this may not matter much where soap is concerned, discourse suffers where it is standardized. And it is not at all clear that publishers, even in their own terms, act rationally where they enforce a market-driven logic of imitation; while popular books may be much alike, the ample evidence of publishing surprises seems to argue against too much attention to the market. This is an old story: By pandering to a preformed conception of what the market will bear, publishers, editors and authors further reduce the scope of literary imagination. The sociologist Robert Merton (1957) called this a self-fulfilling prophecy; yesterday's publishing successes dictate what is published tomorrow. Of course, with the help of advertising, difference can be successfully conjured out of sameness. Last year's blockbuster can be transmogrified into next year's, given the right advance work and promotion, even movie tie-ins. But only so much of this will really sell books. At some level, imitation fails to reproduce popular culture successfully; a modicum (if not much) of innovation is demanded by a restless public hungry for new versions of titillation.

The drab sameness of American popular culture, especially where trade books are concerned, certainly reflects the commercialization of publishing. Most bestsellers resemble each other; they share tone, level, style, worldview. What innovation there is tends to be conjured out of minute differences. Writers are said by industry insiders to have different "takes" on the world; in fact, their takes are much the same because both the market and publishers are homogeneous. Two things are important here: first, writers are constrained by the market and thus public discourse declines. That is the larger theme of this book. But a second theme deserves notice, too. Editors and publishers are responsible for domesticating discourse in response to marketplace norms allegedly blocking innovation and thus reducing literary risk. Where authors face the exigencies of making a living from what they write, editors control access to those very livelihoods. It is to them that we must look as we delve further into trade publishing's contribution to popular culture (Madison, 1974; Powell, 1985).

Here, a postmodern theory of culture becomes dialectical, balancing structural and individual factors. Editors clearly function as important gatekeepers; they select, as well as reject, literary projects. The publishing, television, film, journalism, advertising and academic worlds are not regulated by a *deus ex machina*. The cultural logic of late capitalism (Jameson, 1984b) is not seamless; people and their projects fall through the cracks. Although commodified writing is never simply "writing degree zero" (Barthes, 1970), neither is it entirely "one-dimensional" (Marcuse, 1964). Of course, Marcuse himself in *One-Dimensional Man* (1964, pp. 203-257) makes it clear that, through ideology-critique and political education, people could seize "the chance of the alternatives" and begin to lift the fog of one-dimensional occlusion. The Frankfurt thesis of the eclipse of reason (Horkheimer, 1974) is too often read one-dimensionally; as Marxists, they remained hopeful, if not optimistic, to the end.

Editors themselves are wage workers. They exist within complex bureaucratic hierarchies dominated by the usual management cadres beholden to boards of directors and, indirectly, stockholders. Editors are not publishers; publishers call the shots and editors do their bidding. Editors have to exist because publishers are generally unknowledgeable about book markets and do not have the time to involve themselves in editorial appraisals. Editors in trade houses are responsible for soliciting and evaluating manuscripts for the house; the most successful editors are those who bring in the largest amount of money from sales of the books they acquire. As such, then, trade editors are gatekeepers; they let a few manuscripts in and keep most out. Information provided by publishers indicates that very little unsolicited work sees the light of day; editors and their assistants are the ones who initially reject and select book projects.

Depending on their influence within the house, editors then take the few promising manuscripts submitted by authors or, indirectly, by literary agents to a higher level of decision-making within the house. They must convince other editors, the editor-in-chief, marketing staff and frequently the publisher that a particular title will make money for the house or will otherwise add lustre to the house's list. Editors as gatekeepers must sort through the great mass of unpublishable junk and half-baked ideas to find the few professionally crafted proposals and manuscripts from which they select books to publish. Writers' temptation to demonize editors reflects the real difficulty of passing successfully through the gatekeepers; in a flooded manuscript market, editors more often than not bear bad news. No matter how elegantly couched in politesse, rejections are still rejections. And very few active writers avoid receiving many more rejections than acceptances from editors.

As crucial players in the political economy of publishing, editors are both superordinates and subordinates (Robinson and Olszewski, 1978; Coser, Kadushin and Powell, 1982). They have a large measure of control over what is published. Only rarely can writers convince editors to rethink their initial negative appraisals; even more rarely can writers appeal over editors' heads. Yet it is important to understand the structurally contradictory role of editorial manuscript evaluators. Although editors determine what gets published – better, what is not published – they are directly accountable to executive editors, marketing managers, chief executive officers, even boards of directors for their publishing decisions. Every trade editor knows that most of his or her books must make money for the house; the "good" first novel or midlist book not destined to recoup its investment must be balanced against a track-record of regular profitability.

Successful editors contribute to the overall profits of their publishing houses. Although this does not mean that "quality" necessarily suffers, editors lose their jobs where they indulge their own literary or political inclinations; "good" books by definition are unpopular. Thus, editors unwittingly reproduce a peculiar notion of the popular by their quite reasonable desire to keep their jobs. The equation of popularity with profitability is virtually unavoidable in a business civilization. Therefore, the "best" editors are those who constrain their temptation to publish the "best" books.

The publishing world is full of stories about notorious editors – those who take risks, pamper their authors and fight indefatigably for literary quality (Sheehan, 1952; Commins, 1978). Such editors exist. But they are increasingly notable as publishing becomes a business in which success is measured strictly by profit. An editor for a commercial academic house reminded me that his house "is in business to make a profit", a tellingly inelegant way for him to couch his negative decision on my submitted manuscript. I appreciated his candor just as I lamented the sad fact that books are no less a commodity than Swiss cheese. Indeed, the editor probably thought he was enhancing his charisma when he made a clean breast of things: surely I, as a worldly Marxist author, could recognize the structural constraints imposed on him by the profit system, even applauding his openness in face of this.

My story is not simply about what happens to me and my friends; we have been rejected (and published) more times than we can remember. Notable here is not only that profitability drives publishing, scarcely news to any reader or writer today. It is also interesting how editors act to ensure that their books will turn a profit and thus keep them employed and how writers themselves create the market by anticipating it. We are all looking over our shoulders at the cost-accountants who run the culture industry. In the particular case I just cited, the editor told me that my book was written "with a point of view", patent code for Marxism and critical theory. Of course, the editor was correct; the book was ideologically oriented. The editor assumed, probably correctly, that the book's political tone would put off readers unsympathetic to my sense of the world. He even listed a few publishers in Britain where, he said, my ideological line is more commonplace. Noteworthy is not simply that Marxism does not sell but that editors implicitly reproduce the marginality of the unpopular – here, Marxism of one kind or another – in their reasonable obedience to the logic of capital. Who am I, or anyone, to say that this particular editor should imperil his job by courageously publishing such a book? He has a right to a living, too. Prevailing notions of the popular disqualify the unpopular by definition; only a madperson would fail to screen out the unpopular except as an occasional indulgence.

In this case, the editor assured me that publishers exist (across the Atlantic) who publish Marxist work. Actually, my book was only very thinly Marxist in the ordinary sense of the word. Yet even the patina of leftism is too much for most academic readers and their students. The editor knew this, and behaved accordingly. "Responsible" editors usually soften the blow by saying some kind words about one's work (in this case, the book was called "interesting") and then by recommending more likely publishing opportunities. Occasionally, some of these suggestions bear fruit; at least, they ease the burden of rejection, giving the writer hope and allowing the declining editor to exit gracefully.

I am talking here about a commercial publisher who publishes books for academic specialists and potentially for their students. That is properly a topic for Chapter 6, on academic writing. Most so-called trade editors do not personalize their rejections, typically form letters sent out not by editors but by their assistants, who rifle through the huge stack of "unsolicited" writing that arrives "over the transom" (Menaker, 1981). Simply to save the processing costs of this virtually hopeless way of doing business some major trade houses no longer even consider "unagented" or unsolicited work, proposals and manuscripts submitted in the hope that an editor will give them a hearing. Increasingly, writers must hire agents to help them navigate through the gatekeeping process, thus relinquishing at least 10 per cent of their eventual royalties from sales of their work. In fact, most new writers cannot even secure an agent, thus finding themselves nearly closed out of the publishing world.

Where genteel norms of the academy may inform scholarly publishing (e.g., university presses), or at least seem to do so, trade publishing is unvarnished by a commitment to the life of the mind. Trade editors do not frequently indulge the temperament or values of writers who resist their own commodification. More than editors in university presses, editors in commercial publishing, particularly mass-market "trade" publishing, are directly accountable to their bosses, boards of directors, stockholders, presidents for each project they sign. As such, authors are simply sources of "copy", the peculiar labor power of writers, and not valued participants in the publishing venture. Of course, publishers and editors vehemently deny this, stressing the fragile and important relations between house and author supposedly claiming the time of editors. But, in fact, authors are merely fungible units of potential profit for the company as a whole. Like everyone else in advanced capitalism, writers become commodities because they produce commodities.

Popular Culture II:
The Electronic Media, Journalism and Advertising

Writers who do not write books often compose scripts, news, advertising – the fundaments of popular culture. In this section, I want to consider writers who write for the electronic media as well as for newspapers and magazines. All are important venues of literary production, certainly rivaling trade publishing in their impact on the collective consciousness. Indeed, for the cagey young writer who wants to make a dent on the national, even world, psyche, a career in television or movies suggests itself (Brady and Lee, 1988; Kaminsky, 1988). Compared to cinema blockbusters, even popular books are composed in a virtually private language. For every reader of an obscure academic tome there may be a million viewers of the television and film treatments churned out by enterprising wordsmiths in New York, Los Angeles and virtually everywhere in between (Bluestone, 1957; Harmetz, 1979; Holt, 1979; Blum, 1980; Dahlin, 1980; Bronfeld, 1981; Whiteside, 1981; Kirkpatrick, 1982; Chancellor, 1983; Katz, 1984; Morrissette, 1985; Blacker, 1986; Laskin, 1986; Weaver and Wilhoit, 1986; Clark, 1987; Armer, 1988; Brady and Lee, 1988; Demers and Nichols, 1987; Kaminsky, 1988).

More than ever, aspiring writers do not write books at all but compose scripts, ads and news copy. One might view this in terms of the individual choices people make who calculate their potential payoffs from different kinds of work (Engebretson and Gillespie, 1973; Meredith, 1974; Balkin, 1977; Appelbaum and Evans, 1978). I prefer to view the displacement of writing as a response to an overwhelming structural shift in the nature of the culture industry: increasingly, books do not exist and people neither read nor write them. Of course, this characterization of a bookless world ignores the ocean of trade books currently available in every Safeway check-out line as well as chain bookstore. We swim in a world of books and yet books increasingly lose their autonomy as old-fashioned meditations that acknowledge, even celebrate, their nonidentity to the world as their vital literary resource. Trade books are intellectual fast-food, popcorn puffed quickly and then degraded once cool.

Thus, in recasting themselves as screenwriters and journalists, writers are not simply answering to an inner calling; they are responding to hard-and-fast changes in the social and economic organization of literary life (Curwen, 1986; Horowitz, 1986). If books do not exist in the traditional sense, defying conventional wisdom to replace them with other versions of the world, then writers who seem to "choose" other displaced discourses of popular culture are not really choosing at all: they are merely doing what they know best, writing, in the absence of traditional outlets for public discourse. No matter how glamorized, television, movies and journalism are often the only available outlets for writers who want to write. After all, it is virtually impossible to break into fiction, poetry, even academia and hope to make a living. The writers who survive by writing mass-market trade books are few and far between.

The displacement of discourse into popular culture, particularly entertainment and news, repeats a time-worn pattern. Sometimes this displacement involves the direct transformation of books into scripts (Bluestone, 1957; Morrissette, 1985). Few writers in capitalist countries like the United States have ever been able to make a living from their writing. It is simply romanticism to portray a golden age when freelancers blossomed like wild flowers on the public landscape. It has always been tough to survive off one's literary product. It is even tougher today because discourse has been sublimated into nontextual activities governed by a market logic. Yet the marginalization of writers only continues a long historical trend. Business civilization has never had much use for the auteur, preferring writers to find gainful employment as teachers, journalists, even academics. Where discourse in capitalist societies has never fully flowered, its decline in recent years has been precipitated by its further commodification. I am not indulging in simplistic era-analysis ("age of reason", "culture of narcissism", etc.) but merely pointing to an accelerating trend: things are getting worse for writers because they have fewer alternatives than ever to corporate employment, whether in popular culture or academia.

This is less because people make the wrong choices (journalism school rather than a doctorate in English or a career in fiction) or fail at their craft than because these "choices" are simply disappearing. Any materialist analysis of writers' lives must begin and end with the exigencies of survival; although authorial temperament matters, and although people surely compound bad situations by making thoughtless vocational choices, the more relevant factor here is the availability of gainful employment for writers. Although, as I just said, writers were not substantially better off in the 1930s or 1950s, they are even worse off today where they must face the *increasing* corporate control of words. These massive social and economic forces virtually compel writers to become employees – of book conglomerates, television networks, newspaper chains, advertising agencies, bureaucratic universities. As such, they lose intellectual and artistic independence as well as the freedom from organizational constraint. It is tempting to view the decline of discourse in terms of diminishing authorial craft, to be remedied by hard work, writers' workshops, even literary self-help books. Although craft has degraded, it is not because individual writers are slothful but because the commodification of discourse has made the issue of craft ultimately irrelevant (Sloane, 1983; Burns and Sugnet, 1981). Heroic literary gestures no matter how well-conceived, must prove themselves on the ledger sheet.

Since the 1960s, young people concerned with social injustice as well as personal fulfillment have been confronted with dismal options. Do they simply join the professions and other dominant institutions and try to do their best within them (the German New Leftist Rudi Dutschke's "long march through the institutions") or do they sever their ties with the surrounding society and work from outside? By the late 1980s, this is not a meaningful choice where it is extraordinarily difficult to make a decent living, especially where writing is involved. Young people clamor to sign on with newspapers, television studios and radio stations where, by so doing, they seek to preserve at least a modicum of their personal integrity – and perhaps even "make a difference". Few survive by living on the fringe, sustained by the heroic belief in their special literary merit.

One can view authorial employment in a number of ways. Where for some it signifies survival and thus deliverance from the dire uncertainties of freelancing, for others it requires huge sacrifices of autonomy and creativity to the strictures of editors, managers and chairpeople. It is tempting to accept these trade-offs as the necessary accompaniments of overall social progress; for starving writers suddenly catapulted into relative job security, whether at MGM or MIT, there is some truth to this. But for writers unable to find corporate employment in popular culture or academe, or to stick with it, the displacement of discourse exacts a grievous price. It is always easy to rationalize away one's misfortune from the inside. One might say – "At least . . . I have tenure/a contract/a regular income", the phrase "at least" covering over a multitude of sins. For alienated wage workers it is often crucially necessary to reduce one's pain by rationalizing it away as "necessary", "unavoidable". But just because there are few extant alternatives to writers' corporate employment does not mean that corporate employment is good or necessary. I am not writing a book depicting a literary utopia. And yet it is worth evaluating carefully the sacrifices writers make when they displace their literary effort from the realm of discourse into entertainment and academia. The abundant self-help books for screenwriters invariably portray this literary world as a bed of roses for capable writers who have mastered the essential technical skills (e.g., Blacker, 1986; Armer, 1988).

In the case of entertainment, writers are doubly diminished. First, they are hired hands, responsive to program directors and others who enjoy the proverbial "artistic control" (Brady and Lee, 1988). Being waged automatically reduces freedom, especially crucial for writers, where it requires subordination to a superordinate who controls one's paycheck. Second, when one foregoes the penurious uncertainties of freelancing in exchange for the relative security of employment at NBC, one must accommodate to the vagaries of popular taste (Bronfeld, 1981; Chancellor, 1983; Weaver and Wilhoit, 1986). Simply put, one must write what people "want" to watch or read. Of course, these "wants" are infinitely manipulable by advertising and accessible to market research. And certain programming creates taste as much as reflects it. Yet, on balance, writers who write for the entertainment industry neither ignore nor elevate popular taste (Blum, 1980).

In the case of journalism, writers write the "news", that is, what editors, publishers, advertisers and readers deem newsworthy (Clark, 1987). Electronic journalism is somewhat devalued in comparison to print journalism by serious types who would really rather write fiction or political theory. They recognize that the short "takes" or "bites" comprising the advertisement-punctuated news broadcast are scarcely sufficient to describe the topic of the report thinly, let alone investigate it in any depth. Although journalists seem to answer to a higher calling than entertainment scribes in the sense that they obey the canons of value-freedom and a *New York Times*-like integrity (". . . all the news that is fit to print . . ."), they are no less wage workers, subordinated to organizational imperatives dictated by circulation size and thus advertising revenue (Johnstone, Slawski and Bowman, 1976; Demers and Nichols, 1987).

Although crusading journalists can occasionally make a splash in this post-Watergate era, the Woodward-Bernsteins are few and far between. Even a cursory knowledge of their excavation of Watergate misdeeds indicates how lucky they were to persuade Ben Bradlee at the *The Washington Post* to pursue the unlikely threads of perfidy surrounding the break-in at Democratic National Headquarters. And for every Woodward-Bernstein success story (after all, they had an estimable role in toppling Nixon), there are scores of journalists who dog the local crime, sports and wedding beats, never to do a story of any importance. The "news" in a positivist culture scarcely has room for speculative construction of any kind (Hallin, 1985; Rachlin, 1988). News is merely description, even if post-positivists recognize that there is no mere description; authorial artifice is suppressed in the interest of objectivity (Schiller, 1981). And, if editors, publishers and advertisers did not dictate a news agenda, the postured objectivity of mere reporting would circumscribe the literariness of news writing.

As in entertainment, "creative people" sometimes find their niche in journalism. Even prisoners and street people occasionally compose beautiful poetry and write important prose. The larger problem is that newspeople are compelled by organizational and professional constraints to limit their literary imagination to the exigencies of the "beat". So-called creative people can find a niche almost anywhere, but that does not mean that the work they do is creative or trans-formative. Journalism, like entertainment, is a crucial component of capitalism's cultural apparatus; it exists to structure consciousness away from the bigger picture and toward the abstract particulars arrayed together into the nightly news and front page (Curran, 1979; Gitlin, 1979; Kellner, 1981).

The argument that writers in entertainment and journalism "matter" simply because they reach a huge audience depends on one's sense of political and intellectual priorities. Are advertisements for fast-food chains or cars more significant than academic tomes read by 150 specialist readers because they reach audiences 100,000 times as large? One needs a theory of truth, of significance, before we can decide that screenwriting has more public substance than philosophy or poetry. The numbers, in themselves, do not tell the story especially where popularity may serve consumption and social control. Although politically and intellectually authentic work speaks louder when read by a significant public, readership alone – "ratings" – decides nothing. Indeed, market penetration might well be a sign of unconsciousness where media themselves have contributed to the decline of public intelligence.

The defense of authorial involvement in popular culture – trade books, entertainment, news and advertising – on grounds of potential "impact" is disingenuous, especially in this Yuppie era. Few young writers even care about the displacement of their discourse; indeed, they relish fast-track careers in which they can "have it all" – the experience of creativity along with ample "benefit packages". Young people flock to the professions, including the "creative" ones, in the utter absence of social and political conscience, even consciousness. They are willing to have their writing degraded into fungible commodities under sway of editorial and market imperatives; the cultural archetype of the starving but righteous artist has virtually no currency today. Yet we must not make the opposite mistake and conclude that the moral obliviousness of the post-Vietnam generation is "the problem", either. Discourse is being displaced from authorial craft into popular culture and academia not because writers want it (people can be led to want nearly anything) but because structures of consciousness, culture and economy evolve in a way mandating the decline of discourse.

A sufficiently elevated citizenry would challenge the complexly interrelated power structures enchaining all of us to an unnecessarily truncated version of necessity. It would also refuse the encoded imperatives of consumption and adjustment emitted as metatexts in what I (Agger, 1989a) have called fast capitalism. The displacement of discourse into the moronized languages of popular culture and academia serves both the purposes of cultural reproduction, diverting thought from critique, and of capital reproduction. Advertising is perhaps the most blatant example of degraded, displaced discourse, oriented to nothing more than the creation of false needs, in Marcuse's (1964) terms.

Where entertainment and news deliver a narrow version of the possible and thus placate wounded souls with various diversions from the bigger picture, advertising depends on writers directly to sell products by creating wants (Ewen, 1974, 1976; D'Amico, 1978; Kline and Leiss, 1978; Leiss, 1978; Williamson, 1978). Advertising writers mold text and design into concatenated wholes tantalizing would-be consumers to buy what they did not know they needed in the first place. Although advertising serves the purpose of product differentiation, recommending Pepsi over Coke, or mineral water over both of them, it also crucially implants texts into people's lives directly as the recommendation to live the very lives screened for them (Leiss, 1976.) One learns from ads that owning an Armani suit or Benetton sweater is more than simple acquisition; it is lifestyle itself where the potential customers for these things presently lead humdrum lives in which little of excitement takes place. Armani and Benetton become texts through the careful craft of advertising; they recommend themselves as narrative, not simply as nifty apparel. Obviously, everyone in a business civilization realizes that certain clothes must be worn to white-collar jobs – now, suits for both women and men. But not everyone recognizes the possibility of desublimation, of liberation, within the glassed-in confines of the skyscraper illuminated by distressing light and organized at an unrelaxing pace. Advertising makes texts of Armani suits accompanying the worker to work as a release from the various degradations and drabness experienced in most jobs the world over. And the sale of Armani suits reaps huge profits for the people who produce them as well as diverts the Armanied customers from what is really wrong with their work and leisure lives (Wernick, 1983).

In the past, various movies and stories portrayed "admen" as the most degraded of writers, churning out unambiguously deceptive copy in harness to their clients' instrumental aims. This has begun to change. Advertising writers now appear in a much more sympathetic light; they are young, Yuppie overachievers who refuse to sacrifice creativity for a more regimented professional job (Kirkpatrick, 1982; Katz, 1984; Laskin, 1986). Although they want money, they are somehow less ruthless than the red-suspendered tycoons who hustle on Wall Street. They were communication and art majors in college, eschewing business administration as the choice of nerds and neurotics. They work on the "creative side" of big business, indeed doing the essential work of making products into texts more lifestylized than consumer durable. The issue is not whether intelligent, inspired writers are found in advertising but that advertising is one of the only available venues for "creative" work. They do not write books – fiction, philosophy, poetry – but compose suits, sweaters, airlines, car rental agencies. As such, they degrade themselves and the reading public still further; they also abet fast capitalism (Wernick, 1983).

Recent advertising campaigns reflect this transformation of products into texts, into veritable lifestyles. The Benson and Hedges campaign, showing Yuppie women brandishing cigarettes in various states of repose, is a good example. Another example is the rock video-like campaign for Michelob beer ("The night belongs to Michelob"). Interestingly, in this campaign, a young urban professional in stylish work clothes with longish hair is shown desublimating in a bar after work while downing a Michelob. It is very likely that this is supposed to be a person who works on the "creative side," perhaps in advertising itself, not in the uptight mortgage banking industry. Or note the recent campaign for Oldsmobiles (of all things!) in which hip music and flashy camera-work support the claim that their new models today are "not your father's Oldsmobile." Finally, Pepsi in recent years has assaulted Coke with advertisements decorated by youthful celebrities (e.g., Michael Jackson, Michael J. Fox, "Magic" Johnson) who signify a certain high-tone pizzazz, thus crafting Pepsi into a text of seductive youthfulness.

Academic Discipline as Literary Practice

Finally, if auteurs do not desire to join the hurlyburly of newswriting, scriptwriting and advertising, they can always enter academia. Although academic posts are not ample, some writers do find their niches in the university. Just saying this invites surprise: we rarely think of academics outside of English departments as writers; researchers, perhaps, or scientists – even scholars; but academic writing as literary practice clearly belongs to a discussion of the decline of discourse (Brodkey, 1987). Scientists narrate when they compose their research reports, as do philosophers when they essay (Knorr-Cetina, 1981; Agger, 1989b). It is a prejudice of positivists that scholarly writing somehow defies or transcends literariness; instead they model writing on mute representation, simply disclosing facts existing outside the writer's purview. In this sense, academic writing is thought to resemble journalism; my own discipline, sociology, is sometimes derided as "slow journalism", emphasizing the connection.

In any case, whatever the literary status of academic writing, it is clear that some writers gravitate to the university. Better, writing takes place in academic disciplines, even if it is research reportage modeled on fact-finding journalism. Although typical scholarly writing may be inelegant by literary standards, a lot of it is going on. The libraries are filled with learned journals reporting the latest research. Near them, the stacks of major university libraries are bursting with the thousands of books written by academic specialists. Others have examined the exodus of writers from bohemia and freelancing into the corporate university, a trend accelerated by the influx of baby-boomers into American colleges and universities in the 1960s, precipitating the rapid expansion of the professoriate (Zukin, 1982;

Harvey, 1985a, 1985b; Kowinski, 1985). In fact, academization has become so commonplace that we tend to forget that academics are merely writers, if also teachers and colleagues.

Here, it is important to catalog academic work alongside employment in the entertainment industries as a viable alternative to literary lives on the margins. The fact remains that many would-be writers find their ways into the university and stay there. Whether academization accelerates the falling rate of discourse is a question I take up later. I am less interested in pointing the finger of blame than in understanding the structural conditions under which writers are forced to write writing. Whether writing is "good" or not – stylish, elegant, plebian – is somewhat beside the point. Just as writing for entertainment requires one to sacrifice intellectual autonomy to the imperatives of the marketplace, so academic writing submits thought to the rigors of what is tellingly called discipline. Smart people are to be found both in Hollywood and at Harvard. I am more concerned here with the diminution of intelligence exacted by the increasingly corporate and bureaucratic context of literary activity (Faigley and Miller, 1982; Wells, 1986).

It is nearly irrelevant that creative, critical individuals work in universities or in entertainment. Intelligence never succumbs completely to its institutional negation; one finds it in factories and daycare centers as well as classrooms and television stations. That is precisely the hope embodied in any literary act. But the weight of institutions is born heavily by the mere individual. Much of the bravado heard about the autonomous academic life is an exaggeration. In the university, specialized writing has largely replaced public discourse. This is not, as some pedants would have it, simply because professors write cumbersome, leaden prose but because literary craft in the university setting has been subordinated to the requirements of disciplinary advancement, scientific replication, picayune scholarship. No matter how lucid, the specialist's treatise on Chaucer will be just that – narrow inquiry destined for other Chaucer specialists. No matter how resonant with social and political implications, the mathematical study of income inequality quickly becomes a fetishistic exercise in research methodology and statistical innovation. Academic discipline in its way contributes to the decline of discourse; academic writing is a peculiarly monologic form of discourse, written for the few narrow experts inhabiting the same minute corner of their field. I will return to a discussion of academia shortly. In the next chapter I turn to the seeming frenzy of literary activity today.

Chapter 4

Everyone Writes, No One Reads

Writing in an Age of Instantaneity

In the preceding chapter, I examined the economic imperatives behind the falling rate and quality of discourse. Simply put, writers to write must make massive compromises with the profit and tenure imperatives of their employment in order to survive. I discussed the displacement of discourse from an authentic realm of public speech and literary community to another realm in which writing becomes a good to be bought and sold. Of special concern to me was how this affected writers' sensibilities. In this chapter, I consider whether writing today is actually written "for" anyone else, a public readership. Then in Chapters 5 and 6, I address the displacement of discourse in larger institutional terms. It is impossible to discuss the displacement and decline of popular and academic writing without also considering the implications this has for reading as a literary practice. Indeed, a whole variety of developments in various European theories of interpretation, from poststructuralism to neoMarxist aesthetic theory, make the writer-reader relationship central to critical analysis (Fish, 1980; Culler, 1982; Ryan, 1982; Eagleton, 1983; Fischer, 1985; Berman, 1988).

It has been said recently (Jacoby, 1987) that the age of the publicist is dead; Jacoby talks about "last intellectuals", people able to write for a wide public comprised of educated and self-educated laypeople. Although I agree with much of the tenor of his analysis, we also need to consider the implications of missing publicists for reading and for readers. My thesis is that readers capable of making sense of broadly literate writing disappear not only because writers do not write "for" them but also because readers become writers themselves. Today, many people seem to be writing *instead of* reading; at least, one can quickly form that impression by spending time in Hollywood, in the offices of large New York trade publishers or in the halls of academe. The literary world is abuzz with busy scribes submitting their proposals, manuscripts, treatments, scripts and stories for editorial consideration. Beacon Press, a Boston publishing house known for a high-quality list, receives about 4,000 manuscripts or proposals a year and publishes perhaps one or two of these; the rest of its list is made up of translations, commissioned books and "agented" books (Curtis, 1989).

There are clearly more manuscripts, proposals, scripts and articles than can reasonably be published. Space becomes a desired scarce resource, an object of contest among these busy scribes. After all, their livelihoods depend on finding editors, sponsors, studios willing to publish or produce them. (Three periodicals advise writers how to secure space: *Literary Market Place*, *The Writer* and *Writer's Digest*.) Who is not working on his or her "book", especially those who have temporarily retired from the corporate or political battlefields in order to have time and space to breathe? In this context, writing is busy entrepreneurial activity, as much for the assistant professor at a large state university as for the would-be Woodward and Bernstein slaving away on the dog-show beat in upstate New York.

The difficulty writers have in getting published only increases people's penchants to write. In an age of instantaneity, "getting" published or produced is equivalent to the fame attained by movie stars and sports figures. Although this might signal the healthy narcissism of people with tales to tell in an age of mass media, I submit that it tells a quite different story. As I will explore below, people who become busy writers have little time to read, a necessary ancillary activity. Any experienced writer recognizes his or her dependence on textuality as a literary resource; by reading and rereading inspiring sources, one learns to find one's own voice, perhaps in counterposition, even opposition. But busy writers have little time to read, driven to find their way into print or onto celluloid. Of course, all such generalizations are defied by exceptional facts. Some writers bury themselves in books and journals just as movie directors haunt theaters to watch what others of their ilk are doing. Yet I am talking here about tendencies, not absolutes. Writing has become access to the instantaneity sought by many in the whirling cultural panorama of the electronic age; achieving publication is a full-time job in its own right, consuming both the passion and hours required to read slowly and carefully as one's own expressive resource.

Similarly, writers have less time to *rewrite*, crafting and then revising their arguments carefully. Writing, like industrial production, is a source of income and thus it is regimented and routinized. But the best prose does not come off an assembly-line, nor can writers afford not to read and reread. Postmodern culture speeds up the rate of reception, perception and discourse under sway of literary commodification. Some theorists of the postmodern like Barthes (1970) and Derrida (1976) justify this in terms of the pleasure and playfulness of the text, although neither renounces reading. Indeed, Derrida and Foucault read voluminously and they compose their own philosophies largely in counterpoint to other texts. In this sense, contradictorily, their postmodernisms slow fast capitalism just as they accelerate the rate and carelessness of writing. This contradiction allows one to develop a postmodern social theory either as affirmative ideology or as critical theory, as I suggested in my opening chapter.

The sheer explosion of books is symptomatic evidence (Gilroy, 1980; U.S. Department of Commerce, 1980; Curwen, 1986). Even for narrow academic specialists, the volume of books and articles in one's discipline necessarily occasions compromises and selective omission. Most academics read only what they "do", not what disciplinary specialists across the corridor are reading and writing. There are so many books, so little time to read them, especially when one must spend the lion's share of one's productive time writing. If, as Hemingway said, the first million words are worthless, then one must invest wholly in one's literary endeavor. Otherwise, improvement will be slow or nonexistent. The writer's life is doubly difficult today. Writers must wend their way through the thickets of the literary world, hoping against hope to locate a friendly editor or producer; as well, they must perfect their craft (Sloane, 1983; Burns and Sugnet, 1981; Dillard, 1982). It is a truism that only a few academics publish much of the current research; most American university and college teachers spend their time in teaching, leaving research to the brave and driven (Caplow and McGee, 1958; Crane, 1965; Blackburn, Behymer and Hall, 1966; Lightfield, 1971; Clemente, 1973; Lewis, 1975). Whether or not one chalks this up to laziness, writers must learn how to write and then discipline their imagination with the particular literary resources at hand. As anyone knows who writes for a living, this is far easier said than done. The writer's life is never idle nor unoccupied by the endless tasks of drafting and revision that inevitably await the successful author.

A person with my critical perspective might well regard this explosion of writing as a positive thing: people heretofore disempowered before the printed word are becoming wordsmiths themselves, taking back language as a moment of a general political empowering. But writing is as much product as process; sheer writing, what Barthes (1970) called "writing degree zero" or *ecriture*, is inherently nondialogical. Instead the Barthesian writer, the quintessence of the postmodern literary actor, indulges in "the pleasure of the text", refusing the public responsibility for writing as if one might be understood (Barthes, 1974). Derrida takes this even further in works like *Glas* (1987), which were surely written to be written, not exactly read. The problem with this postmodernist approach to writing is not simply obscurantism or playful self-indulgence, although these are factors, too. Postmodern textuality is characterized by a dogged inattention to the public, hence political, dimension of writing; writing not meant to be read, considered, engaged fails to fulfill its own transformative purpose. Instead, as sheer self-expression, it does not express the passion to change the world – to raise consciousness, criticize, educate (Callinicos, 1985; Eagleton, 1985).

This is especially ironic where Barthes and Derrida take pains to read others carefully as their own literary resources but neglect the "readability" (Barthes) of their own work. In this, their postmodernisms elevate criticism to the level of creative writing. Although I agree with Derrida that the distinction between criticism and writing is blurred, he fails to anticipate that his own work will be the topic of future rewritings. His prose is the apotheosis of discourse in spite of his seeming valorization of discursive textuality.

I will postpone a decisive discussion of an alternative textual politics until my final chapter, where I take up the possibilities, however dim, of literary resistance. Here I want to confront the reality of writing in an age of readerlessness; what *can* writing signify when few read and thus few write to be read? That is the problem in a nutshell: literary standards of public discourse decline when writers intend no audience and thus discourage dialogical reciprocation. This is not simply a matter of overly turgid or technical prose, although these are undoubtedly symptoms. It is rather an attitude, an approach, to discourse failing to hear writing's own echo in a way informing a genuinely public text. Writing meant to be read and understood differs from writing not anticipating its reception. It does not matter that the writer means to block reception, interpretation, dialogue; indeed, readers sometimes accord self-monologizing writing the respect given to religious treatises, exhuming profundity from thoughtlessness. And writers are often oblivious to their writing's lack of a public dimension; they may never have considered technical or entertainment writing as public discourse and hence political action.

I want to approach the readerlessness of writing in terms of temporality, although surely other things are involved, too. Writing lacking attention to its potential or possible audience is crafted differently from writing anticipating its own completion by readers who become writers. Writing done too quickly, neglecting revision signaling careful cogitation and reflexivity, degrades as soon as it is published. This is initially a political-economic problem: Books must move quickly, like all commodities in the marketplace. They are only as good as their exchange value, which falls when books lose their seeming timeliness. In this context, fast writing is not only an economic necessity; it quickly becomes a mode of authorial tempera-ment, the writer rushing to replace degraded significance with new expressions, more *ecriture*, whether or not the market demands it. Alan Sica (1988, pp. 249-262) in his defense of hermeneutics suggests that much academic writing is done too hastily, at least judging from the meager returns paid to readers of academic journals and monographs. Certainly, the economic pressures bearing down on writers to earn a living form a context within which writers must write hastily. On the other hand, the routine of fast writing becomes self-reproducing, beyond any original economic necessity. Writing as postmodern *ecriture* is a compulsion, nothing less.

The decline of discourse hastens its further decline. One thing leads to another: the trade bestseller is imitated in the author's next version; the screenplay becomes Screenplay II, III and IV. But the doyens of postmodern literary culture still try to find aesthetic authenticity, if not genius, in those who participate in this duplicative "creative" process. For example, see the *Esquire* (February 1989) story about Sylvester Stallone – the filmic Rocky and Rambo. The academic journal article is rewritten a dozen times and published in a dozen journals, thus padding one's curriculum vitae. The decline of dis-course has an objective context, the economic fungibility of writing; it develops a subjective context in writers oblivious to the public requirements of their literary craft. Although some first drafts endure simply because they are so vitally composed, the very requirement of revision – re-vision – adds a public dimension to writing, anti-cipating readerly intervention and thus rewriting. Although revision can itself become a fetish, virtually all successful writers recognize that their first drafts are no deeper than the paper on which they repose, awaiting the working over epitomizing literary imagination.

Obviously, trade authors, journalists, copywriters and academics do revise their work; much of this is enforced by editors, outside readers, even market research. But there is a hastiness to *ecriture* that neglects writing's crafted publicity, making a mockery of writing's own responsibility for democratizing dialogue chances, in Habermas' (1984, 1987b) terms. Good writing, carefully crafted to envision the problems and obscurities experienced by untutored yet interested readers, provokes writing in turn. Comfortable with its own authorial signature, its distinctive voice, it solicits its own dialectical completion in dialogue; good writing does not fear critical evaluation but urgently requires it, learning from it its hidden *sens* and, in any case, requiring a community without which it is lonely scribbling (Hymes, 1974; Fish, 1980).

Writers are no less alone than the rest of humanity; modernity is characterized by privatization, and the postmodern is a noisy world in which few listen. Where everyone has a story to tell, the cacophony of authoriality is not stifled by writers who love a story as much as the next person. Those who write public, challenging prose read voraciously; they learn from the voices of their peers and share literary, hence political, community with them. Even in academia, the ultimate combat zone for literary ego, people at the top of their game and thus self-confident enough to go public feel completed by other writers who are also their readers (Brodkey, 1987). Such writers write not for the many, the undifferentiated mass captured by demographic analysis of audiences, but rather for particular readers – perhaps their loved ones, best friends, literary rivals, trusted editors. If a mere five or ten people like my work, then it is worth going public; their criticisms are appreciated and their support taken for granted (Agger, 1989b, pp. 43-49). They constitute my most significant audience, my real and ideal listeners. If my work makes it past them without crumpling under the pressure, I suspect that my more public ordeal will be bearable. Or, at least, I will have pleased the few without whom it is hopeless to persevere.

This suggests another angle to the problem (Iser, 1974, 1978). We cannot trust many people to read us faithfully and then be honest about their reaction. We doubt the authenticity of their responses: either they snow us with unqualified praise or they jealously protect their own fiefs by demolishing our versions with unforbidding scorn. Few read carefully and *thus* few write carefully; at least, writers do not test their versions with honest friends. The more writers can anticipate the trusty criticism of attentive friends, the more they will address a wider public. After all, one's friends, from the vantage of readerly interest, can suggest some of the problems one's work will occasion with readers generally.

This does not mean that authentic writing will try to please or placate everybody (Adorno, 1973a). Frequently, writers who are most adept at anticipating criticism do so not to meet those imagined criticisms but to strengthen their arguments beforehand. That one offends does not mean that one should avoid offending. The domestication of writing through what amounts to market research is not equivalent to writing in a readerly way, anticipating that *one's work will have impact*. The impact does not have to be gratifying, nor must writing kowtow. It is enough that writing anticipate its reception even if that reception will be unsparing or dogmatic. Critics need not be friends, although one needs friends to anticipate criticism and so adapt one's writing to its reception, any reception. In the best of all possible worlds, one's literary work would make friends, build community, uproot injustices (Agger, 1989c). But this is unlikely where few read carefully (because few write carefully) and where so much writing is purposely manipulative and mystifying. A good deal of writing must be demystifying, laying bare the practised falsehoods of what Marx called ideology.

For writing to anticipate its reception opens it to a public, hence a political, dimension unavailable to sheer *ecriture*. Very little writing today is *ecriture* in Barthes' and Derrida's senses, reveling in the pleasure of the word unbidden to an intersubjective standard of comprehensibility. Most hasty, uncrafted writing is designed to earn points in the entertainment or academic marketplaces. Readers are considered only formulaically, as consumers with preformed tastes, not as interrogative reader-writers in their own right. The trade potboiler, like the esoteric academic journal article, avoids literary reflexivity under pressure to enter the marketplace in an unmediated way (Whiteside, 1981; Crider, 1982). Words are not dialectical echoes of themselves but simply the fungible stuff of the literary commodity, whether traded for profit or tenure. In the age of instantaneity, crafted writing goes the way of studied reading, and prepares the way for it in turn. Literary commodities are produced and consumed; thus, *ecriture* is reserved for the few Derrideans in English departments and then cultivated as a topic of endless interpretive "deconstruction".

The postmodern is a myth in this sense. The busy scribes of the day do not trade on elevated postmodern metatheories but hammer out the accelerated literary work compelled by advanced capitalism. Postmodernism, embracing the self-infinitizing labor of *ecriture*, sheer writing, is just another ideology under which people dismiss utopia and refuse the communicative and strategic means of achieving it (Raulet, 1984). Postmodernism is a theory of cultural discontinuity harking back to Nietzsche and refusing Marx and all other transformative "interventions" or "metanarratives" as hubris, impossible in the face of a directionless, meaningless history (Foster, 1984). So-called postmodern writing is the name writing gives to itself when it either sinks deep into the exchange relations of popular and academic writing or eschews the cash nexus in search of absolute textuality, whatever that might mean.

The Obsolescence of Reading in a Postmodern Age

Acknowledging that postmodernism is yet another fad, the political issue here is that, by writing depthless trash, writers destine readers to become dumber – literally, voiceless. Where everyone has a story to tell/sell, whether a potboiler or pretentious "writing degree zero", reading is eclipsed. It is customary to blame the decline of evaluative standards on television and music culture; writers now clamor to be rock critics, an absurd sublimation of literary desire on the face of it. *Rolling Stone* self-consciously shifts gears now that baby-boomers have mortgages, children and white-collar jobs. It recycles rock culture in a softened, depoliticized form; so-called New Music replaces the *Sturm und Drang* of the 'sixties. I am not trying to reinvent the 'sixties as a significant period of political and cultural opposition; for every political rebel attempting to capture the voice of a restive generation, there were hundreds of stoned music lovers. Most of those who attended Woodstock now work in downtown jobs; some of the few among them who theorize themselves culturally embrace postmodernism as the *Zeitgeist* of the moment.

I am not dignifying what passes for literary work today as more than it is; self-inflation is still inflation. Postmodernism as a serious or semi-serious cultural movement is restricted to a few high-tone magazines, galleries, musical genres, architectural movements (Gitlin, 1988a). Many Yuppies watch *The Cosby Show*, saw *Platoon* and, perhaps, read Anne Beattie. The occasional bicoastal culture critic works Barthes or Foucault into his or her repertoires. Those who write, and thus degrade the act of reading, celebrate fast capitalism. The name of the game has not changed since Marx. Labor congeals in commodities that both bear surplus value and deepen unconsciousness. Books are sold and thus read as things today.

Textual politics in a postmodern age amount to little more than the commodification of discourse, a perennial tendency of human labor under capitalism (Lukacs, 1971; Marx, n.d., pp. 76-87).

The political problem here is that discourse itself is the only medium through which consciousness, language and public life can be elevated and educated. Its commodification into journalism, advertising, movie scripts and academic articles cheapens thought and blunts critique. This is a critical problem for those who oppose postmodern cynicism about the possibility of social change. Although American Marxism and feminism rarely communicate effectively about the possibility of utopia, tending to become thoughtless canons themselves, this tendency is not inevitable; the modern is not fated to curve around and swallow its own tail – the so-called postmodern. The myth of the postmodern, history collapsing upon its own spoiled hopes, is no less mythic than the myth of postindustrial society, the galvanizing imagery of the 1950s. Capitalism no more ends utopian imagination than it ends human labor; the plenitude of the future is certainly not exhausted by the miserable present, no matter how much we dress it up in the profundities of a cultural theory to end all cultural theories – postmodernism.

It must not be forgotten that the original modernists (Schoenberg, Beckett, Adorno) were sharply critical of capitalism. They anticipated modernization in a dialectical way: the rapid advances of technology promise to liberate as well as enslave humanity. The cynicism of postmodernism, packaged as world-weary sophistication, is occasioned by the collapse of imagination, not its actualization in a decent social order (Kroker and Cook, 1986). People who dress in black and use their drugs of choice are not culture heroes but ciphers of the *Zeitgeist*; they reflect the darkness and despair of the disappointed modern. New York City is ground zero for postmodern writing only because the publishing and entertainment industries cluster there, side by side with the homeless victims of modernity.

The obsolescence of reading should not be taken to mean that people do not consume writing; the consumption of literary commodities proceeds apace. People plug into expensive home video systems, buy cable television packages, subscribe to newspapers and popular magazines, purchase trade books and acquire academic monographs and journals in record numbers. The rate of textuality rises as the rate of discourse falls. This is not an argument against the commodification of writing per se but only an observation about the seemingly inverse relationship between the displacement of discourse and its decline. Nor do I suggest a mystical notion of hermeneutic interpretation according to which reading signals deep devotion and allows one access to a literary divinity (e.g., Gadamer, 1975). By reading I use the homely term for the considered perusal of literary sources, stretching from scholarship to fiction.

Today people litter their living rooms with magazines, videos, paperbacks, even academic reprints but they seldom pause to really read them. Where Jacoby (1987) suggests that there are very few publicists in an age of academe, it seems to me that reading, too, has declined both as art and discipline. Few of my students pause before textuality in the old-fashioned sense. A casual inspection of books from our university library turns up many *symptoms* of reading, allowing me to reconstruct what is going wrong. Books are frequently larded with underlinings, passages marked by those ubiquitous yellow felt pens, suggesting what is essential to the text in question. Reading truncates writing into these pithy passages scoured for their relevance to the upcoming examination or plundered for their topical significance in dissertation work. It could be worse. At least, the books are being cracked. Yet the utter disrespect for the next reader is compounded by the interpretive destruction (deconstruction?) of complexly interrelated texts, simplified into a few passages highlighted against the implicitly extraneous marginal text (Agger, 1989b).

Reading accelerates in the age of instantaneity. Interpretive pragmatism holds sway where discourse does not present itself in the irreducibly complex pastiches of sense and sentience. Writing ought to be what Levi-Strauss (1966) called *bricolage*, the intertextual assemblage of meaning into the whole cloth of a provocatively reasoned argument. By the same token, reading must match this authorial *bricolage* with engagement fully as constitutive as the original composition itself. Derridean poststructuralism suggests that reading is writing; it is such an active intervention into the text that its difference from writing fades. Better, writing needs to be rewritten to be read.

These are dialectical phenomena; the decline of discourse causes reading skills to decline, too. By the same token, where people do not read intelligently, where one cannot assume their studious engagement with the argument, one's writing must follow suit. Who is to say which came first, lazy writing or lazy reading? It scarcely matters for it is equally difficult to elevate reading and writing. No one knows where to start, except to prescribe more "good" writing and reading. Cultural conservatives deny the dialectical relationship between reading and writing and instead call for more factual knowledge about history and deeper immersion in the so-called classics. Although few would gainsay those recommendations in themselves, it is preposterous to believe that dulled college students, raised on television, music, videos and fan magazines, will benefit from an intravenous injection of western civilization. Knowledge cannot be maintained.

In my own university, our new "core" curriculum, boasting a two-semester World Civilization course, force feeds an encyclopedic history to unwitting undergraduates. The central book is a 1000 page compendium of facts, names and dates from Mesopotamia to the present; fully 30 per cent of the final grade depends on the memorization of these minutia. The rest of the course is to be taken up with original reading in a variety of classic sources; the influence of the left in my university has been sufficiently large so that these "great" books are not only the white-male classics but include minority and marginal voices. Still, it is difficult to imagine this course doing more than assuaging the guilt of faculty about what has happened to depress the level of general discourse.

I teach a large section of our Introductory Sociology course every year and I encounter a cross-section of our lower-division students, exactly the same people who will sit through our World Civilization course. These students can barely read the banalized ninth grade-level textbook, a dozen or so pages a week; they strain to relate my lectures to what they have fathomed from the book. They will not do well with the World Civilization curriculum not only because some of them have poor work habits. They will struggle with the "great" ideas because they have been underexposed to any ideas, having failed to master even basic interpretive and compositional skills.

It is generationally insensitive to suppose that the decline of reading is restricted to the television cohort. Adults are as much victims as their children; indeed, the inability to read and thus write is passed down. Pointing the figure of blame solves nothing, either; we are all in this together. Something much larger, and thus harder to see, is going on. The commodification of discourse ensures its instant fungibility; thus, text has become another product next to the toothpaste and toiletries. Its value endures no longer than the time it takes to flip through magazines and paperbacks while standing at the checkout counter or reposing on the beach. If there are generational differences, they are trivial. A freeze frame of a family at leisure might reveal the children plugged into Walkmen and the parents reading trashy novels, each largely inured to their own possibilities as authors, creators, thus free citizens.

It is unsurprising that most can read those texts but not more difficult ones. Even "serious" literature degenerates into mere cultural description; the flash success of hip young scribes like Bret Easton Ellis and Jay McInerney shows the way. They describe, and thus valorize, a sexed-out, coked-up subculture of urban affluence. Where *Entertainment Tonight* is the emblematic television show of the time, *People* the essential magazine and *USA Today* the modal newspaper, *Bright Lights, Big City* is the paradigmatic novel.

McInerney (1989) in *Esquire* takes on his many critics. He argues that the older establishment WASP critics who reject him, Ellis and Janowitz as representatives of a trivial literary youth movement are just protecting their own generation's cultural turf. Although correct in this, McInerney should realize that one cannot criticize one's critics without inviting further scorn. The critique of criticism, unlike the negation of the negation, does not turn into a new positive; it is read merely as churlish whining, even if it is not. It is self-interested. Actually, McInerney's *Esquire* article is more insightful than his fiction. In any event, books like *Bright Lights, Big City* (McInerney) and *Less Than Zero* (Ellis) offer no redemptive public voice; they are merely ethnographically precise evocations of the dystopian postmodern sensibility of the post-baby boom generation. If there were ever a truly Nietzschean generation, it is the one they write about: upper-middle class urban Americans in their 20s.

These "works" demand little from the reader; they can be perused casually, tossed aside and then reengaged later with little missed. *They are all narrativeless*, requiring little attention to rhetorical structure. Modern magazines are plundered the same way people rifle through racks of clothes at the mall; the articles are essentially interchangeable, requiring little attention from readers too dazed by the surrounding world to keep things straight. If one article or sweater does not fit, it can be discarded. If one medium does not provide gratification, one can switch to another one. This is not an argument for or against popular culture as such. I am interested in how we constitute the popular. An idealist theory of culture would stress the role of taste and authorial intention in determining this realm of easy leisure; a more materialist theory would emphasize the relevance of cultural products as commodities, as I do here. Popular entertainment is insubstantial precisely to engage people in endless, restless consumption. *People* magazine is not a monthly, requiring close attention to the long, convoluted articles, but a weekly. College textbooks are not stupid in themselves but they breed stupidity, larding the page with pictures, simple-minded charts, marginal material emphasizing "key" points and boldfaced definitions.

Whatever the excuse for doing so, writing popularly reproduces popular readers, that is, readers unable to read strongly, even to become writers themselves. The villain is not television per se but the televisionization of text – the way in which we learn to watch books, not read them. Popular culture reproduces itself *through* writers and readers. Although the popular need not be a region of intellectual degradation, today the realm of the popular is governed by a spectacular, televisionized model of communication derived from our reception of electronic media (Debord, 1983; Grossberg, 1986).

Reading is, strictly speaking, obsolescent where books are watched like movies and television. To view a book, like a television show, distances the watcher/reader from interpretive constitution. Whatever one may think about the ultimate politics of deconstruction, Derrida powerfully argues that reading, reception and critique are authorial accomplishments in their own right (Berman, 1988). *Both* the writer and reader must *make sense*, ideally in a democratic way provoking other versions of their topic. The observation that television disempowers is usually taken to mean either that viewers cannot respond to the screen or that viewing otherwise takes children away from more active play. Although both of these are true, televisionization is dulling where it prevents the watcher/reader from engaging in constitutional activity. Who, after watching television or a movie, writes a script and mails it in?

It is credible that the occasional *New Yorker* reader might well be moved to pen a reply to a controversial or provocative piece or even to compose a full-blown article. No matter that the acceptance rate for unsolicited, unagented work is low. At least the "average" *New Yorker* reader has the skills and inclination to turn reading into writing itself. Moreover, whatever their intellectual content, *New Yorker* articles are written not to be sloppily or quickly digested. The endless columns of unadorned print command attention. *New Yorker* articles are not excessively complex and yet, in their heady denseness, they eclipse the daily prose of newspapers and the weekly prose of magazines as examples of challenging public writing.

The New Yorker is only one, and probably not the best, example of "discourse." There are numerous other little and little-little magazines that publish intelligent, intelligible and, most important, provocative prose (e.g., *The Kenyon Review, Salmagundi, Dissent*). The people who read these magazines also write for them. Or, more important, those who write for them also read them. That is the real issue: writers who do not read create readers who do not write. It is important to recognize that the problem is dialectical; it is not merely a matter of "communication", of writing and reading clearly. Clarity sometimes obscures, especially where it diminishes the interpretive work required to raise reading to the level of writing (Agger, 1989a).

My point is not simply to recommend *The New Yorker* and *Atlantic Monthly* over *People* and even *Time*; what people read is symptomatic of their abilities to read in a creatively dialogical way such that their reading becomes writing itself – rewriting. Most people watch, but do not read books as textuality is increasingly dispersed into the built and figural environment. Few books remain between covers; and those that have covers are often not books in their own right, requiring little more attention than television or movies. In a world in which few read, or can read, few write, or can write. To say that the problem is dialectical does not solve it; we must still read and write in new ways.

It is tempting to believe that different books, written with crystalline clarity and intended for the inquisitive public, will elevate the standards of reading (and thus of writing). It is also tempting to believe that better secondary and post-secondary education will solve the problem – more "great books" courses, stricter requirements, additional homework. All of these may be true but none is true alone. It is idle to speculate how to "fix" particular social problems in isolation from the totality in which they reside. By the same token, sloganeering aiming to change everything ends up changing nothing in the meantime – or, worse, only alters the names we give to whole oppressive systems of administration.

The truth is not to be found "in the middle", either. It is on a different plane altogether. The decline of discourse is not something we can remedy in a single book or with a singular agenda of reforms. The problem it represents is a more general one, commodification, and the implications commodification has for the quality of public life. Putting value on writing, as on every labor, degrades writing into an instrumental activity, whether communication, reputation or simply selling books. Writing for money and tenure is not writing in the sense in which I intend the term discourse: neither helps constitute a viable public sphere in which people talk and write to each other endlessly as the sinews of a good community. Indeed, popular and academic writing both contribute to hierarchy and thoughtlessness in their own ways. Not only do they not solve the problem – discourse's, and hence the public's, decline – but they exacerbate it.

Do Writers Read?

I have considered the obsolescence of reading from the point of view of temporality: few pause before the written word. Now let me consider the eclipse of reading from the point of view of writers themselves who, like people everywhere, spend less time reading than before. Of course to say that everyone writes and no one reads is an exaggeration: writers read, just as readers write. And readers read, too. But the more writing becomes a business the busier writers must be in order to keep their heads above water, with enough "projects" to sell in the marketplace. The fact that reading is declining is especially troublesome for writers who rely on reading as their imaginative resource as well as their source of dialogue, hence literary community. When writers cease to read carefully (or at all), literary artifice declines still further.

Although postmodernism is not to blame for this, its apologetic Lyotard version excuses the eclipse of readers; the reader is dead. And Derrida (1978) in his playfulness devalues the reader by devaluing reading, paying little attention to his reception. But textuality intends community, not only self-expression, an issue that postmodernists and poststructuralists too often obscure in their drive to overcome the hierarchical dualisms of writer/reader, philosophy/literature, speech/writing, subject/object, etc. This is where Habermas' (1984, 1987b) reconstruction of historical materialism, particularly his move beyond the monologic subject of traditional western philosophy, comes in handy: his communicative-theoretic critical theory renders philosophy genuinely intersubjective, even if he relinquishes too much of the materialism of traditional Marxism, as well as Marxism's utopian agenda of social reconstruction.

Writers cease to read because they are so busy word processing, hustling, networking, lunching, traveling, talk-showing, conferencing. But a conservative version of postmodernism and poststructuralism tends to endorse this for grandiose philosophical reasons, notably that writing is somehow more worthy than mere reading. This is a very difficult issue because the reprivileging of writing, of self-expressive textuality, is precisely postmodernism's main contribution to a feminist Marxism. It revalorizes reproduction, showing its secret productivity. As well, it empowers the subject, the writer here. Indeed, for critical theory's version of postmodernism, to which I am contributing, the notion of writing becomes a paradigm of all free self-expressive human activity, the way labor functioned for Marx (1961) earlier.

But the downside of this postmodernist reprivileging of writing is that it neglects writing's necessarily public dimension, an especially troubling outcome when the public sphere is collapsing all around us. As Habermas shows, writing, indeed all speech, intends consensus. I would go further and say that writing intends to change the world. Although this transformation passes through the empowered creative subject (akin to the subject of phenomenological Marxism; see Paci (1972) and Piccone (1971)), it must not remain at the boundary of the subject, here the writer. The empowering of subjectivity intends intersubjectivity, real community – a new polity. Writing seeks readers; more than that, it seeks to turn readers into writers but in a way that dialectically ensures that writers read and that readers write. After all, the antidote to a silenced public sphere is not a cacophonous one in which everyone talks and no one listens (see Wexler, 1991). Writing must know when to stop, to solicit responses before it assays its own corrections. That is the essence of a democratic polity, after all.

Postmodernism and poststructuralism tend to invest too much in a monologic model of textuality. Sheer writing, "writing degree zero" (Barthes, 1970), solves nothing if it does not intend and achieve community. The empowering of authorial subjectivity is crucially necessary at a time when writers are becoming obsolete, merely wage slaves of the corporate and academic literary apparatus. But that empowering must be carried out on the model of intersubjectivity, as Habermas (1984, 1987b) insightfully contends. Otherwise, writers will write *only for themselves*, the desperate self-obsession of those who endorse postmodernism and poststructuralism as legitimating ideologies. That model of literary subjectivity capitulates to the cultural and political-economic logic of late capitalism (Jameson, 1984b) precisely in the way it encloses writing hermetically in the individuated, isolated sensibilities of solitary literary workers, rebels only in their own eyes.

This introduces what many cultural creators view as a tawdry, ideological consideration: writing as a model and vehicle of generic non-alienated human activity wants to change the world. Thus, the problem of intersubjectivity is the central problem of left-wing political theory where "subjects" are fragmented into the billion different "subject positions" of late capitalism. Unfortunately, postmodernism and poststructuralism (e.g., Laclau and Mouffe, 1985) valorize this very fragmentation in their defense of difference, otherness, marginality and heterogeneity. As a result, literary language games are judged incommensurable when, in fact, as Habermas correctly argues, they can be adjudicated according to global criteria of reason or what he calls "universal pragmatics" of communicative discourse (Habermas, 1979). To endorse a communicative pluralism is fatal for a communication theory that endeavors to overcome people's isolation as well as to empower them to speak and write, hence to hold power.

We must not confuse the solution with the cause. That reading has declined, even for writers, ought not to be celebrated as the dawning of an age of pure textuality or writing degree zero. Reading and writing belong together both constitutively (how can one write without reading or read without writing?) and strategically, in terms of building political community. The Barthesian and Derridean auteur too quickly gains a monopoly of dialogue chances, creating an ironic deconstructive vanguard composed of university professors. This is not to say that writers must write or read "down" but that a concern for readers requiring writers to read is an essential corrective in democratic social movements. After all, reading humbles as well as edifies; the voluble writer who neglects others' textuality also neglects their humanity. We have enough hierarchy already; the deconstructive left must avoid its own tendency to stratify the writing/reading relationship.

Of course, to return to my earlier discussion in this chapter, perhaps reading and writing have been so transvalued in fast capitalism that it makes no sense to talk about writers reading or readers writing. When textuality is dispersed into things themselves, losing its critical distance from the world necessary for mediative cogitation and hence social change (Agger, 1989a), books themselves become obsolete. True. But these are tendencies, not hard-and-fast realities. Books can still be found in bookstores and libraries. And textuality is all over the place, issuing its subliminal commands to consume and conform. That is why we need a radical cultural studies in the first place, as well as a deconstructive methodology to pierce these implacable tomes seeming to drop from the sky unbidden. If readers, writers and texts were thoroughly archaic, why bother to write, hope, organize? Recognizing the tendency of discourse to decline is all the more reason to resist it, not accelerate it through the apologetic lenses of a postmodernism only ontologizing the eclipse of reason. Modernity is not postmodern just yet. It can be de- and then re-modernized along different, left-feminist lines, notably through the inspiration and good counsel of a different, more critical postmodernism as much dialectical as post-dualist.

Although Marx has been canonized for too long, we can look to Marx in *The German Ideology* (Marx and Engels, 1947) for a model of intellectuality and hence of textuality. His "all-around individual" who rotates social roles without taking on the life-long imprint of any of them remains a suitable model of socialist personality. Writers can read as well as take on the other productive and reproductive roles available in advanced industrial society. A flexible division of labor is crucial to contemporary social change, especially where that helps us overcome the rigid role definitions confining people in the various niches of subservience in which most of us find ourselves. In my concluding chapter I speculate more systematically about the postmodern intellectual or, better, about postmodern intellectuality, notably what it might mean for people to write and read in – and toward – a different social order.

At this point, let me only attempt to distinguish between two possible "postmodern" perspectives on the eclipse of reading. One postmodernism endorses it in the frenzy of writing degree zero, hence only compounding the problem of declining discourse and thus the eroding polity. The other postmodernism traces the eclipse of reading, even on the part of writers, to various tendencies of literary political economy both reducing contemplation and mediation on the one hand and forcing writers to become entrepreneurs on the other. Readers disempowered before textuality hasten the decline of the public sphere, just as do writers too busy to write and read dialogically. I will return to this issue in the next chapter when I consider the contemporary nature of literary lifestyles. Here I am raising this issue in the overall context of a discussion of the fate of reading in fast capitalism. We should protest its fate, not endorse it, as many postmodernists and poststructuralists do. Otherwise, we lose the political edge of a theory of culture that resists the eclipse of public reason both doctrinally and through its own example.

That is my final point here: postmodern writing models a postmodern society, even if postmodernists think they lack social theory altogether (see Kellner, 1988), being somehow beyond politics (Lyotard, 1984). Derrida intends a Derridean world that he prefigures in his own example of a "grammatological" (Derrida, 1976) writer. Similarly, Barthes (1975) models a world order governed by the rule of textual pleasure, exemplified in books like *Writing Degree Zero* (1970) and *S/Z* (1974). At least Adorno (e.g., 1973b) as a Marxist of sorts recognized that his own literary example intended a whole world in his image. His "negative dialectics" differs from Derridean grammatology in the sense that it is a dialectical political posture, at once a critique of ideology and a prefiguration of a certain literary community. Adorno wrote complexly in order to undo the complexities of the world and especially of its ideological cover concepts. He did not practice or defend obscurity for its own sake, as British analytic philosophers often forget (e.g., Slater, 1977). His was a dialectical obscurity, attempting to prise clarity out of obscurity, learning from falsehood by speaking its language, a model of what the Frankfurt theorists have always called immanent critique – paradigm implosion.

We cannot simply live utopian literary lives where to do so ensures that we will not be published or produced. That is as apolitical as acquiescing to the decline of discourse. Our sentences may not all be pretty where we are dealing with difficult, dirty, depressing topics. But we look beyond the present world just as we confront it imaginatively. That is what the Frankfurt School meant by "dialectical imagination" (Jay, 1973) – the ability to live in the present without losing sight of its potential for being transformed into something qualitatively different. Our writing must both criticize and communicate, unleashing political desire and hope while suggesting strategies of social transformation both substantively and through its own example. We best learn not to ignore the reader by reading, thus always remembering the challenge of comprehension posed by every angry and energetic text.

Chapter 5

Textless Books, Busy Bookstores

The Commodification of Publishing

The decline of discourse both reflects and results in its displacement: writers do not write writing (Fish, 1980; Newman, 1985). Instead, they write for the trade market, other popular entertainments, advertising and journalism; or they compose obscure academic treatises and journal articles. That only describes; it does not explain. Having addressed writing's displacement, it is important to dig beneath the surface for the reasons why. My analysis is largely political-economic in nature, although often the symptoms are not. In particular, I address the causes of the decline of discourse in terms of *literary commodification*. By commodification, I refer to the way in which book publishing is increasingly governed by the drive for profit and organized along corporate lines, a theme I pursue further in the following chapter when I address academic writing and publishing (Braverman, 1974). This is hardly new. Yet quantity has turned into quality; in recent capitalism the pace of commodification has quickened to the point that *books themselves have disappeared*, eroding the public sphere essential for democracy still further.

The eclipse of textuality belongs to a larger tendency in capitalism for value to disappear into valued objects (Marx, 1961). Here, I consider the eclipse of textuality in terms of its causes. As a result, standards of literary craft, and thus people's interpretive abilities, have declined. The problem is a dialectical one: we can take no comfort in solutions pretending to remedy things with better books or more elevated readers. Instead, the problem is largely one of structure – the way we have arranged our literary worlds, both in trade publishing and popular culture, on the one hand, and in academia, on the other.

Do ideas have to be bought and sold? My earlier lament for the demise of the freelancer would seem to contradict my analysis here. It it not whether people can sell their writing but rather the scale on which publishing, entertainment and academia take place. In part, this is true. Corporate culture diminishes individual creativity and thus literacy (Whyte, Jr., 1957). But, even in the freelance world, we accept laws of copyright as divine. I want to challenge these laws less for what they are than for what they represent. In assuming that literary work can be bought and sold, we begin the fateful process of literary commodification resulting today in thoughtless books and witless readers.

This is the logic of capitalism, affecting literary creation no less than other types of human labor. Where everything has its price, intrinsic value has no meaning. Even saying this sounds like a diatribe against money as currency, usefully simplifying a host of otherwise impossible exchanges in a complex society (Simmel, 1978; Shell, 1982). But money is a text itself encoding and thus reproducing relations of hierarchy and dominance (Agger, 1989a). Where money buys power, the use of money reinforces power relationships decided in those economic terms. Currency happens to be the currency of the realm; it both encodes and reproduces the salient social relations in capitalism. For book publishing to be governed by the logic of capital means that writing and reading will fall under the sway of capital's logic. Where human relations congeal into relations between objects (Lukacs' (1971, pp. 83-222) "reification", reformulating Marx's (n.d., pp. 76-87) notion of "commodity fetishism"), it is no wonder that literary relations degenerate equivalently. After all, books are societies, too – nucleic units comprising the social order.

Aspects of this critique have been raised before. Culture critics have argued against the corporate nature of publishing and for the preservation of small houses, little magazines and non-profit university presses. These critics contend that intellectual integrity and quality are sacrificed when the life of the mind becomes a business. Who would disagree? Yet criticism has not gone far enough. It is also important to understand the way in which the commodification of discourse, degrading discourse, springs from certain objective tendencies in capitalism. Publishing, writing, reading are hardly immune; one should therefore not be surprised that the book world is run, and reproduces itself, in the same ways as everything else. The life of the mind was never a world apart, nor, perhaps, should it be.

Anyone who criticizes the way in which social relations erode when a price is put on human labor, the essence of Marx's critique of capitalism, must extend that analysis to literary relationships, as I do here. By the same token, anyone who worries about the decline of literary culture must understand it in larger terms; the commodification of discourse both reflects and thus reproduces commodification generally. I prefer to take a structural view of the decline of discourse rather than to lament the loss of an intellectual class or stratum. It is true that this loss only accelerates intellectual, hence political, degeneration generally; yet we should understand the loss not in terms of literary failure of nerve. That only heroizes earlier intellectuals. Whether or not they were heroic in their resistance to academization, McCarthyism or other trends degrading discourse is not the question; we cannot simply choose to be heroes ourselves. Structures of administration affecting the book world no less than most other capitalist institutions deny us the moral as well as literary efficacy to write our way out of the dilemmas, the marginality, in which we find ourselves.

Writers must vigorously resist their own heroization lest other writers, and would-be writers, confuse the symptom for the cause. Literary culture degrades where all culture succumbs to the imperatives of capitalist, sexist and racist administration. These are not just slogans but analytical categories through which to understand how the "choices" seemingly confronting individuals are not really choices at all but contingent outcomes of our overdetermination. It is wrong to presuppose that writers by writing differently – better – can break through the codes of mystification and control entwining all of us in thoughtlessness. Writing differently does nothing to change the fact that major publishing houses are only corporate extensions of huge parent companies. Indeed, as most writers know, they will likely not be published if they write heroic books. Every exception only proves the rule.

It is tempting to point to these exceptions – the occasional author who makes sense, as well as a living, in prose accessible to many. We gigantize the few "successful" public writers who avoid the degradations of trade publishing or the corporate university precisely because these figures are so exceptional. Who does not dream of being Carl Sagan, John Kenneth Galbraith, C. Wright Mills? But these are dreams; those people survived, and made names for themselves, in spite of the tendencies of literary political economy to crush them. They were hard-working; they were talented; but, above all, they were fortunate. Although in this age of instantaneity it is possible to win fame cheaply, it is much more difficult to make a substantial literary contribution without a major commitment of time, effort, ego.

It is tempting to believe that the few hugely successful writers who write discourse and not junk have special talents or work especially hard. Perhaps they do. But it is more likely that their talent and hard work have combined with fortuity to elevate them above all the other talented-and-hard-working wordsmiths who miss the right breaks or otherwise run afoul of intellectual and political administration. We do not live in a meritocracy, even though most of us desperately want to believe we do. Otherwise, we would not bother to put in the effort to "earn" success – preferably the "old-fashioned way". But the literary world, like the world at large, does not recognize talent and thus reward merit. The literary outcomes enjoyed by a few are hardly earned in the sense that they are deserved; after all, most deserving writers are ignored.

The Obsolescence of the Writer

Turned into people who "deliver manuscript", that then becomes "product", writers quickly become obsolete in modern publishing. The "managed" textbook is written by an author team found in-house or hired from the outside. Textbooks in my discipline, sociology, are increasingly composed by a professional academic working with a ghost writer hired by the house; sometimes this "ghost" even finds his or her name on the cover of the book. Just as capital tends to absorb and thus diminish human labor, one of the self-undoing contradictions in capitalist economies, so publishing absorbs, and thus cancels, living authors. The author becomes a minor functionary in a vast team of editorial, production and marketing experts who together "make" and sell books.

This notion of the obsolescence of the writer echoes parallel themes in both the Frankfurt School's critical theory ("decline of the individual") and in postmodernism ("death of the reader"). Books write authors, not authors books. That is, the authorial contribution to literary products is negligible compared to the influences of marketing and editorial experts. Although authors are never wholly eclipsed, for books need the aura (if not substance) of imaginative individuality, they take a back seat to the people who conceive and sell literary commodities. In Hollywood, movies and television shows begin from "concepts", ideas about a cultural product's niche in the marketplace. These "concepts" are derived by the marketing experts who have their fingers on the pulse of popular taste and who in turn constitute it (Gans 1979; Katz, 1984). The sweaty work of scriptwriting is far less important by comparison and is thus farmed out to any number of hired hands. Indeed, script writers are often changed in midstream, responding to the cavils of producers, directors, even big-ticket stars. The death of the author indeed!

Publishers find writers to be virtually expendable where writers are temperamental, independent, idiosyncratic – not team players. Anyone who writes understands the inherent frictions built into publisher-editor-writer relationships (Coser, Kadushin and Powell, 1982). I am not denying that writers are not fractious, self-important souls, for, of course, sometimes we are. But we derive our standards of authorial autonomy, and thus our irascibility, from prevailing organizational standards of conformity: writers who request little in the way of editorial support and literary autonomy are seen to be asking for the moon. As a result, writers want more than they can reasonably expect from publishers and editors.

Writers are objectively obsolete where literary standards have declined; nearly anyone with minimal literary skills could craft the mushy prose sold as trade books or textbooks. The more books appear similar, the more writers become fungible sources of literary labor power. Textbook publishers recognize that every manuscript must go through "development", a telling euphemism for stringent, market-driven revisions. I am not saying that every first draft is as good as the last; far from it. But, ironically, when writers recognize that the "final cut" on their literary work is out of their hands, they lower their standards for their own work. Recognizing that anyone could do their writing for them, they relax their attention to detail, paying insufficient attention to literary craft.

It is easy to see this as a two-way street. Authors victimized by corporate publishing nearly making them dispensable write poorly or, at least, inattentively; editors react with the complaint that literary standards are declining. Both are true together and neither is true alone. I blame the commodification of discourse, and not the particular players in the literary game; after all, editors are little more powerful than writers where they are mere mid-level employees of large houses owned by even larger parent corporations. The system benefits by pitting writers and editors against each other, thus diverting them from the bigger picture: what is really at issue here is not the heroic or conformist sensibilities of individuals in the literary process *but the process itself*, the logic of literary capital turning prose into profit.

The obsolescence of reading, discussed in Chapter 4, is matched, and deepened, by the obsolescence of writing. Literally, writing is here to stay; it is *writers* who are disposable. Where anyone with minimum literary skills could write writing, writers as individuals with special skills and thus artistic rights become obsolete. The more curmudgeonly writers are, the more they obstruct the literary production process, which ill-affords authorial temperament. "Good" writers are those who produce "product" for the market; understanding their own role in the literary process, they do not overreach themselves. Authorial self-importance is an enemy of corporate publishing in the same way that dissidents weaken social control. The ultimate societal purpose is not social control per se but its byproducts, here marketable literary product.

Editors are not the only ones who will protest what they contend is this monochromatic portrait of the deceased writer. Authors, too, want desperately to believe in their own indispensability, the more so the more they try to buck the system and do quality work. Of course, this is part of postmodern ideology: the New Individualism assumes that individuals control their own destiny in a post-political age beyond ideological contention. Yet the giant publishing houses, movie production companies and television networks are less "postmodern" than corporate in the traditional sense. Authorial and editorial ideology notwithstanding, literary political economy reduces everyone on the "creative" side of the culture industry to employees. Writers and editors are allowed the illusion of their own mythic individuality precisely to keep them in tow, ever the function of ideology.

One might suppose that smart writers would want to write "for" the market, maximizing profit and thus their own royalties. Should Saul Bellow crank out duplicative versions of the same basic motif or should he help form taste, both anticipating bad taste as well as the possibility of its redemption? Now, Bellow is a bad example here because by now "Bellow", the name, sells more books than does the quality of his work. Take a lesser example. (The fact that we cannot easily think of one only evidences the power of the literary star system.)

One of my favorite writers, Robert Parker, composes detective fiction, having "created" the character Spenser in a series of nearly twenty interrelated novels set in Boston. Parker cranks out "product" precisely because writing is his business; the books are written to formula, although they are good books with serious moral lessons. Parker would not deny that he is writing "for" the market; in his case, he gets away with a higher-tone version of a formulaic theme than do other detective writers. He compromises relatively little of his aesthetic integrity in return for a reliable income. It is impossible to gainsay Parker's literary choice simply because he is the rare author who makes a decent living by writing; he even resigned his tenured position in English at Northeastern University once his books sold briskly enough.

But if Parker decided to abandon the Spenser motif and try his hand at a more avantgarde form in order to raise literary intelligence, he would be disappointed; although he would probably find a publisher for his first break-the-mold book, it is unlikely he could sustain the sales he has come to expect from the Spenser treatments. All too soon, Parker would come back to his senses. His audience would not tolerate literary revisionism from him. Although his reviews might be good for writing "good" books, his income would be imperiled. Parker undoubtedly resolves this dilemma in the way most of us would: he defends the detective genre as serious fiction, and I, as a Spenser fan, would not disagree with him. But Parker's writing has been commodified: he has very few literary options beyond the formula-like books his fans and editor have come to expect.

This does not mean that the Spenser books are entirely duplicative; plot varies and, with it, character development. Spenser has changed over the years, at least in the sense that he has attained a greater maturity; and his cohort, Hawk, has mellowed, just as his woman friend Susan has come into her own. By now, Parker has evolved a rich collage of relationships, themes, plots and contingencies enticing his readers. Whether or not the books are really duplicative depends on the perspective of the reader: "More" Spenser/Parker is good for those of us who like what we read of him/them.

Robert Parker is a real author. I have seen his picture in *People* magazine, I have read interviews with him and I saw him interviewed on the Today Show; together these definitely constitute ontological proof of one's existence! Yet, for every Parker, there are many failed writers – or, better, eclipsed writers. Through indefatigability and circumstance Parker has persevered to make his books reflect a good deal of his own authorial temperament; he says in interviews that he sends in final manuscript and the publisher prints it after minor copy-editing. Most writers do not enjoy that much creative control over their writing; as "product", writing is not meant to be protected by jealous or surly authors. Writing is increasingly a management decision, a process of "development".

Literary Hegemony: Editing, Market Research and the Homogeneity of Literary "Product"

Where editing is driven by market concerns, it is no wonder that books become commodities. But the publishing world has been relatively insulated from objective appraisal of its own commodification largely through industry norms deceiving publishers, editors, authors and readers about what is really going on. Where faculty and administrators contend that massive state universities with huge operating budgets and football stadia resemble the medieval colleges at Oxford and Padua in their concern for the life of the mind, publishing houses perpetuate the false impression of their own antique self-determination. In fact, both universities and publishing houses are no more or less than bureaucracies, subject to the same hierarchies, flow-charts and narrow job definitions as any private and public sector organizations.

Supply – literary product – is determined by authors' and editors' views of what the trade market will bear. What succeeded yesterday largely governs what will be published tomorrow. The same is true in journalism: it is telling that *Time* and *Newsweek* often come out with similar cover stories and treat the same series of substantive topics from week to week. Surely, insider information largely sets the agenda for reporting in this sense. Even television and movie producers "test" their product before release. It is often part of a show's or movie's story how plots and denouements were changed at the last minute in light of audience response to previews. *Fatal Attraction*, the box-office blockbuster, gained attention because it was widely known that the ending was changed in this fashion. It was decided that, because audiences preferred Anne Archer, as the cuckolded wife, to kill the harlot played by Glenn Close, Archer, not Michael Douglas, would be allowed to do the fatal deed. This is especially interesting in light of the good woman/bad woman theme informing the movie. No major publisher, magazine, network, or studio will invest in projects approaching the outer limits of popular taste. Given mounting production costs, the stakes are perceived to be too high to allow untested or unconventional artists to have their way. Thus, the same people – authors, journalists, scriptwriters – produce the same product, over and over. This both creates hierarchy, for only a few people have their work printed or produced, and reproduces prevailing taste by catering to it. No matter how vigorously editors may lobby for off-beat projects, or even occasionally succeed in seeing these through production, the deck is stacked against authorial autonomy, creativity, vision.

The issue is not simply "bad" writing, whatever that might mean. It is *uninspired* writing – writing that does not challenge the conventions dictating style and substance. Writers today are victims of enormous social control, both externally and internally imposed. Either one's work will be domesticated by outside readers, marketing experts, developmental editors; or one will so fear this domestication that writing becomes an exercise in self-control, anticipating what is bound to happen if one's work does not pass muster according to prevailing standards of convention. Either way, authorial autonomy, and thus the quality of discourse, declines.

This suggests a notion of *literary hegemony*, corresponding to my earlier notions of literary commodification and displacement. The former is the subjective counterpart of the latter, more objective processes: writers come to regulate *themselves*, imposing discipline on themselves before it is imposed on them from the outside. Hegemony, Gramsci's (1971) term, describes the self-reproducing dominance of the dominant ideas in societies based on unequal power and wealth. Domination is deeper than sheer exploitation in that it is added on to exploitation *by the victim*. Once disempowered objectively, the disempowered come to view their own disempowering as natural, inevitable, even good, and hence they deepen it. It is not enough to say that ideology deludes people. Although true, it is important to recognize that cognition is not just a blank slate but rather plays a more active role in this disempowering process. Literary hegemony describes what happens when writers freely check their own creative, rebellious tendencies, believing that if they do not someone else will. This becomes a self-fulfilling prophecy: books write authors via literary hegemony.

Writers are both victims and authors of their own neutralization in a commodified literary world. Few favor the strictures imposed by market standards of taste and thus evaluation; they author their own neutralization in order to attain publication and therefore earn a livelihood of sorts. Academics submit to their own self-imposed criteria of judgment; disciplinary professionals anticipate the likely responses of other jaded academics to their submitted work (see de Certeau (1986, pp. 193-198) on Foucault's critique of discipline). Academic "professionalism" does more than obey these norms; it anticipates them. The most successful academic authors engage in self-censorship before they receive external reviews of their work;

they respond to editorial directives dutifully, without worrying about whether subtle authorial compromises add up to wholesale betrayal.

I and a co-author sought a contractual offer from a major college textbook publisher to write an introductory-level textbook in our discipline. We are not neophytes; we recognize the commodified nature of textbooks and thus the huge amount of administration imposed on writers by the major corporate houses, marketing experts, editors, reviewers. After all, one must not break the mold in the textbook business; one's work must sell to "adopters", other academics who teach the college course addressed by one's book. Indeed, we initially sought a house affording us high-quality support in the myriad small areas of editing, production and marketing together determining a book's success or failure.

We view ourselves as hardened, even cynical, "professionals". We both teach the introductory course in our discipline and thus we have perused the 60-some competing books currently available in the marketplace. We know people who have written these textbooks; we know many publishers, editors and college salespeople. But even we are surprised by the degree to which these major houses want to ensure we are temperate, responsible, responsive writers – able to make revisions to form, to follow editorial directives, to deliver "product" on time. Even though these publishers have courted us, flying us to corporate headquarters and entertaining us expensively, they all make it clear that we must be "their" kind of people: no zealots or crackpots need apply.

The most explicit house in this regard was Prentice-Hall, the largest publisher in the capitalist world by some accounts. The sociology editor at Prentice-Hall insisted we fly from Buffalo to Englewood Cliffs, N.J. before we began contract negotiations so that they could appraise us. Even though we had spoken frequently on the telephone and had provided the house with numerous documents (our book prospectus, a long "sample" chapter, twenty-five reviews of our prospectus obtained by another publisher, our curriculum vitae, etc.), these 'phone and mail contacts were insufficient. They wanted us to meet their executive, editorial and marketing personnel as a way of sizing us up. Although their request to fly to New Jersey was not especially inconveniencing, it told us a lot about their interest in our professional virtues and authorial responsibility. Are we Prentice-Hall people? – that is what they were asking.

This test of loyalty was done for economic reasons. As we were told repeatedly during our visit to Prentice-Hall Inc., the publishing house was risking a large amount of money on our project; hence, our authorial virtues had to be assessed carefully. On one level, this was candid: a full-blown introductory textbook in our field can run upward of $250,000 in production and marketing costs. But Prentice-Hall wanted us to scale back our financial demands, notably for "advance" money to be paid out before publication of the book and charged against subsequent royalties. Indeed, at the end of our visit, we got down to nitty-gritty negotiations with members of their administrative staff about a possible contractual "package". Although a good deal of this discussion had taken place before our visit to Englewood Cliffs, some crucial issues remained unresolved. Indeed, they were never resolved satisfactorily: the next day, on the morning of our return to Buffalo, the editor called us to tell us tersely that the deal was off – this, after weeks of labored discussions, reviewing and editor-author exchanges. We wondered whether we failed the citizenship test or whether our demands were simply too rich for their blood.

An interesting feature of the rhetoric surrounding our quite typical textbook contract negotiations was the way the publisher used the term "risk" in order to undercut our bargaining stance. Obviously, any publishing deal where the house pays authors an advance against royalties (in this case $60,000 plus other nonrecoverable expenses for typing, xeroxing and research assistance to be paid in the form of a "grant") involves risk. After all, a book might not sell well enough for the house to recover the full extent of its initial investment, including authors' royalties. Although the standard publishing contract clearly states that advance payments not recovered through actual sales must be repaid by the author, there are legal as well as ethical ambiguities here. If authors work hard, respond to reviewers' criticisms on route and then deliver the final manuscript on time, publishers usually do not litigate in order to recoup unearned advance payments. This is all the more reason for publishers to try to minimize advance payments, typically, as with Prentice-Hall in our case, by trying to convince authors that they should bear some of the "risk" in an expensive publishing venture by reducing their demands for advance money. No matter that authors' royalties usually do not amount to more than 15 to 18 per cent of the book's net price.

Just as books become homogeneous in a commodified literary world, so too do authors. Authors who deliver product successfully possess similar virtues like punctuality, intellectual temperateness, deference to editorial and collegial authority. This Prentice-Hall person is devoid of the idiosyncracies troubling author-publisher relations; he or she is a company person, a capable wordsmith, a team player. Those writers who succeed are those who possess the most ability to knuckle under to the market forces driving literary work. They are the ones "easiest" to work with, least likely to rock the boat or make waves. I could be describing any successful "player" in the corporate world, any savvy and deferential white-collar employee.

This is why we use the adjective "professional" when describing academic writers with these virtues. Interestingly, "professional" is also an occupational category, referring to someone with special skills to sell. Both are true. Professional writers behave professionally. Their financial rewards and standing in the literary community are affected by their professional comportment in the corporate maze of publishing. One thing leads to another. This is not to endorse unprofessionalism – the absence of timeliness, courtesy, productivity. It is instead to raise the issue of literary professionalism within the organizational and corporate contexts of commodified publishing; professionalism is the norm governing essentially hierarchical relations between publisher and editor, on the one side, and author, on the other. Individuals inevitably behave badly when their relationships are overlaid by structurally contradictory interests. The real issue is whether, in fact, authors and editors collaborate productively. They do, where authors accept the corporate goal of profit; they do not where authors are willing to reduce profitability, and thus their own royalties, in exchange for a certain literary license. Publishing houses want to convince their authors, "Prentice-Hall people", that they share a common interest; this is not a difficult case to make to textbook writers who, above all, seek sales. Yet for people who write more serious books, or simply less potentially profitable ones, these are trade-offs.

Bookselling and the Creation of Taste: On Mediocrity

For their part, publishers and editors will insist that popularity and quality do not oppose each other; of course, everyone hopes they do not, writers especially. But by catering to extant standards of taste, publishers only reproduce them; writers who try to write against, or beyond, popular taste risk being unread or, even more immediate here, going unpublished. We routinely debate this issue in the realm of network television (Williams, 1975; Gans, 1979; Rubin, 1985). Critics' laments about pedestrian, dispiriting television shows are illogical given the logic of network profit. Shows succeed where their popularity justifies certain profitable advertising rates. But exactly the same problem occurs in every other literary domain: by writing down, we reward literary incompetence and thus lower standards even further.

This is very much a dynamic process; either taste is getting better or worse. The longer we perpetuate listlessness among readers and viewers, the harder it is to rehabilitate interpretive skills. The more we challenge the audience, the more authorial risks we can take, thus legitimating further risks. Apologists for declining popular culture pretend the issue is elitism: how can one disdain others' standards in the absence of an objective standard of quality? Marcuse (1964), representing the Frankfurt School in this, answers in the following way: we know that needs are "false", and taste decadent, where needs, values and standards are not arrived at freely but instead are composed by the very market research tapping the nature of the popular in the first place. Marcuse does not object to particularly "bad" books or shows in themselves but understands mediocrity as an objective outcome of a commodified literary world in which taste is manufactured.

Marcuse provokes the criticism that he inflates his own standards into a universal (MacIntyre, 1970; Schoolman, 1980). But he does not offer a definitive agenda of taste; he merely reveals taste to be the cultural and political-economic product it is. The logic of capitalism requires producers to create markets in order to ensure profits; this is especially problematic in an advanced stage of capitalism in which most basic human needs can be met relatively easily. Taste is manufactured in order to protect capitalism against overproduction and underconsumption, two sides of the same coin (Mandel, 1968). Reason, for Marcuse, is the absence of external constraints, not a narrow list of tastes, jobs, titles, lifestyles. In this, he and his other Frankfurt cohorts rely on early Marx's (1961) image of socialism as a free-for-all of creative activities chosen in an economic system blurring the line between productive and creative work.

Mediocrity is the objective outcome of manipulated taste and lit- erary production strictly matched to that taste. Critics who bemoan the mediocre typically fault authorial or editorial judgment, as if that were the whole problem. They fail to understand the structural con- ditions under which mediocrity is reproduced by literary producers for reasons of profit and control. Bad cultural taste is the absence of taste arrived at in rational ways; its nature is to be imposed. It is also tempting to blame advertisers themselves for hawking the mediocre, as if they could do differently in a market economy. One of the coping skills of the late-20th century rationalist is to decode evaluative claims, whether offered blatantly in advertising or encoded in critical praise, for what they are – commercial boosterism.

The fact that virtually everything has its price erodes judgment as well as the things themselves. Goods trade through mere appearances and the discursive claims both constituting and reinforcing these appearances (Leiss, 1976). Literary goods are no different: people who rely on best-seller lists or particular mainstream reviewers look to the wrong sources of quality control. One can only "read" best-seller lists or critical notices deconstructively, that is, in terms of the cultural, political and economic interests of the reviewer. Although even falsehood educates, it does so dialectically, requiring us to think back and forth between false claims and the topics or objects they smother in falseness as a way of getting at their real nature.

One must think about the subtext of critical evaluation as well as advertising, the story being told (and to whom it is told). It is not enough to know "good" or "bad" but *whose* "good" and "bad". Is the review intended for Yuppies, beer-drinking rednecks, homemakers, Cadillac-driving golfers? Can we read the reviewer's praise or disdain to be the opposite of what it appears to be? Ultimately, we acquire "our" reviewers, advertisers, products, books, television shows and movies. We make them our own in terms of implicit criteria of *what lies, disappoints, displeases least*; we are conditioned to expect the worst – claims that challenge credulity shamelessly. In expecting exaggeration, we value modest claims over hyperbole. After all, every publishing season seems to bring forth the Great American Novel.

The problem of mediocrity is that it expands endlessly; writing reflecting a certain taste reproduces it, deepening it over the long term. It is important to recognize the structural roots of mediocrity: it follows from the commodification of discourse coupled with its enslavement to a market-based notion of popular culture. The popular today is equivalent to mediocrity simply because prevailing standards of taste drive publication and production decisions. And these standards dialectically derive from the standards yesterday, which in turn both reflected and reproduced the standards the day before yesterday. Mediocrity is not merely bad taste but the conflation of popularity with value, contingent marketplace outcomes inflated into ontology itself. It is not a question of whether "the people" are always right, or never right, but of what constitutes the popular structurally. Today, as yesterday, the popular is derived from exchange principles governing a capitalist marketplace: what sells reflects inherent standards of populist excellence.

Culture critics and other elitists suspect this conflation to be false; *The New Yorker* and *New York Review of Books* reviewers know impoverished culture when they see or read it. But bourgeois criticism has by and large failed to understand the imbedded mediocrity in "postmodern" capitalism objectively – that is, in terms of structural forces, both cultural and political-economic. Instead, we blame authors or, through them, the *Zeitgeist*. The orgy of postmodern and poststructural theories of interpretation respond helplessly to standard bourgeois criticism mistaking authorial outcomes for aesthetic design. That is, a range of critics from Barthes to Derrida have attempted to deprivilege authorial intention as a way of understanding how language itself – better, culture – determines and overdetermines meaning.

Although there is something to be learned methodologically from deconstructive criticism, notably about how to discover ideology in surprising places, by and large postmodern theories of culture merely invert bourgeois notions of literary intention. Instead of tracing taste to writers' conscious designs and moral choices, deconstructive critics register what Barthes called "the death of the author" in certainty that authorial intentions have no place in cultural outcomes. This is as undialectical as the Leavis-era criticism placing every literary outcome at the feet of authorial sensibility (Leavis, 1973). And, for their part, orthodox Marxist theories of culture fail to comprehend the non-identical relationship between aesthetic process and product, reducing interpretive judgments mechanically to class background (see Brenkman, 1987).

Here, literary hegemony is reflected in the decline of taste. A postmodern theory of culture lays the blame for the decline of taste, and hence the whole decline of discourse, less at the feet of individual subjects – readers and writers – than at the door of literary commodification generally, what the Frankfurt School called the culture industry. Not that "subjects", readers and writers, do not matter at all: we do, but only at the margin, where the occasional heroic reader becomes a different, more public sort of writer, and then influences others in the same direction. Postmodernism becomes critical theory where it analyzes and criticizes the desubjectified cultural world in structural terms yet without neglecting the possibility of new, powerful writing and reading. This is not an either/or: people can make a difference, even if few do today. Indeed, that is precisely the topic of postmodern cultural studies.

Authors are compelled to write the way they do by economic exigencies. At the same time, authors who fail to recognize their external determination reproduce it thoughtlessly. Writing is always an act of freedom, yet most writers in abdicating that freedom lessen freedom for the rest of us. Cultural criticism must understand mediocrity as a dialectical outcome of literary intentionality and the structure entwining intentionality in the overdetermination of the literary marketplace. One can write "what" one wants only in the constraining context of the publication outlets and readership available in the moment. After all, unpublished writing has no constitutional impact whatsoever, nor does it put bread on the table.

Too much bourgeois cultural criticism scolds authors and publishers for various failures of literary nerve. If only it were that simple. Instead, we are all disempowered "players" in a larger structural game virtually guaranteeing a certain outcome – one might call it mediocrity even at the risk of seeming to pose absolute standards of taste. The critique of mediocrity is important in an age of instantaneity (Bourdieu, 1984); when our cultural superstars are so inept and shallow, one must reflect seriously on the nature of taste. This is especially important in a market-driven literary world: Taste directly determines what writers will write. If literary product does not move in the marketplace, no amount of aesthetic authenticity will redeem the broader culture. There are all sorts of "serious" writers but little serious writing. Good writing has been reduced to an efflorescence of literary *attitude*.

Celebrating Postmodern Capitalism

Critics of postmodern capitalism have tended to become its celebrants (Berman, 1982). The critique of New York corporate dominance of our literary and entertainment worlds quickly becomes a paean to New York's vibrant zaniness; "serious" writers who denigrate the prevailing standards of the popular haunt clubs, bars and restaurants, seeking the elixir of cosmopolitanism. Although New York is not the issue, the transmogrification of postmodern criticism into the affirmation of the postmodern certainly blocks serious social and cultural criticism going beyond the ephemera of style and sensibility. "Who" writes, and how they do, is much less important than *what writing is, what it can only be, in postmodern capitalism*.

Lyotard's postmodernism is essentially a perspective on cultural discontinuity disqualifying utopian philosophies of history, whether capitalist-enlightenment or socialist-feminist (Huyssen, 1986). This is not to say that most postmodernists strongly theorize capitalism; they do not understand the problem that way. They resist millennial social change strategies in favor of decentered eclecticism; intellectually this amounts to an epistemological and substantive relativism inured to the various versions of the absolute. But although one cannot posit definitive utopias without risking their own degeneration into that from which they emerged as counterpoint, one can and must condemn the present world absolutely. Postmodernism is too world-weary, too faddish, too avantgarde, too apolitical, to do this. Instead, it rejects politics in favor of galleries, movies, restaurants. Midwestern mediocrity is counterposed to urban chic. The political ethic of affirmative postmodernism is *to be cool* (Kroker and Cook, 1986).

Postmodern criticism is not political resistance. Critics who lament the decline of discourse prefer to blame the sensibilities of those who write, publish and produce discourse rather than the logic of commodification engulfing all of us. Chic is not a proper political metaphysic; not only does it not encode a vision of utopia but it does nothing to subvert existing power. Imagine the trendy New York intellectual chatting about movies, armed with the latest version of poststructuralist film criticism, either inspiring a vision of a better society or leading others into action. This urbane postmodernism strikingly lacks utopian imagination. There is an almost irresistible tendency to equate analysis of the postmodern with its endorsement.

Yet there is another postmodernism (Jameson, 1984b; Kellner, 1988; Wexler, 1991) that heats things up, rejecting acquiescence as a viable political strategy. As I indicated in my opening chapter, this postmodernism functions effectively as political critique or "negative dialectics" (Adorno, 1973b) precisely because it refuses to short-circuit history into the falsely sufficient present, instead arguing for a standard of the post-modern continuous with the various left and feminist modernisms proposing one concept of progress or another. This disaffirmative postmodernism is hopeful; hence it rejects the glib cynicism of contemporary cosmopolitanism for its ahistoricity and its insensitivity to its own colonial hierarchy over the non-cosmopolitan. In fact, it argues, history is open (Merleau-Ponty, 1964a, pp. 81-82), if not open only to the linear vector of capitalist "progress". Like the left-existentialism and Frankfurt critical theory with which it shares a common grounding in a political version of Nietzsche and Freud, this critical postmodernism does not tremble anxiously because history has no guaranteed teleological endpoint. Instead, it uses history's indeterminacy as a resource of imaginative reconstruction.

This is why it may be worthwhile to periodize capitalism as modernity and then open up a discourse of social change that breaks clearly with the aggrandized "modernity" of technological, class, sexual, racial and environmental degradation: the post-modern. Although Habermas' (1981b) argument for modernity and against the trendy neoconservative postmodernism of Lyotard (1984) is cogent, it is extremely difficult for any critical theory to claim modernity or modernism without laboriously disentangling itself from the false meanings of the capitalist-sexist-racist "modern" so prevalent today. What is in a name? Everything and nothing. At least, we must attend to the hidden implications of eschatological naming for a critical theory that recognizes clearly how discourse has become a form of domination today, even on the left.

Literary Lifestyles and Work Styles in Postmodern Capitalism

Commodification turns us all into objects; we relate to others and the world on the basis of exchange value, not intrinsic utility. The lives we lead are constrained by the physical and metaphysical possibilities available to us. Thus, in a depressive age littered with the junk and ephemera of a "postmodern" popular culture, we are bound to spend our lives filling ourselves with postmodern culture objects and, if we are writers, adding our own literary wares to the rubbish heap. Although it is important to know what writers write, it is also important to know how they lead their lives in the postmodern context. Like many people, postmodern writers spend most of their work time doing anything but writing: they network, self-promote, hang out – the ancillary activities of the literary life that have some-how become its central preoccupations. After all, to exist off one's work, whether writing popular entertainments or academic articles and monographs, one must attend to its publication and production and otherwise locate oneself in a postmodern cultural space.

I am not as concerned with describing the average literary life as with evaluating changes in writers' lives between yesterday and today. Of course, this begs the question 'When was yesterday?'. One could casually respond that postmodern literary lives are lived sufficiently differently from modernist ones that we can notice the difference. In short, writers today spend less time and effort on their actual literary work. They are not simply lazy if, by laziness, one means deep-seated tendencies to avoid work at all costs; people who write to live also live to write – they could, as well, have chosen safer careers in accounting or plumbing. Rather, the sublimation of discourse into commodified media of literary exchange entails the displacement of literary work time into other activities supporting the literary life – dealing with agents, publishers, editors and producers as well as hobnobbing with the literary set.

These activities are especially important in a crowded literary and entertainment marketplace. The busy market itself explains why writers must spend so much time seeking publication and production outlets. One must scramble to find publishers and producers, taking the time necessary to scout out leads and network. By now, we take these things for granted. All academics who publish know what it takes to "place" one's work in journals and with publishers. One must write letters, make calls and attend annual professional meetings. Even to get to the first stages of writing our aforementioned sociology textbook, I and my coauthor had to spend inordinate amounts of time doing lunch, having breakfast, taking meetings, talking on the 'phone. This time could have been better spent doing the actual writing. But we must attend to our literary work *as a business* for, after all, that is what it is.

Just saying this invites scorn: I seem to posit a literary golden age or utopia when writers could "just write" and leave their literary and personal affairs to others (notably women). That is a patrician and patriarchal model of literary activity, the sort of image purveyed by those, even the left, who lament the decline of the public sphere, public "man", public writing, etc. This image returns to Greece's golden age and to its political philosophy suggesting a redemptive, even self-creative notion of politics as praxis. Now this was a driving imagery for Marx himself. Yet the valorization of public life, as well as the critique of its decline, too frequently leaves untheorized what happens in "private", notably in the realm of housework, childrearing and the other unwaged support jobs millennially done by women (Lasch, 1977; Sennett, 1978).

One can sustain a non-sexist and socialist notion of publicity; after all, it is within that framework that I elaborate my own critique of the decline of discourse. (Indeed, one of the central projects of a feminist critical theory (Marshall, 1988) is to develop a feminist concept of public life not beholden to the "male" dichotomy/hierarchy of public-private.) When writers are encumbered with the host of support activities animating the successful literary life, they lose the time to write; days only have twenty-four hours in them, and energy is not limitless. The decline of public speech and prose is hastened by a *literary entrepreneurship* ripping writers away from their studies and studios to spend time in self-promotion. One can understand this in pragmatic terms: to live the literary life one must sell one's work. Or one can understand the postmodern literary lifestyle less in political-economic terms than as a cultural requirement of successful authorship: one soaks up cultural vibes by *hanging out*, the preferred mode of jaded urban postmodernists. To "be" a writer one must have experiences typifying life in the big city.

As my version of cultural studies demonstrates, a dialectical cultural studies can explain both cultural and economic aspects of this busy self-promotion on the part of writers. They must do it in order to publish; and it becomes a way of life itself, what Bourdieu (1984) called *habitus* or simply lifestyle. This leads to a larger discussion of *cosmopolitanism* as literary political economy borrows from, and feeds into, urban political economy (Harvey, 1973, 1985a, 1985b; Castells, 1977, 1983; Zukin, 1982; Feagin, 1989) as well as communication studies (Rachlin, 1988).

As soon as I reduce my analysis of the decline of discourse to individuated terms of literary self-promotion I must immediately reverse my field and locate that entrepreneurship in the dense web of the capitalist city and culture industry, what Foucault (O'Neill, 1986) called the "disciplinary society". The peculiar character of life in the literary fast lane derives from the concentration, centralization and urbanization of cultural capital, whether in New York, Paris, London or Tokyo. Of course, New York is first among equals as the ground zero of postmodern cosmopolitanism. Where Bennington and Oberlin graduates used to flee to the Left Bank upon graduation, perhaps working their way across the Atlantic on a freighter, today they point their Saabs in the direction of Manhattan, the cultural lodestone. They would mortgage their souls for a job in the culture industry.

This image of literary entrepreneurship, of the literary lifestyle generally, is purveyed in popular organs. From *Vanity Fair*, where the literati sparkle with bon mots and attractive mates, to *The New Yorker*, where public lives are laconically dissected and celebrated, the literary life is portrayed as a lifestyle – a mode of urban existence typifying the postmodern rejection of political passion. These successful literary people are presented in terms of their abilities to avoid the pitfalls of celebrity – too little sleep, too much cocaine, even too much self-importance. Celebrity is celebrated for both pragmatic and cultural reasons; it is what happens to writers who enter the literary firmament and become notorious, if not, exactly, important. We are all taught that too much notoriety, like too much of any good thing, can be perilous. But we are not instructed in the artistic, let alone political, price of living one's life on the literary fast-track. (Although Tom Wolfe's *Bonfire of the Vanities* is not explicitly about the literary crowd in New York City, he captures life in the big city through his penetrating ethnographic lens.)

Celebrity is enjoyed by very few. For every Steven Spielberg there are hundreds of would-be Hollywood stars. There is only one John Updike, Bob Bernstein, Carl Sagan. Precisely in its rarity literary celebrity is sought by youthful writers and other arrivistes. Magazines like *Esquire* trumpet up-and-coming young writers and artists, predicting good things for them in the years ahead (and thus ensuring it). Every star-system is a byzantine hierarchy. People are arrayed on one pecking order or another. I was recently told by a chairperson in a sociology department to which I applied for a job that I made the second half of the "short list", the bottom six and not the top six. The top six are what he called "small stars", people who were cited by other scholars "25 or 50" times in the past year in the social science citation index. Of course, to know that I am not even a "small star" tells me exactly where I stand. Citation equals reputation.

Living a literary life today takes too much time away from one's writing. At some baseline level, one must write and write and write some more. One's literary "product" cannot pass muster in the marketplace unless it achieves a certain level of technical and rhetorical competence. The time and energy it takes to write seriously is, of course, different for different people. Yet the more one invests in building a literary career, the fewer resources one will have to do creative work – time, energy, affect. As a discussion of tendencies, this suggests that writers are writing less than before *and* that this has serious implications for literary standards.

Although it is relatively easy to find exceptions to this rule, the good young writers are exceptions. And in order to parlay their writing into careers they will have to make artistic sacrifices to keep their business flowing. Postmodern writing is business, cultural mythologies notwithstanding. Authorial intention does not change the fact; commodification ensures it. Just as Russell Jacoby (1987) wrote about the missing generation of social and political publicists under the age of forty-five, so one could offer a similar analysis of a missing literary and artistic generation. I doubt that the results of this analysis will differ significantly from Jacoby's findings: Everyone succumbs to the rule of commodification, writers no less than academics – anyone whose worth is identical to the value of one's labor power.

This depiction particularly offends those who believe that the cultural marketplace is fair and rational. Although occasionally cream does rise to the top, too frequently it curdles and writers either sell out or languish in a tortured, self-doubting obscurity. Of course, the people who believe that good work will emerge victorious are precisely those who have the most to lose by an unmasking of corporate cultural production as commodifying and hegemonizing. So be it. My real concern is that writers and readers, the people at the bottom of the literary ladder, reproduce the culture industry by failing to see through the ideology of literary entrepreneurship designed to keep them in gear. It is to them – us – that my book is addressed. Although in my closing chapters I do not simply urge a literary Great Refusal (Marcuse, 1964), where writers throw down their pens and unplug their computers, it is imperative for critical literary workers to recognize that they have choices and that they are presently making the wrong ones. Heroic resistance is easily crushed or diverted. But when writers organize their protest into new literary arrangements they begin to subvert the culture industry, even create a new culture. Unfortunately, these remain abstractions, especially for those without a background in European social theory. In Chapters 7-9, I hope to concretize these notions in terms that appeal to writers and readers concerned to make a political difference beyond the catechism of left political orthodoxy.

Freelancing Yesterday and Today

In light of what I just said about the construction of a literary lifestyle into a veritable form of entrepreneurship, I seem to be contradicting my earlier claim that the age of freelancing is long past; instead, the commodification of literary activity has made writers into veritable employees in either the entertainment or academic industries. I use the term "entrepreneurship" advisedly; I am not saying that most writers freelance, or can freelance, but that aspects of entrepreneurial self-promotion definitely inform the building of successful literary careers. After all, one can do corporate or bureaucratic work and still promote oneself and network; some would say that the bureaucratic work setting more than any other provokes that self-salespersonship (Maccoby, 1976).

Freelancing was never a secure existence for American writers. One was always at the whim of unpredictable, sometimes haughty editors. Yet *the past was better*: one could write more of what one really was, unbidden to the corporate imperatives of profit. And one could expect more civility, more sensitivity, from publishers and producers; sometimes one received carefully crafted, even informative, rejection letters. Today, every writer knows that one's treatment by the literary "industries" will be impersonal at best; many people submit work suspecting that they will not receive a reply, even a form letter. Those publishing houses that refuse even to consider "unagented" work accelerate the degradation of literary relationships; the beginning writer will have little success even finding an agent.

The literary world is as cut-throat, as dehumanizing, as any business in a business civilization. Although some effete editors and authors would still believe that the literary and academic worlds are worlds apart, this is window-dressing if not downright self-justification. The Saul Bellows, the lucky few, might enjoy leisurely lunches with their editors in Manhattan as well as other courtesies any worker should expect in the workplace; the rest of us recognize that our power disadvantage with respect to publishers and producers both reflects and reproduces our overall powerlessness. We have to spend so much time simply finding a publication outlet that we cannot afford to lunch languorously or pick and choose among publishers. We take what little we can get.

The literary industry might view this phenomenon differently. It could be said that the frenzied competition in the literary and academic marketplaces reflects a lot of good writing, a resurgence of a literary class. But this impression is largely conjured by publishers and publicists who placate writers they reject and sustain the illusion that marketplace competition results in the best possible "product". But, as in capitalism generally, spirited competition need not raise standards especially where the market's own logic prohibits substantive innovation; there are many brands of toothpaste but who can really distinguish them? There are many books in the bookstore and yet they all seem alike; at least, the principles governing their publication ensure a certain fungibility, an unrelieved self-sameness.

Again, the temptation to gild the past is nearly irresistible: "before" (whenever that was), books were *really* different; authors left a heavy imprint on their literary work because they were not as relentlessly driven by the logic of the marketplace and the implications this holds for literary homogeneity and conformity. Although publishers still publish loss leaders, books they know will fail but whose prestige elevates their list, these are rarer; now, nearly every mass-market book must be a "profit center", holding its own in the marketplace. Even university presses increasingly publish trade books as well as specialized academic monographs; they are expected to be self-sustaining, especially in a period of declining university budgets. This analysis of the literary effects of commodification is made good when one glances at *People* and finds a story about a writer who wrote a book for a prestigious university press on American "First Ladies". An Oxford University Press book just appeared entitled *Baseball Anecdotes* (Okrent and Wulf, 1989)! Today, academic presses like Oxford have their own trade departments where "yesterday" this would have been unthinkable.

Publishers will interpose the caveat that much of this is inevitable where publishing costs have skyrocketed. Perhaps. Yet at issue is not whether publishers should chase profit per se but how *large* their profit margins should be. Business logic flattens every enterprise into the same nearly irresistible mold; every book must do more than recoup its investment. Houses that accept lower profit margins are dinosaurs, either sustained by the sheer prestige of their lists or bound to fail. As in every capitalist industry, publishing is increasingly standardized, centralized, hierarchized. Nothing should lead us to suspect that publishing would be exempt from the logic of commodification, centralization, concentration.

The lowest person on this totem pole is arguably the reader; after all, the hungry reader who wanders into Waldenbooks or Follett bookstores has few alternatives to the regular fare. Even university bookstores are increasingly nationalized and operated on a profit basis. Few college towns or cities boast even a handful of good bookstores, as Ithaca (Cornell University) does. My own city, Buffalo, has a left-counterculture bookstore squeezed into a delapidated space. It has limited stock, even though the owners genuinely support the intellectual project and try to order serious writing for serious and politically conscious readers. But this sort of bookstore is an anachronism. It simply cannot stand up against Waldenbooks and Folletts.

Publishers respond by saying that they are only giving readers what they want. That is the standard capitalist argument for the standardization and banalization of commodities. Indeed, there is ample evidence that people busily consume the trade properties offered in the chain bookstores and the jumbo movies released by the huge Hollywood movie outlets. *But this is because they – we consumers – have little choice.* The fact that we buy, read and watch schlock, indeed that some of us *write* schlock too, only indicates the extraordinary extent of literary hegemony. Our frenetic consumption is less a sign of literary commodities' validity than of their inauthenticity, their failure really to satisfy (Leiss, 1976). That we patronize "bad" books, movies and television shows does not mean that we endorse them. We simply have few alternatives.

Formerly, freelancing was no bed of roses; checks were unpredictable and meager. Yet corporate discourse, although somewhat more regular, is dumber, constraining writer and reader into formulaic language games. We readers are offered little in the way of real variety, nor are we challenged; and we writers are prevented (and thus, fatefully, prevent ourselves) from breaking the mold. Perhaps yesterday and today are equally repugnant, although for different reasons. Scholastics who count angels on pins lose sight of the bigger problem: the pins are sticking in their own flesh. This is much the same discussion people have about whether early entrepreneurial capitalism was more or less humane than the corporate capitalism into which it evolved. Perhaps it is only a sign of my nostalgia that I favor the ethos of frontier America; compared to Lewis and Clark, literary individuality is but a pale copy. It takes little gumption, but perhaps some irrationality, to strike out on literary careers today. Writers gladly exchange their ambition to write "serious" prose for jobs in advertising agencies and television. In a world in which everyone and everything has a price, writers have a lower price than many. We trade the hardscrabble existence of freelance writing for the relative comforts of the academic and entertainment industries. That is the important point: discourse is a business today.

Chapter 6

Academic Writing as Real Estate

Getting Tenure

Those who exchange the uncertainties and modest literary freedoms of the freelance career for the job security of academia are now on easy street, at least if they have tenure. Tenure protects one against the caprice of university administrations and intolerant colleagues, affording a relative degree of academic freedom, and it insulates one to some extent against the vicissitudes of university budgets. There are clearly two classes of employees in American universities, those with tenure, or on tenure-track "lines", and those ineligible for tenure. As in the economy generally, universities are moving quickly toward part-time and impermanent employment, reducing fiscal risk by allowing the institution to maximize organizational "degrees of freedom"; sudden downturns in university financial fortunes can be checked by simply laying off the growing cadre of non-tenured staff members (McPherson and Winston, 1988).

To the extent to which tenurable employment still exists in the university system, there are some well-researched strategies one ought to pursue in order to achieve tenure (Lewis, 1975; Reskin, 1977). One needs to combine regular, if modest, productivity (so as not to threaten one's more laconic colleagues) with a genial collegiality and interpersonal temperateness. After all, universities, like other bureaucratic organizations, reward obedience and punish rebelliousness. This is an overriding feature of academic hierarchy: one must "fit in" just as much at the University of Michigan as at Exxon or the IRS. It has been shown that "charm" contributes to success more than any other single virtue.

In addition, there are literary requirements for tenure. *What* and *how* one writes is perhaps more important for academic success than *how much* one publishes. "Publish or perish" is a rough rule of thumb;

yet the overachiever, as in any modern organization, will be widely perceived by one's colleagues as a rate-buster. And one must not just publish but publish what is judged to be legitimate academic scholarship – refereed journal articles, academic monographs and chapters in academic books. This is really the issue here: the decline of academic discourse is hastened by the narrow literary requirements of academic scholarship. One writes narrow specialist prose to "earn" tenure, not for general comprehension and enlightenment.

In the commercial literary world academic prose is the butt of jokes; it epitomizes self-important, self-referential writing. Most academics have had little or no training as writers and they do not usually attend to the stylistic dimensions of their craft. Being published in the legitimate organs of one's discipline is much more important than either form or content; academic publishing is a game played by clear rules known to all. Above all, inattention to form is thought to signal seriousness of content and thus evidence adequate academic professionalism. Where tenure is the prize, academic writing is governed by the same market logic as mass-market publishing or entertainment. One writes "for" publication, not for real readers who carefully consider, and then respond to, one's argument (Agger, 1989b).

On the surface, though, the practised obscurity of academic writing contrasts with the formulaic popularization of writing for mass culture. Yet I am claiming that both academic and mass-market writing contribute to the decline of discourse in fundamentally similar ways, even though the one seems much less accessible than the other. What these discursive forms share is an insensitivity to the *dialogue requirements of public speech and prose*, notably the way good discourse not only anticipates but provokes a response as a way of constructing a democratic polity. The lusty potboiler, no more than the esoteric scholarly journal article, fails to provoke this type of discourse precisely because it is scripted in order to make money, not to turn readers into writers. Although academic writing is generally not profit-oriented (save for textbook writing, a subject I consider below), it is driven by the equally disciplining requirements of academic disciplines themselves: academic writing is written not for general readers at all but in order to build one's curriculum vitae and thus advance one's career in the bureaucratic university, in the process contributing to the elite language games of one's particular academic field. In this sense, the commodification of popular writing is matched by the disciplining of academic writing: neither defies the hierarchical relations between writers and readers in postmodern capitalism. Both accept that writing is a product to be consumed by non-writers, in the case of popular culture the everyday trade consumer, while in the case of academic scholarship the manuscript reviewers and editors who sift through submitted manuscripts for the few "publishable" ones.

Unlike trade writers and those who write for television, movies, newspapers and ad agencies, academics writing for tenure accept the agonizing uncertainty of the pre-tenure period in exchange for the prospect of a "job for life". Although the other displaced literary activities I just mentioned involve varying degrees of job security, academic tenure is easily the most secure of all. And, perhaps as a result, it takes longer to earn tenure (typically six years) than it does to find relatively secure positions in the professional and business worlds. Universities want to hedge their bets for as long as they can before they reward junior academics with lifetime job security; after all, tenure is a gamble that a moderately productive and pleasantly collegial faculty member will keep up both pace and face in the many years ahead before retirement. Indeed, some universities are increasing their probationary periods before tenure from six years to as many as ten; in other universities, it is often uncertain whether academic positions will result in tenure at all, either because the school's finances are uncertain or because there is competition among junior faculty for tenured jobs.

Writing for tenure is intense; one has a stipulated number of years to make one's mark, finding one's way into print according to whatever standards of productivity apply in one's own department and university. It must be kept in mind by non-academic readers here that there are no *formal* guidelines indicating exactly how much, or what, the successful tenure candidate must publish; standards are notoriously vague in order to afford universities leeway in dismissing productive but irascible colleagues and keeping relatively slothful but pleasant ones. For this reason, in large part, women and minorities denied tenure increasingly sue their universities for wrongful dismissal based on sex and race discrimination, respectively. They must show that white males earning tenure at the same time had less illustrious publication and teaching records, a case relatively straightforward if not always legally successful (Brodkey, 1987, pp. 8-12).

The absence of clear and public standards for tenure only intensifies academic writers' anxiety in the probationary period before tenure. One experiences anxiety in the first place because *it is difficult to get published in legitimate academic organs*. There is no getting around the fact that the academic literary marketplace is extremely crowded, the more so the more universities stiffen tenure standards, thus forcing junior faculty to compete for space in a limited number of prestigious journals. In my own discipline, sociology, there are three leading journals (*American Sociological Review*, *American Journal of Sociology*, *Social Forces*) all of which have article acceptance rates of about 10 per cent. (In natural-science disciplines acceptance rates are somewhat higher; there is more agreement in these fields about what constitutes legitimate scholarship, framed by a common paradigm.) Typically, few have their work accepted upon its initial submission. Instead, work showing promise, according to anonymous peer reviews, is returned for a "revise and resubmit" by the author or authors. If one fares well with the rereview of one's revised work, one's work may eventually be accepted for publication.

Although this seems like a straightforward system, with clear informal norms about what and where to publish (e.g., the three leading journals I just mentioned), the process of article and manuscript submission is notoriously slow and often capricious. Sometimes it takes three months or more even to receive an initial appraisal by an academic journal. Even excluding revision time, it might well take another two or three months for a final evaluation once one resubmits one's work. And, after all that, *one might still be rejected*, forced to search elsewhere for a publication outlet for one's work. This is compounded by the fact that academic journals typically prohibit "multiple submissions", the submission of the same paper to a number of different journals at once. Academic publishing houses are sometimes more relaxed about this requirement, although some compel authors to sign a commitment giving that house the right of first rejection (or some other promise that one's work is not being considered elsewhere) (Powell, 1985).

In the case of academic books, the review process might be much lengthier than for journal articles. Notoriously understaffed university presses take months simply deciding whether to review one's book manuscript at all. After that, it may take many more months to receive an initial publishing decision and then to revise and review one's project. Obviously, for academics who work in "book" and not "article" disciplines (e.g., English, history), the stakes are very high: a single accepted book, frequently one's doctoral dissertation, is sufficient to earn tenure for the author; but lack of success in securing a publisher gives one little on which to fall back. Many university presses have acceptance rates even worse than the leading academic journals; the publisher for two of my books, the University of Illinois Press, estimates that in 1988 they received about 1,500 manuscript proposals or manuscripts and accepted around 100 of them (Malley, 1989). This is a typical acceptance rate at American university presses (which commonly publish books mainly by untenured authors struggling to hit the tenure jackpot).

For these and other reasons, getting tenure is an anxiety-producing and obstacle-strewn process. Professional academic socialization requires untenured faculty to be blasé about tenure, to show evidence of self-confidence. This only intensifies their secret anxieties and perpetuates the mythology suggesting that academia is meritocratic. Junior faculty learn to mouth the words they hear from senior faculty: "If you are good, you will get tenure". Of course, what constitutes "good" is precisely the issue: no one knows, or rather, everyone has an idea (after all, many people vote on a person's tenure; in academia one has numerous "bosses").

Even if academia were run by meritocrats according to objective criteria of excellence, untenured faculty would still have doubts about their own worth. Virtually no academic fails to harbor secret feelings of inferiority and inadequacy; a system in which excellence is praised but not explicated promotes these self-doubts. Of course, they may eventually realize that that is precisely why they are being made to jump through tenure hoops: corporate academia, just as much as Exxon, wants its employees to obey authority. Professional self-confidence is a posture for most academics; it conceals a deep fear of failure.

Few can do their best work, or any work, under these pressures. The academic system is littered with the bodies of people who did not measure up, especially those who washed out before their ultimate tenure verdict. It takes so long to learn how to balance teaching, writing, departmental obligations and personal life that untenured faculty frequently waste the first years of their probationary period. And, as I suggested, this is seriously compounded by a publication system forcing one to wait a long time for the evaluation (not to mention actual publication) of one's work. And given that journal and book acceptance rates are low, one is inevitably faced with having to submit one's work to a number of publication outlets before one wins acceptance (Powell, 1982).

In this light, it is not hard to understand academic publication as a valuable form of real estate. In my discipline, publication in one of the three leading journals is like landing on Park Place. Not only is publication in these journals highly valorized but it also introduces one to scholars across the discipline who then cite one's work in their own writing, thus helping one build reputation. Where tenure and promotion decisions are often made on the basis of the number of one's citations by other academics, the value of publishing in leading outlets is doubled. Acquiring academic real estate by "placing" one's work in leading journals and with prestigious publishing houses is essential for tenure and, beyond that, regular advancement through the ranks.

Like all real estate, the values people place on academic publication outlets are entirely subjective. That is the nature of value in a capitalist society; worth is always extrinsic, not intrinsic. Thus, the aspiring academic must carefully scrutinize the conventional wisdom in his or her discipline about which real estate to acquire. Just because one finds a particular journal or publisher worthy does not mean that one's colleagues and administrators share those views. Academic real estate is valued in terms of a hierarchy of legitimacy. Indeed, in my own discipline, as in most others, the contending journals are actually *ranked*, like football teams, on the basis of their perceived quality. Tenure committees frequently *weight* one's publications, affixing coefficients to them on the basis of *where* they were published.

Every junior academic quickly learns the value of this real estate. In addition, one learns that some properties have no value whatsoever, or so little value it is pointless to try to acquire them. Some disciplines and departments value journal articles but not books; others require junior faculty to publish books before tenure; still others balance the two modes of publication. Within these categories, articles and books, further hierarchies are elaborated. Articles must, of course, be "refereed", that is, evaluated on the basis of double-blind readers' reports, reviews of their quality by academics working in the same field and chosen by the editor or editors for their expertise. The referee system reinforces the impression that academia is an open marketplace of ideas. Publication in "nonrefereed" outlets, whether the local newspaper or monthly mass-market magazines, is almost universally disqualified in American academia.

Books are divided roughly into academic monographs and textbooks. Often the line between the two is somewhat hazy. In general terms, academic monographs are books published by either university presses (e.g., University of Illinois Press, University of California Press) or commercial monograph houses (e.g., Sage, Praeger, Academic Press). Like refereed journal articles, they are written for other academic specialists. As I said earlier, many university presses are moving quickly into trade publishing, bringing out profitable books for a general readership in order to stay "in the black". If one publishes a trade book with a university press, one may have to make a case for its academic legitimacy at tenure time.

Textbooks are books intended for adoption in undergraduate and graduate teaching. The big-selling textbooks, like the one I and my colleague intended to write, are those designed for introductory-level courses. These books are almost universally disqualified as "academic" publications; they may have value, though, in teaching-oriented colleges where tenure decisions are made more on the basis of pedagogy than publishing. Textbook writing may be seen as evidence of pedagogical commitment. But upper-division textbooks, those destined for disciplinary majors in the junior and senior years or for graduate students, are often harder to evaluate in terms of their academic legitimacy. Frequently, authors of upper-division texts are given more intellectual latitude in their presentation of material, making their own "arguments" by synthesizing information. In these cases, academic worthiness is usually decided in terms of the author's own argument for the legitimacy of his or her book as well as the general reputation of the house. An upper-division "text" with Knopf will probably be accorded more legitimacy than a lower-division book with Scott, Foresman.

Finally, a third mode of academic presentation falls between articles and books. Edited books are those comprising articles written by a number of scholars in the field. The issue of academic worthiness here involves both the contribution of the editor and the contributions of the chapter writers themselves. In general, people who write these "book chapters" receive some sort of academic credit. Sometimes these chapters "count" for as much as journal articles, sometimes less. It may depend on the reputation of the publisher and on whether the articles are clearly "refereed", passing through dispassionate professional scrutiny. Inasmuch as books with university presses are almost invariably refereed (as well as scrutinized carefully by their own academic editorial boards), chapters in such books may pass muster with tenure committees more easily than chapters in books with commercial houses. This depends very much on disciplinary norms.

As for the editors of these books, there is real ambiguity about how much weight editing a book should carry. In departments that make tenure and promotion decisions with regard to stringent norms, editing a book counts for very little, perhaps not even as much as a single refereed journal article. In other departments, editing a book is tantamount to writing one. Some faculty pad their vitae by listing the books they have edited under the heading for "Books", thus strengthening their cases in the eyes of unwitting or simply unprofessional readers. Most experienced academics do not regard editing books as particularly worthy in value, even if this activity makes a real scholarly contribution, bringing together specialists for focused work on a particular topic or problem.

Sometimes the publication of conference proceedings also bears academic value. Again, the issue is arguable. The presentation of conference papers indicates ongoing professional activity but does not count in the conventional sense until they are published in journals or as chapters. Frequently, academics "try out" their work-in-progress by presenting it at professional meetings.

Within this general topography, academic real estate is further differentiated. Variation across department, university, discipline is rampant; what "counts" at one place or at one time may not count elsewhere. This is frequently the bone of real contention in departments where the struggle for scarce tenure has become very competitive. Candidates are pitted against each other both within and across departments and thus they scramble to *make their cases*, attempting to squeeze as much value as possible out of their curricula vitae (Lewis, 1975). Although my sketch of academic real estate suggests general consensus about the norms regulating academic reward, in fact the issues are often muddied simply because people's accomplishments are incommensurable and because colleagues have real intellectual differences over what constitutes legitimate scholarship. Comparing the work of an article producer in psychology with the work of a book author in comparative literature is devilishly difficult, especially where the evaluators cannot read intelligently in both disciplines. After all, what should count is quality, not quantity, or even the prestige of one's publication outlets. But most highly specialized academics can barely keep up with developments in their own fields within their home disciplines, let alone developments in other fields or, indeed, other disciplines.

Evaluating Academic Writing

Thus, the evaluation of scholarship is inherently ironic: given both extraordinary intellectual specialization and the lack of specificity in prevailing tenure standards, it is difficult to make credible judgments. Complicating this even further is the irony that faculty from one generation, when academic norms surrounding the definition of productivity were very different, evaluate younger faculty from a relatively more productive generation. After all, academic labor market competition is much stiffer than it was in the early 1960s; there are fewer positions available and more qualified applicants. The generational irony of intercohort comparison leads to distorted readings where unproductive older faculty evaluate productive younger faculty from the point of view of their own persistent insecurities, even defensiveness.

When this happens, the tables are often turned: the heavy producer might well be turned down for tenure; those who pass muster may be intellectual lightweights who possess enough interpersonal politesse not to offend their elders. Even at best, tenuring is an ambiguous process. When generational irony is added to the picture, junior faculty frequently become victims of generationally-invested evaluation. In the long run, this produces bizarre results: relatively unproductive senior faculty promote junior faculty *like themselves*, those unlikely to rock the boat or threaten egos.

It is for this reason that most studies of the tenure process conclude that productivity, which is difficult to define in any case, is frequently not the most important criterion in personnel evaluation (Finkelstein, 1984). This is no comfort for junior academics: apart from becoming good departmental citizens and joining the suburbanized university "family", junior faculty must still publish work defined as legitimate. Except for those faculty attempting to earn tenure in "teaching schools", where good teaching is more important than published scholarship, junior faculty cannot relax their vigilance; they must attempt to acquire as much publishing real estate as possible.

Commodification of Academic Publishing I: The Academic Commodity Form

Inasmuch as space in academic journals and monographs is valuable real estate, it is possible to analyze academic publishing as a process of production and distribution. Academic editing is similar in many respects to trade editing and movie and film production, notably in its self-reproducing logic: what was published yesterday will be published tomorrow. It is different, too, in that the goal of such editing is not profit but the distribution of journal space, a scarce resource desperately sought, especially by the untenured. One must route one's work through and around academic editors quite differently situated from trade editors and entertainment producers in the sense that *they are usually academics, too* – or, if they are editors at university presses, they are accountable to purely academic criteria of excellence.

Academic book editors are more powerful than trade editors in that they are not directly accountable for publishing profitable books (Coser, Kadushin and Powell, 1982). Although they are not academics themselves, they spend their careers in the ivy-covered institutions housing academics who write the books they publish. University press publishing is genteel, governed by the same academic mythology surrounding the tenure process. Books are accepted for publication by university presses on the basis of their academic quality, not their vast audience. Indeed, most university presses in the U.S. publish their books in very short print runs, sometimes as few as 500 to 1,000 books at a time. Unlike trade publishers, they keep their books in stock for a long time, catering both to libraries and to single-copy purchasers. Although trade houses pump large amounts of money into advertising, they do not usually allow less-than-huge successes to languish on their current list; their books go out of print quickly if they do not fare well in the mass market.

Inasmuch as editorial decisions at university presses are invariably made on the basis of peer reviews, editors may be somewhat constrained by these written reports. Unlike the double-blind process of journal reviewing, it is common for reviewers to know the names of the authors whose manuscripts they review but not for authors to know their names. This is an inherently disempowering and possibly prejudicial process especially in narrow academic subfields in which "everyone knows everyone else". Editors determine who their reviewers will be, thus in effect loading the dice in favor of the prejudgments they may have already made about the publishability of submitted manuscripts.

Inasmuch as editorial decisions at university presses pass through editorial boards composed of academics in the sponsoring institution, editors are further constrained in their judgments. Some university presses are relatively unburdened of directive oversight in this regard, where others are closely supervised by press boards who not only read the manuscripts' reviews but even peruse manuscripts themselves. Norms vary widely here: some university presses are intrinsically attractive to authors because their editors are known to have a free hand in deciding what they will publish. Other presses are known to have meddlesome, unpredictable press boards who often make trouble for sponsoring editors.

In any case, editorial decision-making at university presses is driven by the peer-review process. Commercial academic monograph publishing may also involve external manuscript review, although here publication decisions are guided more by profit. But the stakes are much lower than in trade publishing; commercial academic houses (e.g., Praeger) might well print a very short first run and then keep the books in stock until another printing is warranted. The profit imperative exists, but it is somewhat muted by the house's commitment to publish books for the long haul. Many commercial academic houses (e.g., mathematics and science publishers) publish highly technical work intended for hundreds of knowledgeable readers, not hundreds of thousands. These houses fall somewhere between university presses and trade houses in that they have mixed motives for publishing; the purpose is profit, to be sure, but editors are less constrained by the bottom line than in trade houses or television.

Academic journal editors are academics themselves. They are selected by the professional associations sponsoring various national and regional journals; they serve for fixed terms, and their home institution supports publication of the journal either through direct cash outlays or by offering the faculty editor some release time from teaching, secretarial support and supplies. Obviously, academic professional journals exist for the dissemination of knowledge, not for profit. Although journal editors seek to stay afloat financially, or at least avoid egregious fiscal shortfalls imperiling the very existence of their beloved journals, their editorial motives are not monetary. They publish work they, and their peer reviewers, deem good.

As with editors at publishing houses, journal editors have complete control over the reviewers they choose. Given the extraordinary diversification and specialization within single disciplines, many journal editors rely on editorial associates and editorial boards composed of other academics to help them process submitted papers and, particularly, to select appropriate reviewers. This is *the* most crucial juncture in the regulation of academic real estate. One's chosen reviewers have extraordinary control over one's ultimate professional success: good, sympathetic reviews, leading to eventual publication, make careers, where bad reviews seriously obstruct the quest for tenure.

Even in themselves good reviews do not necessarily ensure publication. What is "good", especially in a very crowded academic literary marketplace? The market is so glutted with submissions that editors who commonly receive quite positive praise for submitted articles still turn them back because other articles are supported by even more enthusiastic reviews. My colleagues who write for these mainstream refereed journals routinely tell me about how they receive two (or two and a half!) out of three enthusiastic reviews but are still rejected.

Even more important, the evaluation of reviews is deeply problematic. Here journal editors enjoy all sorts of latitude; they can "read" basically positive reviews in an unfavorable light, or vice versa, depending on whether they want to publish the piece or not. Or if they genuinely have not formed an opinion about a submitted article, they may simply misread the reviews, either exaggerating or muting the positive. I have seen many examples of editorial misjudgment, where editors simply do not read the reviews carefully enough to distinguish text and subtext and then to arrive at an overall sense of the competence of the reading.

It is common for editors to accept work with relatively unenthusiastic reviews and reject more positively reviewed work simply because they prefer one article over the other. Inasmuch as editors rarely accept anything at face value, instead sending promising articles back for revision and resubmission, they can exercise a strong editorial hand in guiding these revisions. As such, the second round of reviews may count for relatively little in the editor's decision about publication. *Editorial readings at every level of publishing, and especially with respect to the evaluation of refereed scholarship, are deeply constitutive*; these readings are what poststructuralists would call *strong readings*, contextualizing reviewers' evaluative comments in terms of the editor's own interests. As one of my book editors said to me, his most important job is to know *how* to read reviews – that is, in terms of his knowledge of the reviewers' perspectives and in light of his own editorial interests.

This editor makes strong prejudgments about works' publishability but still leaves himself open for surprises once he reads reviewers' comments. I know other editors who use reviewers simply to support publication decisions they have already made. Still others do not even read submitted work until the reviews are in; this is particularly true of journal editors who simply have too much to read to be able to do a great deal of prescreening. The more experienced editors are, the more they can filter what seems promising from what seems unpromising and thus save both time and money, on the one hand, and carefully construct the review process in terms of their editorial interests, on the other. There is nothing really nefarious about this as long as editors and writers know what is going on: the allegedly value-free and merit-based review process is bent to editorial purposes; the game is played on the editor's own field and reviews do not mechanically drive publication decisions.

This raises the even more interesting question about what constitutes editorial interest in the first place, especially in academic publishing where the motive is usually not profit. Editors who have a large amount of authority in what they publish use their power in non-arbitrary ways; even if they only "publish their friends", that is a telling interest and probably helps explain some of the "networking" that clearly goes on in academic publishing circles. Unlike trade editors and producers constrained by a strict profit motive, academic editors of journals and university presses exist to *perpetuate the discipline – perhaps, better, just discipline itself.* They edit work that they believe both entrenches disciplinary boundaries (e.g., sociology as against non-sociology) and furthers the state of existing knowledge (Agger, 1989b).

Although these seem like laudable goals, they raise further questions, notably about *whose* discipline is being defended and advanced and *for what* reasons. By definition, editors of mainstream journals publish mainstream work, thus implicitly defending a hierarchy of mainstream as against marginal scholarship. The interesting issue is what the prevailing notion of the mainstream *excludes* – not just bad sociology, in the case of my own positivist-empiricist discipline, but, even more important, non-sociology: today, Marxism, feminism, critical theory, poststructuralism, postmodernism etc. Once we agree that what constitutes disciplinary work is not self-evident, nor what constitutes good and bad work, then we can see that journal and press editors exercise considerable power in reproducing prevailing notions of disciplinarity. Nor does this assume that editors as individuals necessarily understand the essentially political nature of their selectivity; after all, they probably believe that they are dispatching professional duties in professional ways. I am not implying conspiracy if, by that, one means a quite self-conscious effort by editors to screen out unconventional work; rather, editors and reviewers add value to prevailing standards, thus diminishing the chances that people in the future will redraw, even reinvent, disciplinary lines or otherwise reformulate what it means to do good work in a particular discipline.

As guardians of disciplines, editors guard discipline itself. Michel Foucault, an important voice of French postmodernism, suggests that western societies have invented standards of deviance in order to enforce external social control without which, it is thought, internal controls would be absent (Foucault, 1977). Disciplines that reproduce themselves also reproduce the social order to which they are attached through the relationship among higher education, the state and economy. In particular, disciplines reproduce *disciplinary discourse*, the peculiarly private argots of academics constrained by the prevailing "literatures" in their fields. Thus, if nothing else, editors, by screening out certain types of work, add value to the prevailing discourses in which disciplined professionals compose their work.

The essential feature of disciplinary discourse is its restricted linguistic code (Bernstein, 1971; Mueller, 1973). A literary political economy of academic discourse indicates that rhetorical specialization serves both to establish a standard of publishability and to keep outsiders out – general readers and writers as well as polemicists and poets. Foucault's (1977) sense of discipline suggests both these functions of disciplinary discourse. Of course, this is not public discourse in that it discourages readers from becoming writers, hence public citizens. Indeed, as I said, few academics outside the narrow ambit of one's own subfield of scholarship actually read academic journal articles and monographs, fragmenting disciplines even further. Scholarly writings are to be entered into one's curriculum vitae and perhaps cited in the literature-review sections of future scholarly articles and monographs. They discourage their reading as essays, arguments, rhetoric (Agger, 1989b). They exist merely to be counted as tangible proof of scholarly productivity, reflecting the bureaucratic Taylorization of academic life generally (Bendix, 1974). If academic writing is read, it is only to instruct other academics (and student apprentices) how to write in the future, hence reproducing discipline.

The exemplary nature of academic discourse is immensely powerful where it establishes the kind of work people will do in the future. Published work exemplifies the work people should write; thus, what is published today both reflects what was published yesterday and what, in all likelihood, will be published tomorrow. This is not to say that editors are particularly idiosyncratic in their judgments about disciplinarily appropriate work; indeed, they are usually only ciphers through whom a discipline's standardized body of knowledge and means of conveying it are elaborated. Journal editors agree to take on editorships out of professional obligation and in order to move the discipline forward in their own image. University press editors responsive to academic reviewers and university-press editorial boards serve not profit but discipline (in much the same sense as journal editors).

Academic editing, then, is double-edged, even ironically so. On the one hand, editors have enormous say in what gets published. On the other hand, the choices editors make about "what" they publish usually only reflect the existing status of knowledge and discourse in particular disciplines. Rarely do editors break the mold; they usually only strengthen it. Editing reproduces prolix academic discourse and thus editors are powerful within their own frames of reference. And yet editing paradoxically does little to change the shape of existing disciplines, bodies of knowledge and discourses. Editors as individuals are relatively unimportant, and yet editing itself has profound impact on what people write (and do not write). Authors must write to please editors who exist primarily to reinforce the discipline's own thought of itself, the way it presents itself narratively to other specialized professionals. In this sense, the postmodern deaths of writer and reader might be matched by the death of editors, too!

What, then, is the academic commodity form? Journal and book space count for the establishment of academic careers; they also matter institutionally inasmuch as particular disciplines offer guidance for people at the upper-levels of power, wealth and politics. Academic commodification involves the self-disciplining of literary work according to certain norms of academic discourse. The "how" is as important as the "what"; academic writing is distinguished by its narrowness as well as by its self-referential quality. After all, academics write *for themselves*, and for others like them. They write not to be read but to command space, the basis of value in the academic world. Or, if they write to be read, they solicit productive readings that generate citations, the peculiar evidence of having been read by other academics. Citations warrant the authority of writing, showing their impact on one's argument.

Like any commodity form, academic writing is given value through exchange; in effect, academics themselves decide the value publication in particular outlets is to have. As I noted above, where the currency of academic value production is journal space, journals are arrayed hierarchically in terms of their prestige. Journal space is real estate that, once acquired, congeals as value in the careers established on its basis. Academic writers compete with each other over scarce resources – access to the most prestigious publication outlets. Heavily regulated by editors, this work is bent to the requirements of the academic marketplace, decided in terms of the evaluations of work by "peer" reviewers.

Thus, regardless of the content and style of academic writing (both of which matter for my analysis here), the commodification of academic writing structures quite differential career outcomes. Some people's work is "less" worthy than that of others simply *by virtue of where it appeared, not what it says.* This fact alone causes discourse to decline; instead of styling intelligent arguments decided in their own terms, academic writers attempt to clone whatever standards of literary presentation obtain in their own literary marketplaces. If one wants to turn one's writing into career capital, one must attend to the discursive implications of one's work, particularly to the relationship between one's literary choices and outlets and eventual career outcomes. It is this simple: some work gets published readily (and well), while other languishes, either published in obscure (i.e., devalued) outlets or simply left to gather dust in desks and on bookshelves.

Commodification of Academic Publishing II:
The Literary Norms of Academic Writing

Just as trade writing reproduces itself through a market-based logic of imitation, so academic writing reproduces other versions of itself. Although one could simply say that academic writing is the writing done by academics, we can say more than that: academic writing embodies particular features of turgidity and self-referentiality notable for their antithesis to discourse and dialogue. The cliche about the low level of academic literary skills is, at bottom, true. Most academics, to establish careers, write specialized, pedantic, pointless prose in the styles to which they have become accustomed by the people who write for, edit and manage leading journals and university presses. It is important at the outset to understand the self-reproducing nature of the academic production process: published academic writing exemplifies the writing people are taught to do in the future thus reproducing itself.

This is exactly what academic writing has in common with the rhetorics of popular culture: both are crafted hastily, without much artifice designed to provoke thought and even a response, let alone community. Academics justify this on the ground that their writing reports research and thus should not compose itself gracefully. Trade writers write inelegantly because they serve the extant level of taste in the dulled readership at large. Both types of writing are done quickly, in order to acquire the rewards accruing to publication, whether tenure or royalties. Genuinely public discourse composes itself more slowly and carefully not necessarily to be the last word but in consideration of readers' likely responses (Iser, 1978), hence of the difference its own voice makes to the public world at large.

Academic writing and publishing proceed according to certain literary norms:

1. Academic writing reflects what has already been published; people who submit their work to academic journals and presses are highly constrained by the "literature", what has been published in the recent or distant past (Kuhn, 1970). Academic writing is necessarily scholastic in the way it locates its argument in a tradition of published scholarship giving it meaning but also constraining it from defining its problems in a distinctive authorial voice. Academic disciplines contribute to discipline at large by subordinating writers to extant traditions, literatures, speech communities largely dictating one's intellectual problems, methodologies, solutions. Academic writing, by definition, is highly constrained by the mountains of citations that must lard one's writing. As such, intellectual innovation is discouraged.

To be an academic writer one must try to resolve, or at least cope with, the literary irony of deriving one's topic and method from established literatures while claiming the distinctiveness of one's approach to the topic. That is much easier said than done, as even a casual perusal of mainstream journal literature in almost any discipline will indicate. By now, disciplines have such irresistible momentum that it is virtually impossible for writers to establish a unique literary signature; it is even more unlikely that a single writer will undo, or otherwise redirect, the forward-march of disciplines. Today, apostasy amounts to tenure denial, not to mass mobilization.

2. Just as all academic pieces must begin narratively with preliminary scene settings, "literature reviews", they also engage their topics in highly specialized and differentiated approaches within common disciplinary rhetoric. Technical writing inherently obscures, preventing interpretive access from outside the discipline (Wells, 1986). The technical codes littering academic discourse are media of power, inclusion, exclusion; they are rhetorically unnecessary in the strict sense. This is not an argument for so-called ordinary language only encoding the structured stupidity of what Marcuse (1964) aptly called "one-dimensional society". It is simply to notice the universal tendencies of disciplinary discourses to become what Bernstein (1971) called "restricted codes", established to reinforce the hegemony of disciplinary talk and the world it buttresses.

This is not mainly a matter of style; most academics could

write well-crafted English if pressed to do so. Academic discourse declines not because of busted syntax or the proliferation of prolix prose; it declines because it semiotizes concepts into prose, figure and number in order to frustrate dialogical challenges to it, and to its world. This is done in the name of *methodology*, a logic with which writers reconstruct their own research program in order to convince readers rhetorically that what they did makes sense (Phillips, 1971; Feyerabend, 1975). If methodology is read as rhetoric, the intent to persuade, that is one thing; indeed, that is the way I try to read academic prose. But methodology is assumed to solve intellectual problems in its own right, whether in chemistry or English departments. Methodology mystifies the narrativeness of academic writing, instead pretending that what is being argued has verisimilitude simply because it is printed in academic journals or books and thus bears a disciplinary imprimatur.

3. Academic writing is to be done by disciplined professionals, people who have institutional affiliations, are networked within the power groups (speech communities (Hymes, 1974)) of their discipline, and write in the appropriate technical argots established as legitimate. Although this seems obvious, it is curious that the people who publish in sociology, history, physics are assumed to be sociologists, historians, physicists. Indeed, this assumption grounds another assumption: work published in disciplinary journals is unequivocally borne of that discipline, and reinforces it. Thus, we sociologists are supposed to know, and thus reproduce, what counts as sociology. If we write other work veering away from our disciplinary boundaries, we are to submit it to journals outside our own discipline. Of course, doing too much of this sort of work will reduce the value of own's professional resume.

4. Academic writing is not meant to be read in the sense that it is supposed to start dialogues and create non-authoritarian speech communities. Academic ideology would deny this, of course, suggesting that refereed academic publication ensures the smooth functioning of John Stuart Mill's "marketplace of ideas" in which the best scholarship emerges victorious in contest with less worthy scholarship. But the extraordinary specialization of academic discourse, coupled with its disciplinary duplication, ensures that most academic journal articles and monographs sink in the vast Sargasso Sea of scholarship.

The commodification of academic writing ensures that people write to get published, not to be read, meritocratic ideology notwithstanding. This is an empirical question: do articles and books typically produce debate? No. And those rare ones that do generate critical enthusiasm, both con and pro, tend to be products of fortuity as much as excellence. Good promotion and self-promotion may count for more than anything else in determining one's reception in the academic community. This is why academic authors relentlessly complain that the university presses publishing their books spend insufficient money in publicizing their work: they recognize that reputation, in all its capriciousness, is largely self-manufactured.

The commodification of discourse meets an interesting fork in the road: people who write for popular culture write "for" readers, the bill-paying public. People who write for tenure write *not* to be read in the same sense; at best, they write to be cited. Their forbiddingly technical prose keeps outsiders out, instead merely adding value to the disciplines whose iteration their narrow work supports. Even if academics lust to be read, thus to become "stars", academic discourse frustrates publicity. Only the Carl Sagans, with their popularizing television shows, hit the big time, crossing over from the academic world to popular culture.

Academic Writing: Written by Writers or Through Them?

As a materialist of sorts, I vigorously resist dehistoricizing analyses; as such, there is no single "academic writing" but only academic writing in certain social and historical contexts. Given my critique of academic writing as purposely obscurantist, can academic writing be done differently? Can intellectuals (Johnson, 1988; Parini, 1989) be reborn as guardians of democracy and community? This is the topic for my three concluding chapters. Here, let me suggest that the heroic concept of a solitary, struggling author is increasingly problematic in light of the administered nature of academic scholarship. Indeed, for people who work in empirical research disciplines, the image of a struggling writer secreted alone in a quiet space, scratching away with a quill on linen page, bears virtually no relationship to what, and how, academics really write: increasingly, writing is done through them, not by them. At the very least, they serve a very minor function in the academic production process, merely drafting work elaborately worked over in the various stages of editorial mediation and domestication.

Imagine the typical multi-authored academic journal article reporting research findings (Knorr-Cetina, 1981; Mulkay, 1984; Agger, 1989b). Sections of the paper, comprising only a few pages, might be drafted by individual writers in the research team and then heavily revised by the other authors. The paper is sent around to colleagues in the field before it is submitted for publication to an academic journal. If the journal is at all interested in publishing the work, the journal editor mediates between the writing team and the several manuscript reviewers who have sent in comments about how the paper could be improved. Most papers that are not rejected outright go through a number of drafts and editorial appraisals. By the time a single paper has been published, it may bear little resemblance to the first draft with which the author team started.

This is not to say that papers are simply scripts prepared by editors, publishers, manuscript reviewers. The irrationality of commodified academic writing is just that. There is no simple or single compact on the part of the people who manage publishing to standardize product or reduce intellect; these things are merely by-products of writing for profit and tenure. In academia, the market is not book buyers but the editors and academic reviewers who domesticate papers and monographs, bending them to the conventional methodological norms of their discipline. Reviewers can influence what is published, especially where editors are uncertain about a work's quality.

Ironically, academic reviewers are also academic writers; people who review work also submit their own work. Peculiarly, it would seem from the outside, academic writers accept their double status as reviewers required to disqualify much of what they read. This is peculiar inasmuch as reviewing reproduces itself in a subculture of literary norms determining what is appropriate reviewing behavior. Bad reviews encourage other academic writer-reviewers to review work badly; nastiness and carping criticism all too quickly become the norm in academic reviewing. "Good" reviewers are those few who are able to praise work they would not do themselves; much intellectual intolerance emerges from writer-reviewers' narcissism: they disqualify work with which they disagree or would do differently. Such reviews intolerantly rewrite.

Academic reviewing becomes even nastier in an extremely competitive marketplace. As I discussed earlier, it is no longer enough in many disciplines to have two strongly positive reviews and one lukewarm one; all three must be sterling given the rate at which writers submit papers for publication. In this climate, reviewers learn (and teach themselves, circularly) not to read generously but to target the smallest issues in their overall evaluation. And many of the seemingly technical issues raised by reviewers when they evaluate submitted work cannot be decided definitively; as a rhetorical device, methodology can be done in many legitimately different ways. Frequently, academic reviewers subvert papers and monographs on specious methodological grounds when, in fact, the reviewers are either narrowly intolerant of difference or simply wrong.

In this context, it is questionable whether academic writers really write their writing. Of course, on one level they do. They put their names on the work they submit and they are responsible for the subsequent generations of revision the work may have to undergo. But when academic writing intends to claim valuable real estate, it is clear that one must write "for" academic reviewers, trying to anticipate their objections and then allow their suggested revisions to guide them in revision. This both domesticates arguments, making them more hesitant than they need to be, and empowers reviewers and editors with unusual literary power. Although it might seem harmless for one's submitted academic work to be appraised by other "experts" in the field, the nature of reviewing is such that reviewing is far from the value-free process John Stuart Mill first envisioned; instead, reviewing is frequently done out of petty jealousy, ideological interest or simply incompetence. By now, in most academic disciplines, reviewers tend to review harshly, trying to dismiss submitted work whenever possible.

It is to be expected that the review process would drive college textbook publishing, movie production, even trade fiction. Those types of literary work are commodified in terms of their sheer exchange value. Academic commodification turns on its real estate value, its existence as cultural capital (Bourdieu, 1984). And this real estate value is established through editorial and reviewing processes basically inimical to public discourse, even to academic freedom. Although reviewing can be extremely useful, alerting the solitary writer or writing team to both stylistic and substantive issues unforeseen by them, too frequently reviewing and editing determine all authorial choices; the revision process becomes a *subversion of original authorial craft*, capriciously undermining literary originality. We academic writers put up with one-sided power relations between ourselves and editors and reviewers simply because we view this as inevitable, something to be born tiredly in the hurly-burly of the competitive academic marketplace. Most of us are too beaten down to challenge the often arbitrary, sometimes downright pernicious and always disciplining directives from reviewers and editors.

Many of my colleagues who write empirical social research for academic journals are experts at the quick literary fix. Their first drafts are inevitably turned back for rewriting, pursuant to the journal editor's mediation of reviewers' criticisms. Most of them obligingly follow even the smallest demands from editors and reviewers and then resubmit their work for further consideration. They realize that publication hinges on their willingness to make the kinds of changes dictated externally. Thus, most academics are inured to the indignities (not to mention the sheer intellectual irrationality) of review-driven scholarship. On the contrary, academic "peer review", as it is called, is assumed to be absolutely necessary for the advancement of scholarship.

Trade editing and academic editing share a certain constitutional authority in what gets published trade editing responds to the prospective readership where academic editing responds to *other academics*, manuscript reviewers. Although this makes sense in the abstract, for academics are in fact the main readers of academic journals, the review process drives editorial decisions in a basically irrational way. After all, the two or three manuscript appraisers chosen by press and journal editors to review submitted work may not, in fact, represent the readership in general (i.e., all academics who work in the particular area within which the author of the submitted paper writes). Nor is it certain that they are even competent or fair-minded, capable of making objective appraisals of work that is not their own. Although academics who write soon become reviewers for journals and presses, thus learning the role obligations of professional academic referees, there is no guarantee that they review *well*, exhibiting the generosity of spirit I talked about above.

Although trade editing and entertainment production may miss, or misunderstand, the potential markets for submitted work, profit-driven reviewing is much more likely than academic reviewing to be conducted rationally – that is, with a more representative sample of prospective readers, polled scientifically. When movie moguls test out provisional cuts of their films on selected audiences, hoping to learn where to make changes before entering into mass distribution, they use a large, selectively sampled pool of "reviewers", members of the movie-going public itself. While trade book editors may not test their "products" in the same way, they are more likely than academic reviewers to have a keen finger-sense of the particular segment of the book-buying public they hope to address with the work they publish.

Take college textbook publishing as an example here. Major houses deciding whether, and how, to publish introductory-level college textbooks often do huge amounts of advance planning and market research, designed both to drive "developmental" (i.e., editorial and revision) decisions and to create a pre-market among the many academic reviewers of the project in question. The textbook I and my coauthor considered writing would be guided by an extraordinarily exhaustive exercise in preliminary market research; as many as *1,500* reviewers would be contacted and asked to review our plans for the book. From this large pool, prospective manuscript reviewers, and thus potential book adopters, would be drawn later on. Houses that invest hundreds of thousands of dollars in development and production leave little to chance. Unlike academic editors and publishers, they require hundreds, even thousands, of people to appraise their potential and actual "product", not the two or three reviewers casually selected by journal editors and academic press editors to scrutinize submitted scholarly work.

Thus, commodified commercial writing and commodified academic writing are both driven by editorial decisions made on the basis of outside reviews; these reviews serve to curb, even replace, the author, who is increasingly degraded into a low-paid functionary responsible only for the initial draft or drafts but not for the ultimate execution of the project. Many college textbooks initially begin as authors' projects but end up being collaborative efforts where the house decides that the author has insufficient literary skills, is too slow or needs other sorts of editorial assistance and thus hires a professional writer to help complete the project.

Academic writers who write for tenure and advancement, not profit, are increasingly fungible – or, at least, subordinate to the evaluations of editors and the manuscript reviewers they select. Academic authors laconically change their manuscripts according to the desiderata of outsiders; they either realize that these changes are indispensable for publication or they deeply believe in the process of peer review as an objective and elevating one. Although any smart writer not only welcomes but requires readers, some of us are too gun-shy to suspend our cynicism about the degrading effects of manuscript reviewing. We hope to find editors who intervene least in the gestation of our work – who read reviews flexibly, who allow revisions to be "author induced", and who recognize the inherent arbitrariness, sometimes even capriciousness, of the review process itself. After all, some of the important books and articles are unpopular precisely because they are path-breaking, challenging, demanding. The literary and academic worlds are full of stories about books that were widely rejected but that, once published, acquired pre-eminence in their fields. Initial rejection did not daunt their intrepid (one might say foolhardy) authors. They persevered, and eventually found publishers. Many potentially important "books" never see the light of day simply because the authors tire of rejection, run out of stamps or become cynical about the literary production process. After the eighth or twelfth publisher has turned them down, they give up. Only the hardiest souls persevere through numerous rejections, eventually finding the one house that will publish their work.

This whole discussion of the disempowering of the academic author owes a great deal to poststructuralist notions about the death of the subject as well as to the Frankfurt analysis of the culture industry. When I say that books write authors I am summarizing the empirical ways in which the culture industry dictates writers' literary agendas, notably in academia. Journals, publishers, editors, reviewers and one's disciplinary colleagues all erase the distinctive authorial signatures connoting literary imagination. Work is so highly processed through the editorial and publishing gatekeeping systems that it inevitably takes on a certain homogeneity: just as trade books and jumbo mainstream movies seem unrelievedly similar, so academic journal articles and monographs could have been composed by the same dispassionate voice. In academic writing, discipline is the real author, an insight owed as much to Foucault, Barthes and Derrida's deconstructive analysis of the death of the subject as to the Frankfurt School's analysis of the culture industry. Together, these theoretical traditions combine to form a very powerful version of radical cultural studies, explaining the decline of discourse subjectively, in terms of what happens to diminish the imagination of individual writers, and objectively, in terms of the institutional processes of literary disciplining.

Getting Published

Getting published commercially is a topic tackled by all sorts of self-help writers; nostrums abound about how to "fix" manuscripts sufficiently in order to find publishers. In the academic world, informal intelligence instructs young faculty members about the ways and wiles of finding journal and presses with which to "place" one's work: the more influential contacts one has, the better. Just as with trade writers, though, the time and energy it takes to get published drain energy better spent in writing and research themselves. Many academics, even at the top levels, spend more time seeking publication than they do writing. Like everything else in a commodified world, the value of their work declines as they become enmeshed in the exchange relationships required to have their work accepted for publication. As a result, their scholarship suffers.

This is not an iron law; people who must hustle to find publication *can* do good work. Indeed, it is sometimes the people doing the best, most inspired work who are most highly motivated – driven – to get published. Yet anyone who writes in the academic literary marketplace knows how deenergizing the quest for space quickly becomes. Not only is academic publication almost inevitably a process of serious literary compromise for writers driven to revise by editors and reviewers; it is also a huge expenditure of time spent submitting, revising, networking, conferencing, xeroxing, telephoning. Whether or not the good-old-days ever existed, when one could just "send in" one's work to a trusty and intrepid editor, today one must work as hard to achieve publication as to write, perhaps even harder.

Although things become easier for accomplished academic writers with track records as well as abundant contacts and sponsors, virtually no one is assured publication. People who appear in print repeatedly are those who have the best contacts, write quickly and well and possess the most energy; every manuscript submission is a struggle to be endured. Academic seniority and reputation make it somewhat easier to publish and perhaps ensure that one will have fewer revisions imposed. Ultimately, this is an empirical question: what are the intellectual compromises required to acquire the valuable real estate of mainstream journal and university press publication?

My portrait of academic writing and publishing in this chapter will be denounced as monochromatic by academics and editors who emphasize exceptions to the general trend of intellectual degradation. True, renegade books and articles do occasionally see the light of day. But they are dwarfed by the self-same academese rolling off the presses, larding curriculum vitae, building careers and reproducing itself. Indeed, an early draft of this book was rejected by a number of editors at commercial academic houses not on grounds of market but because the editors were offended by my portrayal of them and of the academic literary world. Two in particular, working at prestigious east-coast houses, were especially miffed, proclaiming that academic editing and publishing do not correspond to my dismal portrayal of them. Although understandable, their defensiveness is telling. Works like this hit a raw nerve where editors, academics and reviewers want to believe that they are the exceptions, vigorously promoting and defending quality. My response to all this is that individual good-will is quite irrelevant: the culture industry grinds us all down. Indeed, in the next three chapters, I consider whether, and how, individual writers and publishers can begin to subvert the culture industry from the inside. Without giving away the whole story, let me say only that there are no ample grounds for optimism. Of course, neither is that a reason not to struggle, write, edit, as I am doing here.

Chapter 7

New Journals, Better Bookstores?

Heroizing the Literary Individual or Indulging Postmodern Cynicism?

I have offered enough of a diagnosis: driven by the political economies and resulting literary hegemony of popular culture and academia, intelligible public discourse has declined; people who write
to live must make numerous compromises that, in effect, negate
the autonomy, as well as political efficacy, of the literary life. They
neglect the public sphere and hence only reinforce a general lassitude,
thus powerlessness. In this and the following two chapters, I turn to
solutions, if any exist. Better, I raise the question about what it might
mean to recreate our literary culture in meaningful terms. At once,
my argument suggests that it is not enough for mere individuals,
whether writers, editors, booksellers or producers, to decide to live
differently outside the enveloping structural contexts within which
commodified writing is now situated but, at the same time, that we
cannot neglect the contribution of good writing and reading to
making the world into a democratically public place, Habermas'
ideal speech situation. Although one inevitably hopes that a few
heroic books and movies could change things significantly for all
of us who write and read, my analysis suggests that this rarely
happens for reasons that have to do with the large structures of
literary political economy. The struggle between good public writing
and the culture industry is no contest.

Yet, for all that, it is also inadequate simply to register the inadequacy of social reform. Lyotard's (1984) postmodernism is fatalism,
hence political quiescence. Although in these times one must muster a good deal of apparently irrational exuberance in order to
resist the preponderant forces bearing down on all of us, writers
no less than welfare recipients or political prisoners, the fact remains

that *people struggle* in the various locales within which they pursue their everyday concerns (Freire, 1970; O'Neill, 1976, 1985). Writers struggle no less (or more) than others who lead lives not fully self-determined. My critique of postmodern cynicism is unsparing; real literary work, real resistance, cannot be traded for an urbane literary lifestyle. Cosmopolitanism is precisely the cultural logic of literary commodification, centralization, concentration. Unfortunately, in the madness of the literary marketplace, writers must promote themselves shamelessly in order to gain publication outlets let alone make real reputations. The tendency to substitute literary networking and posturing for literary work is nearly irresistible when manuscripts become "product" and editing is largely an exercise in market research.

Thus, there is plenty of responsibility to pass around. Instead, the issue is not to indict individuals who shrivel in face of literary star-systems or editors who must "make target" but to understand *our common plight* – the ways in which our literary activities are dominated by forces largely inimical to intelligent creativity and thus public political reason. Writers indict editors and editors pass the buck to their corporate bosses. Capitalism has always subsisted on divide-and-conquer; the powerless fight each other instead of their common enemy (Adorno *et al.*, 1950). Yet what exactly can it mean for editors and writers to unite in order to confront the civilizational tendencies of commodification – world capitalism – turning all of us into mere utilities as well as sources of labor power?

I have no patent solutions. The notion of solutions implies that the causes of the decline of discourse can be readily isolated, and then eradicated. Where capitalism is the cause, particular reforms are either co-opted or deflected. Just understanding this helps us reject what are *false solutions* to the decline of literary culture – heroizing the solitary auteur, who holds out against insurmountable corporate odds, or reducing the literary effort to a postmodern cultural mien, an "attitude" as much as a work style. This is a false option: to enter the modernist writer's garret, scribbling madly alone, or to hang out with the smart set, reducing one's literary effort to networking. As tempting as these options are, they must be debunked. "Good work" solves little if it goes unpublished, the modernist mirage. And literary chic sacrifices the Dionysian in one's literary project; "cool" is the antonym of "warm", thus of aesthetic and political passion. In the rest of this book I begin to suggest a perspective on, if no hard-and-fast blueprints of, a literary culture that is "post"-postmodern.

Many of us viscerally respond to the gigantism of literary institutions, whether mammoth Manhattan trade houses, newspapers and studios or bureaucratic universities, with heroic images of our own integrity. Holding out for the "right" publisher assumes that there *are* "right" publishers today, houses somehow outside the networks of literary commodity exchange. It also assumes that the literary world is, at bottom, a meritocracy: someday, one will be "discovered", published, lionized, rewarded – even change the world. But the single writer is fading fast, his or her autonomy crushed under the market pressures turning books into profit centers and editors into accountants. Although we might hope to return to a literary world in which unfettered competition existed, and thus more authorial opportunities, there is no turning back: CBS, Prentice-Hall, *The New York Times* are here to stay.

Of course, people with historical perspective doubt that yesteryear was really any different or any better. Even if it was, the literary world has gone corporate. Can writers resist, even fight back? Empirically, few do. Most writing is derivative and shallowly formulaic because writers have not been able to resist the commodification of their literary imagination. These are not theoretical issues but empirical ones: if discourse has declined, can singular authors, or even publishers, heroically reverse it? In general, the answer is no although, in my last chapter, I will come down on the side of literary heroism more than on the side of literary chic, the postmodern miasma. By and large, it is far-fetched to suggest that writers can write "good" writing, find publishers or producers, and thus make a living. Meritocracy is an ideology invented to justify inequality: those on top "earned" it the old-fashioned way, while those beneath them are either less talented or simply lazy. Although "good" writing gets published, it is not the norm, nor does *writing* "good" writing ensure publication.

That is the nub of the issue: if writers could expect to be rewarded for their hard-won talents and honest effort, then one could propose to change the literary world from the ground up. Writing workshops, editorial nurturance and lots of patience would be tickets to success, even to social change. Unfortunately, the vast majority of people who try to write for a living simply fail, and not because they are untalented or lack promise. Corporate publishing needs little "good" writing, indeed discourages it, where there are few "good" readers and thus little demand for it. Writers are prized for their "professionalism" – punctuality, agreeableness, technical writing abilities, even their willingness to help market their book actively through personal appearances. The good writer today is like any obedient corporate citizen, ever willing to please.

Postmodernism dismisses heroic responses to corporate publishing and production as ineffectual; instead, the postmodern writer, recognizing the futility of "good work" as an ideology with which to defeat literary institutions promoting mediocrity, disdains the mediocre: postmodern writing seeks a literary thrill-a-minute, hyping itself as a cultural form of life somehow unbidden to corporate imperatives. Clearly, this embodies a kind of entrepreneurialism, too, yet not the pastoral one of the American frontier. Postmodern writers "circulate and motivate" in bars and at writers' conferences, recognizing fully that their work is "product" and that they are the best shills for it (e.g., Ueland, 1987). Even if these writers want to write serious work, they end up fatigued, dispirited, spread too thin – overstimulated and undergratified, as one of the Yuppie slogans of the times has it.

Heroic writers want to improve the culture, where postmodern writers want to *make it*. Of course, these are broad archetypes; many literary workers fall somewhere in between, or beyond, this simple dichotomy. People like Jacoby (1987) clearly choose the heroic route, even if he, as a Marxist, recognizes the enormous institutional blockages to living a real writer's life, notably the decline of urban bohemias and the academization of literary work. I, too, resonate with literary heroism as a spirited antidote to the commodification of writing. Yet, like Jacoby, I recognize that literary heroism is nearly hopeless; even if one can survive by writing "good" work (getting it published, making a living), one's voice will be quickly swallowed in the cultural din of the moment. The fate of Jacoby's book, compared to that of Allan Bloom, shows the way here. Even though Jacoby found publication, even wide critical notice, *The Last Intellectuals* scarcely makes it easier for people under 45 to be "intellectuals", in his terms.

Given the difficulties of writing intelligently in a corporate literary world, whether trade, electronic or academic, postmodern literary chic seems the only available option; few could argue against networking as a means of getting published, noticed, famous. Yet rubbing shoulders with the literati, editors, agents and reviewers does not warrant its inflation into a full-blown cultural style, whether based in New York or Los Angeles. Postmodernism is the demise of political hope; instead, postmodernists insist on the eternal discontinuities of history, falling back on a cynical, blatantly self-serving version of rugged individualism. In particular, post-modernism, as yet another assault on Marx's modernist utopianism, disqualifies committed literature (Sartre, 1965), indeed all political action, as irremediably futile, even counterproductive. The hordes of cynical avantgarde arrivistes posturing as auteurs reinforce the *Zeitgeist*: postmodernism says, again, that ideology has ended, and none too soon.

Nevertheless, we can reconfigure postmodernism, as I do in my concluding chapter, in a way that releases its critical energy and thus enlists it in the struggle to create a vital public culture. If postmodernism is the cultural logic of late capitalism, as Jameson (1984b) claims, we can plot a post-postmodernism, a post-capitalist postmodernism, that does not betray intellectual and hence substantive democracy. This depends on our literary and political commitment as well as on our imaginative ability to depict a better world in believable, attainable terms, something that even the most rebellious modernisms (e.g., Marx, Adorno) have ceased to do. Although, with Habermas, Marcuse, Adorno and Marx, I value enlightenment over myth, enlightenment has become so mythic (Horkheimer and Adorno, 1972, pp. 3-42) that to speak its language is a betrayal. We have to reinvent the vocabulary of liberation at a time when freedom is merely an empty slogan used by advertisers and politicians, not just political theorists.

Only in America are expressive possibilities exhausted by singular heroism, literary Lewis and Clarks conquering the barren wasteland of popular culture, and by the self-promotion of writers who dress up their "work" with the pretentious posturings of postmodernism. Today, in fact, we hear about postmodernism everywhere we turn: office buildings, writing, film, the *Zeitgeist* itself. Unfortunately, this dichotomy – literary purity "or" lifestyle – excludes writing destining itself as a moment of social transformation. By now, drab Marxist aesthetic theory seems to discredit any attempt to approach literary work from a progressive political perspective (Hauser, 1982). The byzantine debates among left aesthetic theorists, from Brecht, Benjamin and Barthes to Derrida and Kristeva, suggest the hopelessness of finding political hope in interpretive skirmishes of interest to the few hundred people in literary theory, not to the billions trampled by the *Zeitgeist* – capitalist, state-socialist, racist, sexist. Yet, although aesthetic theory itself will not change the world, the possibilities of political literature are not exhausted by the debate over postmodernism (e.g., Adorno, 1978a; Benjamin, 1978).

If aesthetic and interpretive theory is recast as a version of the critique of ideology, then it is easy to see its political relevance.

Although individual writers might not matter much, certainly popular culture does, as the Frankfurt thinkers suggested half a century ago (Horkheimer and Adorno, 1972). Although capital's contradictions subsist at a bedrock layer of the social totality, they are now highly mediated by the state's interventions designed to forestall economic crisis and by culture's ameliorations of psychic crisis. Culture can be a battleground of the political as long as culture is neither reduced to economics nor so divorced from it that we try vainly to "take writing on its own terms", whatever that might mean. Although, against deconstruction, the world is not all text, text itself is a world, a nucleic "language game" both reflecting and reproducing domination.

But these are portentous considerations. For writers themselves, the issue is survival before all else. Although political writers want to extend their writing into full-blown social criticism, politics follows survival as a priority in a commodified literary work. Derrida does not put bread on the table; in this sense, the postmodern literary lifestyle is a more reliable ticket to survival, if not a more lasting type of success. Of course, the Manhattan crowd dabbles in deconstruction, mouthing words like "Derrida" as a means of accumulating cultural capital. Indeed, fads like deconstruction, situationism, even critical theory carry value when they surface at the level of the Sunday *New York Times* and *New York Review of Books*. As slogans or cliches, this heavy intellectual baggage gains access to the conferences, clubs, restaurants and gallery openings frequented by other would-be "stars". No matter that the work being shown or promoted is hopelessly atheoretical, having as much to do with serious intellectual or aesthetic construction as corn flakes have to do with haute cuisine.

Surviving Survival: Alternatives to Literary Gigantism

On the one hand, then, these ponderous aesthetic, intellectual and political concerns are quite irrelevant to, even hinder, literary survival. Mass-market writing addresses people in Portland, not Paris; and the percentage of academics who care about critical and cultural theory is extremely small. On the other hand, my interest here is not to offer cookbook advice to struggling writers but to consider how the struggle to write real discourse – world-constitutive literary work – intersects with sheer survival. To pose seriousness and survival as a polarity may only describe the present; yet this reflection quickly becomes a rationale for choosing "either" one or the other. I am interested in the choices available to writers that do more than sustain literary lives, yet without denying that the issue of literary work is, at bottom, a question as much about work as about literature.

Precisely because I reject the heroic response to cultural commodification I consider textual politics from the point of view of material interests; thus, I insist that "what" people write cannot be divorced from "how" (i.e., under what circumstances, and for whom) they write. The commodification of discourse has enormous impact both for people who write discourse and for discourse itself. Literary capitalism cannot be ignored as if it did not exist; the solitary writer, no matter how good, cannot change the structures enmeshing publication. Although there may be Updikes, Cheevers, Bellows, Malamuds just waiting to be "discovered", they will surface much more by dint of their own exhausting self-promotion than through editorial scouting and publishers' risk-taking. The Updikes of the next generation will probably find themselves working in ad agencies, law firms and colleges, squandering their imagination and thus impoverishing all of us.

Whatever one may think about high cultural theory, whether postmodernism or my critique of it, *writers write*; they attempt to steer clear of the maw of administration reducing them to keyboard pounding and calculator punching in the entertainment and academic industries. Jacoby exists, as do his counterparts in art, fiction, music. This book is hopeful, even though I suggest structural and empirical blockages to hope. Writers live to write, to make a difference, auguring, in their own example, a good polity or aesthetic community comprising equal speakers and creators. This much is essential for those who endeavor not to drive cabs or write ads, nor to spend their valuable creative hours hobnobbing with gliterati in bars and clubs. There are "honest" writers out there who recognize the ironies of survival, indeed who want to *survive* survival and live to write another day. Of course, at the limit, this raises the question about whether people who write are "really" writers if they are not published as such. The well-meaning, generous answer is yes; but for those who exist on the fringes, it is harder to sustain the literary self-identity required to perfect one's craft – let alone make ends meet.

Let me turn to what serious writers actually do about the dilemmas imposed by literary commodification. My polarity of heroic literary individualism versus networking and posturing is not exhaustive; there are flesh-and-blood literary workers attempting to beat the system and survive yet without compromising their intellectual and political integrity. One of the criticisms of Jacoby's book is that he failed to search carefully enough for writers under 45 who refuse to succumb to academization or the postmodern literary lifestyle. He acknowledges that there are artists, poets, fiction writers, notably people of color and women, who defy the crushing corporate literary institutions and manage to survive with integrity intact (Jacoby, 1987, p. x).

In general terms, one alternative to literary gigantism and corporate control, whether in the entertainment or academic industries, is to conceive of and foster *actual institutional alternatives*: thus, some heroic writers and editors start journals and publishing companies, establish bookstores and form literary circles as alternatives to the establishment cultural institutions (Gottlieb, 1987). These efforts defy the commodification of literary activity, resisting the demeaning norms of these large institutions, particularly the reduction of literary activity to market relationships. Indeed, my critique of the commodification of literary activity would suggest that we should refuse to put a dollar value on our writing, insisting that ideas, and the people who conjure them, should not be bought and sold. Thus, publication and production alternatives are sought *beyond* the commodity circuitries of McGraw-Hill, CBS, Harvard.

In practical terms, of course, material survival dictates the usage of currency – actual dollar bills exchanged for one's literary output. In a money economy money is the universal medium of barter, not just a literary fiction easily defied by the impecunious or rebellious. The effort to start journals, publishing houses, bookstores, production companies, newspapers and magazines as alternatives to the dominant literary institutions does not dispense with currency but decentralizes literary production and distribution in such a way that writers and artists have more control over their product. This attempt to go beyond the dominant literary institutions is venerable; the utopian socialists and then Marx stressed workers' control and ownership as means of mitigating the horrors of capitalism. And, in the 1960s, co-operativism gathered momentum as a blow against a whole host of food and cultural conglomerates.

People who start little-little literary periodicals, radical academic journals, small self-managed publishing houses and community-oriented arts theaters are the same people who shop and work at food co-ops, visit neighborhood health clinics and buy second-hand clothes. These pragmatic efforts to sustain people's real lives without rewarding, and thus succumbing to, huge institutions thwarting creativity and autonomy are the most tangible examples of literary and political resistance today. American political culture has always contained a thread of radical populism sympathetic to this latter-day co-operativism. For the most part doctrinally non-Marxist (or, as they would often claim, post-Marxist), these efforts trace their roots backward to Tom Paine and Thoreau and forward to the commune movement, peace movement, women's movement and environmentalism. The attempt to do honest work and consume authentic products converges with what amounts to a moral indictment of all gigantism, both capitalist and state-socialist.

Like Jacoby, I celebrate home-grown American radicalism of this sort. Mark Kann in his *The American Left* (1982) and *Middle Class Radicalism in Santa Monica* (1986) articulates a genuine American progressivism-socialism with roots more in Debs than Gramsci. These efforts combine material survival with moral and political education; they were given powerful momentum during the 1960s as large groups of middle-class Americans arose to protest racial and sexual inequality as well as the war in Vietnam. The Michael Harringtons (1962) and Betty Friedans (1963) are American radicals in the best sense, even if they do not join dialogue with more recondite European traditions of radicalism. These traditions have much to offer literary workers precisely because they afford practicable alternatives to "mainstream" literary institutions, whether Simon & Schuster, Yale University Press, Metro Goldwin-Mayer or ABC. Publishing or producing with small, politically and socially conscious outlets offers subsistence, if not substantive social change.

Media caricatures of a selfish Yuppie generation, born during the birth spurt between about 1947 and 1960, are monochromatic. Very few baby-boomers are now resplendent in high-powered, high-pay jobs to which they travel in BMWs wearing Brooks Brothers. In fact, baby-boomers raised to view the world as their oyster suffer severe economic disappointment in a retrenching economic climate; Yuppies who (by some journalistic definitions) make $2,000 for every year of their age are few and far between. In addition, the media portrayal of a generation raised on Spock but now embracing neoconservatism is also one-dimensional. Just as many baby-boomers are working-class, not upper-middle class, so some live "alternative" lives beyond the dominant economic and cultural institutions. They do socially relevant work, raise non-patriarchal families and do not depend on the mainstream cultural outlets for their entertainment.

Demographers, pollsters and census takers rarely detect these marginal souls simply because they are captive of the traditional categories into which to slot people – marital status, income, level of education, political affiliation. Our social-science discourse has largely prevented us from recognizing non-traditional radicalism, what Habermas (1981c) calls "new social movements". Instead, we plot all difference on the established grid of middle-class conformity. And this explains why cultural producers continue to ignore the very real audience for, and suppliers of, non-mainstream cultural expression. Instead, the publishers and networks deliver the same old dreary product reproduced for putative Yuppies, never mind that Yuppies scarcely exist.

As such, many young writers and artists have managed to fall through the cracks, defying their own commodification. Many of these are "undiscovered", and will remain so, given the nearly impenetrable networks of publishers, editors, reviewers. At most, they can hope to be published by small presses, off the beaten track. They live in Toledo and Eugene, not Manhattan or Boston. For many of these people (us!), small is beautiful. Where we give up the promise of the fast-track, we gain a measure of control over our literary existence. There is less hassle dealing with small outlets than large, corporate ones. Editors are more responsive, accessible, committed to a democratic intellectual project. And thus one has more control over one's editing and production, both crucial issues for writers who compose serious work.

This alternative mode of literary presentation and production refuses to accept commodified literary relationships as given, nor the profit and status definitions assigned to them. It is both morally and politically forward-looking and practicable; after all, no one objectively needs more than *some* basic material, spiritual and political resources – how much is another question. All sorts of Americans are content to scale down their lives, to write poetry and grow squash without the desperate allure of the big time or big town. Populism, in its best formulation, is about popular control and thus is implicitly a radical critique of gigantism, here corporate literary production and the bureaucratic university system (Agger, 1979a).

Much of this pragmatic-populist tradition has a counterpart in Europe, particularly among poststructuralists and feminists (and especially poststructuralist feminists like Irigaray (1985) and Kristeva (1980)). Derrida and the French feminist poststructuralists stress "difference" as a political metaphysic, valorizing the heterogeneity of human groupings as well as intellectual tendencies (Eliasoph, 1987). In its Marxist formulation, this stress on difference suggests that what appear to be only dichotomies (e.g, urban-rural, big time-small time, man-woman) are really hierarchies. This helps alert us to the power relationships concealed in the pluralist illusions about heterogeneity: deconstruction defrocks liberalism by showing the power-imbeddedness of social relations.

This feminist-deconstructive theme is very much like radical populism in its insistence on real, not phony, "difference" – freedom of choice, substantive work and leisure alternatives, diversity in personal and intellectual expression. Difference theorists, like radical populists, insist on workers' and consumers' control as a means of reversing the hierarchical relationships between people on the margins and corporations and states in the mainstream. This is not a far cry from certain heterodox or "western" versions of Marxism, where the critique of centralization is broadened into a full-blown critique of capitalism, patriarchy and racism (Agger, 1979a). It is one thing to call for thoroughgoing societal transformation; it is another thing for individuals to try to carve out decent lives for themselves somehow contributing haltingly to social change. Marxism and feminism may aim too high, thus abstracting too much, for people inhabiting political cultures basically hostile to European emancipatory themes. In the U.S., after all, Marxism is typically conflated with the Soviet "evil empire", making Marxist struggle that much more unlikely.

Just here, left poststructuralism, especially feminist poststructuralism (e.g, Ryan, 1982; Weedon, 1987), fertilizes left postmodernism – if they were ever really distinct at all (Agger, 1990). Poststructuralist difference theory can inform a left-feminist poststructuralism where poststructuralism is broadened from a critique of epistemological dualism into a general theory of culture and society. Although poststructuralism assiduously resists becoming science, even social science, it can become an agenda of critical cultural studies, as Denzin (1991) has shown. I draw upon this perspective in my blend of poststructuralism and critical theory, already recognizing the filiation (through a left reading of Nietzsche) between critical theory and poststructuralism, as Ryan (1982) has suggested. This risks becoming alphabet soup: at some point, critical theory, feminist theory, postmodernism and poststructuralism combine into an overarching emancipatory social theory, of which this book is an application in the realm of cultural studies. (I have attempted to synthesize these traditions in my *Fast Capitalism* (Agger, 1989a).)

Difference theory, deriving from postmodernism and poststructuralism, has a down-side, however. In line with Lyotard's aversion to totalizing metanarratives, it tends to denigrate the sort of world-historical comprehension and transformation urged by Marxism. Feminist postmodernism quite self-consciously breaks with Marxist and feminist totalities but in the process enfeebles itself politically. I believe that Adorno handles this problem best where he preserves the notion of difference-within-totality, what he (1973b) calls the non-identical. Sartre (1976), too, addresses the complex mediation between person and group as the backdrop of his totalizing historical materialism. Without aiming for totality, difference theory is merely a form of liberalism and pluralism. This is a radical hermeneutic circle: without changing particular things, the totality will not change; but everything must change for particulars to be transformed.

Can Writers Resist the Monolith?:
On the Cultural Logic of Capital

Survival can be survived; writers can eke out livings and still do relatively autonomous, serious work. Yet for every successful attempt to start a non-mainstream journal or open a co-op bookstore, thus winning vital personal space for struggling literary workers, many such efforts fail. The logic of capital, commodifying all human activity and thus reducing human relations to relations between things (Marx's famous "commodity fetishism"), tends to chew up counterhegemonic activities, no matter how well conceived. Although only a tendency, as Marx carefully noted in his *Capital*, commodification feeds on its own successes. The ingestion of small publishing houses into huge "parent" companies makes way for more of the same. That is the logic of capital, according to Marx: profit requires more profit, and thus more exploitation. Socialism would be a rupture in this continuum of domination, an active outcome on the part of an underclass so impoverished that there is no real alternative to mass political action. Of course, the crisis tendencies of capitalism today may differ significantly from the ones sketched in 1867 by Marx. That is, the precise pivots around which the system turns, and thus can be redirected, must be addressed in fresh empirical ways. As always, capitalism tends to sow the seeds of its own undoing: profit producing more of the same also impoverishes the very workers whose consumption is required for productivity to be converted into profit, Marx's "surplus value".

Thus, the effort to resist literary commodification is both theoretically and politically precarious. It is theoretically so because, as Marx correctly indicated, capital's logic, like the proverbial science-fiction monster, compels it to gobble up everything in its path, both workers and businesses. It is politically so because, alas, there are few examples of genuinely non-traditional literary enterprises that resist their absorption into the commodified mainstream. Many, like Pareto, Michels and Weber, have theorized this as the inevitable tendency of opposition to become entrenched and hierarchized over time; history is littered with examples of "revolutions" that end up as revolting as the ancien regimes they initially opposed. But for Marxists power does not inevitably corrupt, especially where power is theorized and thus enacted as both process and product. Western Marxists insist that oligarchy is not an iron law, nor is joining the establishment.

Iron law or no, most heterodox literary efforts either fail outright or are co-opted. Even if the inauguration of new journals, presses, bookstores and production companies does not change the world but simply lets individuals subsist in somewhat more sane ways, we cannot assume that they will survive. The external world is simply too threatening – rents too high, start-up costs immense, suppliers wary. Where economics does not doom alternative publication outlets, the lack of energy does: it is enormously taxing to challenge the mainstream literary producers on their own terrain, just as any restauranteur knows who opens a business in an already highly competitive market. One needs amazing energy as well as ego-strength; one also needs friends and counselors who offer both assistance and help test reality when tunnel vision sets in.

And even if such heterodox literary outlets manage to avoid early mortality, other, even more dire, threats loom. Success can be the kiss of death, too: "alternative" outlets, like health-food stores, can quickly go mainstream where the lure of big money is irresistible. Either literary "product" is slowly altered to fit the standard molds or else one is too tempted by buy-out offers from mainstream houses or studios that know a good thing when they see it, recognizing the corporate rationality of both product diversity as well as vertical integration. *Ms.* magazine is a good example of an "alternative" publication engulfed in the surging mainstream. What began as a magazine devoted to a sharp critique of patriarchy in America has now become, in effect, just another "women's" magazine: a recent series sang the praises of the family, as if that hallowed institution needed more cheerleading on its behalf. Although *Ms.* limps along financially, it has already sold out, differing little from other magazines for women that started squarely in the middle of the road but have sagely added something of a feminist perspective in order to capture an even wider upscale audience (e.g., *Glamour*).

Selling out is not moral failure but a built-in tendency, as inexorable as the tide of corporate takeovers. Being inside is much more alluring than being outside, especially when one has already tasted the sweet fruits of "success". Fanon's (1966) notion of the "revolution of rising expectations" suggests that the people most likely to commit revolutionary deeds are alienated members of the bourgeoisie, who possess education and a universalistic worldview. Conversely, those who "make it" tend to make it *over* others, and stay there. Radicalism has been commodified, too, with the star-systems and ample salaries of the university left. Few who manage to inch their way "in" stay outside for long. Of course, they may justify their self-establishment in all sorts of "political" ways. Tom Hayden, the founder of the Students for a Democratic Society (SDS), has now gone suburban as a California state legislator, family man, little-league coach. His recent memoir *Reunion* (Hayden, 1988) chronicles his voyage from fringe to center; his wife Jane Fonda even apologized for her intemperate partisanship of North Vietnam during the war. Their marital split-up is delicious fare for the gossip magazines. It is to be noted that Hayden's book was published by a major trade house and is doing well. The Yuppification of the New Left is only commodification, radicals tumbling to embourgeoisement.

But the opposite of co-optation is not a visionary purity; I have already dismissed heroic literature as yet another myth of bourgeois individualism. The opposite of co-optation is simply *not* to be co-opted, a notion that gains in substance what it lacks in specificity. Whether or not this takes inordinate moral or political courage is an empirical question, answered only in terms of the contingencies of the moment. Yet deconstruction instructs us that the dichotomy "co-optation-heroic isolation" does not exhaust all the possibilities. Sometimes refusing to be captured in simplistic categorical oppositions is the truest stance of all or, at worst, the least likely to be swallowed by the logic of capital. It is enormously difficult to resist the tidal pull of what Adorno (1973b) called "total administration", the reduction of every aspect of one's existence to instrumental, quantitative, money terms. Just to resist is often the most that can be hoped for; more positive heroic gestures risk the catastrophes that usually befall true believers.

But just because counterhegemonic efforts ultimately fail does not mean that they were moral, theoretical or even political failures.

Defeat should not be ontologized into defeatism any more than "success" should be uncritically valorized. Capitalism has defeated socialism and feminism for over a hundred years. This does not mean that socialism and feminism are illegitimate or impractical goals but only that they have to be tried again. Careful empirical study of resistance's defeat is an antidote to both defeat and the deenergizing tendencies of fatalism. That is a way to read this book.

The Illusion of Literary Difference

It would appear obvious that certain heterodox literary efforts succeed and others fail. Renegade writers occasionally achieve publication, establish magazines and presses, keep their bookstores and studios solvent. Yet literary difference is often an illusion concealing the drab sameness of the corporate literary world. Difference is a social construction, an emergent outcome; it must be rendered objective for discussions such as these to have meaning. Unfortunately, there are no yardsticks with which we can measure difference. "Difference" is usually gimmicky, insubstantial.

The illusion of difference is directly functional for outlets emphasizing their varied repertoire of literary products – a book or movie video for "everyone". Writers themselves are often tempted to view their work as substantially innovative, serious, authentic. After all, they labor for so long that, perhaps inevitably, they come to believe in their own uniqueness. This reaches absurd lengths where college textbook writers in their prefaces announce the "real differences" their books reflect. Any study of college textbooks reveals an unrelieved sameness. Authors learn to cope with their own degraded fungibility by lionizing their literary efforts. Of course, this is easy to do when adjectives like "new" and "different" are cheap and uncontested. It is the rare literary product that is not published with all the hoopla accompanying the discovery of the Salk vaccine.

The dustcovers of books are adorned with celebratory and testimonial claims, usually garnered from big names whose word carries currency. Similarly, movies are advertised with great fanfare: noted movie reviewers rave about everything and anything, decorating their byline with the numerous "stars" they award to mainstream blockbusters. Although the "smart" reader can sometimes read through and around this puffery, such decoding skills are hard-won; one has to know who is saying what about particular literary products and then try to interpolate between their words or somehow reduce their bravado to manageable interpretive proportions. But such hermeneutic intelligence is rare, especially in times when the appearance of commodities is equivalent to their "essences", their real natures. Marx carefully distinguished between commodities' use and exchange values, products' utility as against their market value. Today, their utility is constructed *through* literary media, particularly advertising, assigning them differential value relative to other products available in the marketplace. Without these differential indications of cultural commodities, it is nearly hopeless to make informed decisions as consumers and critics.

Public relations, including advertising, is itself a literary medium. Large numbers of people are employed to write literary products in a way that assigns them these differential significances; the advertising industry is crucial in the realms of publication and production (Ewen, 1976). Knowing only this fact alone would raise the very real question about whether literary products are different from any other products in that they have value or meaning apart from the labels through which they are offered to the public. As always, this is an empirical question: the extent of real literary difference must be established by actually reading books and viewing films and television. By now, most of us even slightly inured to the grandiose claims made on behalf of literary "product" suspect that "difference" is generally constructed out of thin air and that, in fact, most literary products are much more similar to one another than they are different.

This is the ultimate problem with the attempt to expand alternative outlets for literary work: commodification eventually runs roughshod over literary difference, pulling all products and activities into the vortex of capitalist exchange value. The value of work quickly becomes its market value, which in turn dictates what will be published and produced in the future. Capitalism in this sense is circular: innovation is highly constrained by the nature of taste, which is a social product in its own right. John Stuart Mill's marketplace of ideas in which literary work automatically finds its own level of value is as fraudulent as the notion that the capitalist labor market is regulated by a fair exchange between workers and their employers. Markets are *made*; thus in reproducing themselves they reproduce writers in turn – even writers who fight hard to avoid the perils of literary commodification. Either their "alternative" literary enterprises simply fail or else their product becomes standardized, resembling mainstream literary product in most significant ways.

We are all caught up in a self-reproducing system reducing our freedoms of action: editors are accountable to their employers, authors to their editors, writers to studios and universities, all of us to that abstraction called "the market". We neglect to observe that we create the market and that it, in turn, conditions the choices we make aesthetically and intellectually. Marxists call this a "dialectical" process, as good a term as any to describe the ways in which we reproduce business-as-usual without really understanding our own complicity in what is going on.

This is not to say that change will come easily; understanding the structural sources of the decline of discourse suggests that we should change those very structures and not hope for heroic resistance from the hinterlands. At the same time, individuals matter: we write, publish, produce, purchase. We could do all of these things differently. Ultimately, we must establish some evaluative standards, both intellectual and political, with which to determine whether, in fact, our literary activity is genuinely different in the sense that it breaks through the market-driven logic of publishing today. For the most part, fringe efforts to enhance "difference" fall by the way or are sucked under. We who write and publish desperately want to believe that we are different – that we march to the drummers of excellence and social justice. But the literary world perhaps more than any other is dominated by hype, the self-inflation attached to work notable only for its unrelieved homogeneity.

Just naming something "different" does not make it so. Indeed, the savvy consumer today recognizes that all such claims are dubious; merely having to make them indicates a kind of bankruptcy. That raises the question about how, exactly, we will make critical evaluations in a different society: how will people sell books and review movies once the fateful cycle of commodification has been broken? Although I have few patent answers, as my concluding chapter will indicate, we can at least consider the fraudulence of self-proclaimed literary difference as a social problem in its own right; the more we presage our work with the promise of difference, the more we contribute to the problem of meaninglessness in its own right. When adjectives like "revolutionary" attach to hamburgers and automobiles, we are all in trouble. Better, we must understand how and why the impoverishment of language is a definite outcome of the way we have chosen to organize our literary culture. Although this risks being yet another oversimplification, we can conclude, at the very least, that capitalism drags down the rate of public intelligence by turning ideas and imagination into commodities subject to the nature-like principles of economic exchange.

The Debate Over "Standards":
Different Formulations of the Problem

Cultural conservatives like Allan Bloom have something to say here, even if their articulation of the problem gets in the way of a real solution: we have lost the categories with which to make critical distinctions (Arendt, 1958); instead, the good is equivalent to goods, to what we can buy. Greek thought interrogated the nature of the good as the fundamental problem of philosophical and social inquiry: the good lies in the gentle talk it takes to get there, even if "there" always to some extent eludes us. Today, we do not expect our literary commodities to interrogate these weighty questions but merely to divert us, even if certain postmodern cultural theories would give diversion the patina of a world-weary sophistication. Let me address the different ways in which people cast the debate about "standards", offering resolutions of it in accord with certain central assumptions about the nature of cultural life today.

Cultural Conservatism

People like Bloom argue for a return to academic "standards" of yesteryear – the assignment of "great books" to undergraduates in particular (Hirsch, 1987). The underlying values and precepts of western civilization will be learned from careful exegeses of these texts. Cultural conservatives argue for a return to elite standards of evaluation, as well, decrying the revisionism of the '60s. They rail against moral and intellectual excess, joining the growing chorus of traditionalists who want to return to the patriarchal family, religion and Cold War geopolitics as nostrums for all variety of social problems. The New Left and women's movement in particular are blamed for the moral morass of the present; as well, cultural conservatives generally support the nuclear family and oppose sexual promiscuity, family planning and abortion as outcomes of our failed moral nerve.

Postmodernism

Postmodernists suggest that history is going nowhere and thus that we have lost all secure moral and intellectual values. Postmodernism borrows from an eclectic grab-bag of names, traditions and cultural styles in arriving at a version of appropriate contemporary comportment. Postmodernism is supremely suited to the Yuppie generation: after the desolation of the post-'60s decades, we not only describe the meaninglessness of social life; we embrace it. In fact, describing it embraces it. Thus postmodern cultural projects seem at once vividly indicting and celebratory: resignation is puffed up into a metaphysic. Postmodernism is clearly an attack on Marxist millennarianism, disqualifying left-wing and feminist utopias as heavy-handed. Instead, postmodernists judge political systems in essentially stylistic terms: are people modishly dressed, appropriately irreverent, turned off the old "isms", whether right or left? Postmoderns fight bad totality by rejecting all totality – concretely, left political theory and practice.

Critiques

There are some, like me, who reject both cultural conservatism and postmodernism but possess no definitive standards with which to replace them. Cultural conservatism is needlessly elitist and arbitrary: after all, why are certain books and values "great"? Although we argue for intellectual rigor, both in writing and pedagogy, we insist that cultural conservatives are not the only ones who favor these things. One can approach cultural degeneracy from a radical and critical point of view, as well, casting cultural and moral rehabilitation primarily in terms of overall social and economic changes.

Critics of postmodernism suggest that the seeming collapse of absolute values ought not to signal a cultural theory acquiescent to Nietzschean meaninglessness. The death of God ought to have surprised only the religious; the absence of theologically-vouchsafed moral standards does not mean that there are *no* standards, albeit ones penned by people. Postmodernism confuses cultural enlightenment and expression with lifestyle; to "be" a writer or artist means to dress and eat like one: cultural choices are, in effect, about consumption, whether books or clothing labels. Lyotard's postmodernism is *attitude and affiliation*, not a substantive perspective on cultural experience and evaluation. And the particular attitude of postmodernists is a sense of resigned disappointment about the seemingly inexorable flow of world history: in the absence of useful guideposts to social action and cultural evaluation, the knowing postmodernist just shrugs, letting it all wash over.

In this context, it is tempting to prescribe a whole new set of values or standards; at least, this would offer counterweight to cultural conservatism, on the one hand, and postmodernism, on the other. Where people like Bloom obviously favor white-male elitist "Republics", postmodernists respond that politics is useless, certainly not the most salient arena of human concern. Yet critiques of both cultural conservatism and postmodernism tempted to legislate their own absolute values will fail, too. Ultimately, they will be seen to be as arbitrary as the standards inflated by Platonists into universal values. Postmodern cynics will be no more convinced by left-wing proponents of absolute values than by right-wing absolutists.

Yet this does not disqualify the critique of cultural conservatism and postmodernism out of hand. Just because one criticizes certain cultural and intellectual taste does not mean that one has a definitive list of "better" tastes. Instead, critique might indicate the absence of values arrived at freely and thus cast doubt on both the conservative and postmodern cultural projects. "Good" values are those arrived at through optimally democratic processes, unconstrained by power. This is the Marxist position on cultural standards, and one that must be repeated at a time when, for most of the world's billions, "Marxism" represents one form of tyranny or another. From Marx to Marcuse and beyond, false needs or false values are precisely those imposed on unwitting individuals by the overwhelming state and cultural apparatuses teaching us what to want and thus circumscribing the realm of possibility.

This neoMarxist perspective on needs denies that popular culture is "bad" according to certain invariant standards; such standards do not exist except in people's minds. What *is* bad is the way in which people are led to value *what presently exists*, and thus to define themselves and their own needs in terms of attainment; people thus clamor for more money, goods, status without considering whether these things are what they really want, or even whether they are good for them at all. Marxists hope that when people are finally and fully freed from these cultural constraints determining their own needs from the outside, they will choose wisely and in ways maximizing the collective good. Marx's utopia, sketched in his *Economic and Philosophic Manuscripts* (1961), was not a rigid list of cultural and political desiderata but simply the *absence of external constraints* on the choices people make about their work and leisure activities. This is what Marx meant by the Greek word *praxis*, simultaneously self-expressive and productive activity chosen freely by people.

Opponents of Marxism frequently accuse Marxists of harboring their own authoritarian list of correct values and political behaviors. Although many, perhaps most, Marxists are authoritarian, and thus disingenuously attack right-wing elitists, this is not the logic of Marxism. Marx wrote a freedom theory, a perspective on intellectual, cultural and political values stressing the innate good sense – the reasonableness – of ordinary people once unchained from either outright political tyranny or the friendly fascism of advanced capitalism. Marx believed in reason,- although he held himself open to the possibility that in a condition of social freedom people would make different, even surprisingly self-defeating, choices. Marx was optimistic that people are rational; in any case, he rejected a priori counterpositions about people's inveterate venality on the grounds that, for all of world history, people have been unable freely to determine their own needs and political options.

This sounds like a labored effort to avoid the prescription of evaluative standards and values. In a way it is. I agree with Habermas (1984, 1987b) that people through unconstrained and democratic dialogue conducted in their various lifeworlds will arrive at a workable standard of public reason. In that respect, a critical postmodernism has faith in the polity shared by diverse philosophers from Plato to Rousseau, Mill and Marx. Although Habermas is on the run for his unexplicated faith in the lifeworld as an antidote to its colonization by "system", his is the optimism of every democratic utopian. There is little more he can say beyond this: people in a rational polity will behave rationally and communally. Only then will we be able to develop evaluative and interpretive standards with which to assess competing truth claims. Indeed, commitment to the ideal speech situation is a procedural standard of sorts, helping us prefiguratively create the very world that seems so distant today.

Cultural conservatism is anathema to this perspective on reason for its arbitrary assumption that the good society is hierarchical. Postmodernism is rejected for its arationality, if not downright irrationality. Postmodern capitalism deflates people's expectations by arguing that happiness (if such a concept makes any sense at all) will be found in the intimate geometries of people's everyday lives and not in the large machineries of state and economy. Postmodernism raises individualism to a new level, resolving Nietzschean meaning-lessness with reference to personal temperament – an '80s version of the '60s refrain "If it feels good, do it". Today the postmodern personality would revise this: "It won't feel too good (or bad), but do it anyway".

Rethinking the Postmodern

Many commentators on what Lyotard (1984) calls the "postmodern condition" miss the fact that postmodernism is yet another attempt to avoid political theory – retreating from the region of politics in order to satisfy people's needs elsewhere, here in the realms of personality and culture. But numerous Marxists since the 1920s have argued convincingly that culture cannot be divorced from politics especially when cultural intervention, "popular culture", crucially prolongs capitalism by diverting people from what is really happening to them. The seeming dichotomy, culture "or" politics, is false; the Frankfurt School theorists, among others, have shown that politics is displaced into the cultural sphere: the region of the political is found everywhere *but* in political institutions proper (Habermas, 1975).

The single point of agreement between cultural conservatives and critical theorists is that authentic discourse is a crucial bond of community; the good is equivalent to the talk it takes to get "there", even if "there" ever eludes us. Platonists and their critics would organize discourse differently; Platonists would deny dia-logue chances to non-citizens, notably women and slaves. Yet the postmodern sensibility justifies the displacement of discourse from discourse proper into either popular culture or academia on grounds that *politics, like God, is dead*. Public meaninglessness will not be made good by more of the same; politics added to politics is worse than no politics at all. Clearly, people are retreating rapidly from participation in public institutions because they perceive that these institutions do not serve them well. "Society" has become an abstraction extremely remote from the everyday lives of most people (e.g., Berger, Berger and Kellner, 1974).

In this sense, postmodern culture peculiarly divorces culture from public life. It is a retreat from politics to self-expression, notably to attitude. But the politics of chic abrogates the choices usually found in political disputation; thus, postmodernists are interested less in ideological or party affiliation than in the aesthetics and attitudes of public actors. Political journalists in the U.S. were much more interested in Gary Hart's sexual positions than in his political positions, such as they were. By the same token, reportage about the unsuccessful political campaign of Michael Dukakis was notable for its fixation on his inability to project a "warm" personality. Few observed that perhaps he does not have a "warm" personality; in any case, his script writers should have turned him into a "warm" political commodity. His failure was their failure. Style not only replaces substance in postmodern capitalism: it is substance itself. The "how" is more important than the "what", especially where literary expression is concerned.

But no matter how much people struggle to divorce culture from politics, they fail. Cultural choices both reflect and reproduce political ones; the flight "from" politics is politics itself, leaving open the terrain of political choice to those more invested in traditional ideological contestation. As always, value-freedom (Weber, 1968) is a ruse; the supposed freedom from values is perhaps the deepest commitment of all. The postmodern only appears to be "beyond" the disputes of modernity. In reality, ideological conflicts are sublimated, reappearing in other forms. Where all political parties are basically the same, ideological tension is displaced into other arenas, especially the literary world. Devotés of postmodernism hope against hope to disrupt political discourse for its ridiculous innocence; really hip people recognize that the atomic age conflates seeming political differences into a general insanity. However much this is true, difference still exists, at least as a possibility.

At root, these are empirical questions. Whether we are beyond, or within, modernity, and what this implies for literary practice, must be argued in light of evidence, not assumed. Difference is attainable, and thus the rate of discourse's decline slowed, even reversed. What this takes politically is a combination of indefatigable literary work plus a careful appraisal of the opportunities for what certain Marxists call "counterhegemony" – innovation. In general terms, literary heroism overemphasizes the likelihood of creating difference through sheer authorial will, where postmodernism underestimates the possibilities of literary, hence political, difference. Perhaps idealism and cynicism, embodied in these polar alternatives, are two sides of the same coin. Of course, these are only labels, as such only accelerating the falling rate of intelligence where they do our thinking for us.

Nevertheless, discourse's decline only continues where we analyze discourse's structural context inadequately. Literary heroism and postmodernism together assume that *the individual matters*; I agree that the individual ought to matter but rarely does today. Whether we believe we are composing the Great American Novel or that our unique individuality will win us Warhol's fifteen minutes of fame depends on our literary and political investments. Postmodernism is the dominant cultural style today or, at least, the one that dominates cultural criticism (and thus informs cultural creation backhandedly). I want to rethink the postmodern in terms of concrete literary practices and the institutional conditions giving rise to them. That is the subject of my concluding chapter. By so doing I hope to sketch a version of literary practice grounded in real possibilities as well as to reconceptualize the postmodern problematic in different terms.

Critics of postmodern meaninglessness nonetheless come to endorse postmodernism as an inexorable cultural movement. Positivist description gives way to evaluation and exhortation where the adjective "postmodern" seems to do useful analytical work. Although there are definite contours of the postmodern landscape, notably the refusal of politics and thus the possibility of social change, postmodern cultural criticism is less criticism than affirmation (e.g., Kroker and Cook, 1986). Trendy European categories appeal for exactly the same reason chic urbanites borrow shamelessly from epochs as well as cultures in fashioning their own postured individuality. Where people prefer Gray Poupon mustard to the standard American variety, they are likely to prefer cultural analysis done under the aegis of Derrida and Foucault: French commodification is preferable to the tired American variety (or the obscure German one, including Marx and Marxism). Postmodernism endorses trendiness profoundly, thus accelerating it.

We pose the postmodern problematic precisely because we lack a clear analysis explaining the host of cultural, political and economic ephemera today. Where American Marxism has been deemed dead (or, more accurately, never lived), people fall back on something with which to organize their analysis and criticism. Postmodernism suggests that anything goes precisely because we lack clear evaluative standards with which to judge the goodness of both cultural and political arrangements. But it is clear that not "anything" goes; the failure of efforts to break through literary and cultural commodification, whether by starting journals or establishing presses and bookstores, indicates just the opposite. The illusion of vibrant postmodern heterogeneity, Japanese food consumed in the middle of Manhattan by Benetton-clad people venturing out to see a "retro" movie, is an ideological artifact of the same culture industry that packages political candidates and dispenses mainstream entertainment. Culture is increasingly standardized and administered, even (no, *especially*) in its seeming diversity. People led to believe they have "options" do not opt for radical politics and cultural counterhegemony; they play the game according to the rules dictated by global capital.

This much is apparent: there are depressingly few ways to do literary and cultural work without buying into the dominant world, thus adding value to it. Most efforts to transcend artistic commodification either fail or are co-opted. Neither cultural conservatism nor postmodernism is equal to the task of understanding what is going wrong. Marxist political economy seems tediously familiar by now; Marxism cannot compete against French intellectual fashion any more than food co-ops can resist giant grocery store chains. But the decline of discourse pivots around literary political economy – the textual politics of postmodern capitalism. A revivified Marxism addresses these phenomena in a concerted way, neither succumbing to sheer heroism nor to the self-mythologizations of the postmodern. This is not to suggest a singular or simple-minded Marxism; Marxisms are as abundant as ethnic restaurants. The study of literary political economy is only as good as the work it does. As I have have shown in this book, that is a good deal. I will now turn to the literary possibilities available to those who would defy commodification from within.

Chapter 8

Writing Resistance:
Toward the Post-Postmodern

The Public Book I: Writing as if Readers Exist

Jacoby in his *Last Intellectuals* (1987) diagnoses the decline of discourse in terms of writers' inabilities to write broad-gauged public
books, accessible to a host of intelligent but nonspecialized readers. This diagnosis has drawn fire if only because it disqualifies
99 per cent of the literary work done by academics, whether in
obscure specialist journals or in the narrowly-focused monographs
published by university presses. I agree with Jacoby's symptomatic
description, although I want to theorize so-called public books in
a way that follows from my analysis of literary political economy.
This is not simply to "recommend" that writers write a certain kind
of literary product. Although apt, that advice is not enough. People
who scribble are not authors but writers; authorship is conferred once
they are published. Many who write the sort of accessible, intelligent
book recommended as genuinely public discourse do not see the light
of day simply because the market researchers who control corporate
publishing make publication decisions: if people have not read those
books in the past, they will not in the future. Thus, such books are
not published.

It is said that "public" readers do not exist, much as the television
networks justify schlock in terms of ratings. Public broadcasting
demonstrates that some people prefer not to watch stupid television.
Just the same, there are readers who want access to informed public
discourse, even to write themselves. Yet where the commodification
of publishing makes it necessary for every book on a list to be a
"profit center", the small audiences addressed by PBS, *New Republic*
and European cinema – precisely the sort of people who read public

books – are deemed *too* small by corporate standards. The economic logic is a compelling one: if a publishing house want to plow as much money as possible into potentially profitable projects, "iffier" ones are turned back. Thus, good books are not published.

Over time, writers and publishers begin to believe that "good" readers *do not exist*. Circularly, the logic of literary commodification has ensured this. The absence of public books convinces publishers that this "sort" of book is not profitable; in imitating their competitors' behavior, they reproduce it. The absence of public discourse reduces readers' interpretive abilities. Writers despair about getting published, or even read. Although the absence of public discourse is basically decided at the point of literary production, writers ensure their own demise by giving up the sort of writing that might make a difference. Only the lucky few, the Blooms, live to write another day. Most would-be writers quickly come to understand the market exigencies dictating their own literary choices. After a few rejections, they "come to their senses", as an editor I know puts it. Their work duplicates prevailing literary standards and thus only compounds the problem.

There are exceptions, as both Jacoby and Bloom indicate. And these exceptions demonstrate the very possibility of public discourse, composed to create a democratic polity in which fundamental decisions are made directly by people. Postmodern cynicism should not be indulged, even if heroic resistance is insufficient. At the very least, writers ought to imagine that publishers might publish their work and sympathetic readers read it. Of course, this is exactly the literary heroism I rejected earlier as unrealistic. I am not saying that authorial attitude will make much difference; yet it is patent that unless *some writers write discourse* we writers will ensure that publishers do not publish it. After all, our work might luckily fall through the cracks and see the light of day. After trying many times, and with many different projects, we might succeed in finding the sort of publisher willing to take a chance, thus contributing our own small voice to overall discourse.

This route is the literary long road. By itself, it will not succeed; the capitalist publishing world swallows nearly everything whole (Kostelanetz, 1974). Yet I am concerned here not only with the probabilities of achieving publication, and an audience, but also with changing the *Zeitgeist*, now prevailingly postmodern – resigned to chic meaninglessness as a plenitude of existence. Although individual writers may be ground up in the logic of capital dominating all of us, even singular resistance can dent the prevailing ideologies and practices governing our cultural and political life. This is not an argument for sheer self-sacrifice; after all, writers must live, too. But writing books *as if* people would read them and publishers publish them at least halts the otherwise inexorable logic of literary commodification and stupefaction. Resistance is just that: it does not pretend to remake Rome in a day but at least to register its voice of protest. The hope is that one day enough writers write public discourse, resisting literary commodification, that cultural life will change substantially, thus changing political and economic life as well.

Where in the preceding chapter I offered ample reason for pessimism, here I want to defend pessimism as an empirical precondition of forward-looking engagement: at least pessimism is an estimate of probabilities and, as such, betokens a task-oriented pragmatism. Poststructuralism is literally wrong: subjectivity is not utterly in eclipse, only individual subjects. Even to recognize this indicates the presence of subjectivity as well as human subjects; similarly, Marcuse's (1964) indictment of one-dimensional society helped reverse it. Here I want to consider the possibility that readers and writers can and do make a difference, if a small one, as a way of broadening this discussion from subjectivity to intersubjectivity – organization and mobilization – in my concluding chapter.

These are distant hopes; there are few empirical grounds for optimism today. But pessimism should not be allowed to become ontology, a veritable theory of being not only disqualifying, but ridiculing, literary and political resistance. Postmodernism does not disdain political action because it has concluded carefully that action is likely to fail or even be turned against itself in unforeseen authoritarian ways. Rather, postmoderns simply *assume* that public discourse is hopeless and that urbane literary attitude should replace ideological effort or investment. Postmodernism is not empirical political theory; it fails to really research the possibilities of literary resistance but disqualifies politics as tawdry. Postmodernism blithely dismisses public standards of reason as hopelessly groundless in a world governed by movie actors and terrorized by the threat of nuclear winter.

Reason is threatened from all sides, it is true. Yet the absence of reason is not cause for endorsing its demise. Postmodernism mistakes fact for necessity, "is" for "ought". That urban life is threatening, intimate relations degraded, politics corrupt and culture moronic does not mean that forward-looking theories of social change should be discarded. Indeed, the evident facts summarized cynically by postmodernists ought to be viewed dialectically, that is, in terms of their potential for being transformed. Post-mod culture instead only accelerates the decline of discourse by endorsing the collapse of absolute standards of value. Another approach would argue for new values in terms of a philosophy of history. One need not itemize a definite list of "good" values, practices, institutions but simply indicate the impediments to realizing freedom in the present (Habermas, 1981a). That is precisely the route taken by Marxism, right-wing caricatures notwithstanding.

Writing "as if" readers exist who can understand the argument, and publishers to publish it, offers resistance against the market logic of the corporate literary world. Postmodernism only capitulates to that market logic, albeit stylishly and apolitically. Ultimately, people have to *do something* to indicate that their critical faculties are still functioning, inviting others to join with them in fanning the embers of reason. Even if one does not make a regular income from work of this kind, composing it in spare time, one at least makes contact with readers, other writers and even editors who share one's vision of what is possible. In my own academic work, I invariably find myself exchanging tales of woe with like-minded academics who share my version of the good literary community and who, with me, protect each other as best we can.

This is especially crucial in the literary marketplace. One needs sponsors, referees, friends who can serve to further one's own interests. Virtually all the success I have had in getting published has been through friends and colleagues who point me in the right direction and even intervene directly in the manuscript adjudication process. I return the favor, thus developing an ethic of mutual aid with which we leftists can protect our own livelihoods and worldviews and ever so slightly reverse the powerful momentum of the mainstream literary and political institutions. Not only does this help individual writers stay alive; it also creates the embryonic communities of equal speakers required to transform the present qualitatively into the future. Public books help create the public, even if these books remain manuscripts circulated informally among groups of friendly writer/readers.

Community must begin somewhere, if only between a handful of intimates. *Samizdat* publishing in the USSR demonstrates the power of this sort of resistance. Eventually the self-published, dog-eared manuscript takes on a life of its own as it is passed along from household to household and nurtured by word of mouth. The history

of Bolshevism is a story of the literary grounding of political community, even though traditional historiography concentrates on political
tactics, military maneuvers, sectarian intrigue. The Bolsheviks were
nothing without their manuscripts, tracts, thick journals, meetings,
speeches. Discourse started the Russian Revolution as surely as did
the first cannon shots from the battleship *Aurora*. Similarly, Marx's
Communist Manifesto and Paine's *Rights of Man* were harbingers of
other revolutions, as powerful as any bullet.

Unless we understand the public as a community to be built we
indulge in overabstraction. Publics are composed of people who
live individual lives and relate to others like themselves. The
commodified literary world denies writers much access to, and
certainly no equality with, the huge conglomerates that publish
books, print newspapers and produce movies and television. They
require *alternative literary communities* within which to nurture their
own talents and create the prefigurative lifeworlds sustaining the
intellectual project, as such transforming politics itself. Where
postmodernists accept the colonization of the public sphere by
the media, corporations and government, instead playing by the
rules of these dominant institutions, those of us who reject these
standards of intellectual and political worth must resist them. We
begin by writing to others with whom we are in sympathy. Only this
way can we create "the public" whose absence we so lament today.

The Public Book II: Reading as if Writing Exists

Not everyone writes, even though it often seems that way. Far more
people consume writing than compose it. Thus, it makes sense to talk
about their responsibilities for literary resistance and reconstruction.
Writers can only do so much. Readers must read creatively, too, thus
making their own contribution to creating a genuinely public literary
space. In particular, readers can refuse to valorize popular culture
and academic obscurantism simply through the literary choices they
make. In addition, readers themselves can attempt to write, thus
breaking through the hierarchy of those who produce culture and
those who merely consume it. As with writing, this is easier said
than done. Yet monologic literary relations only reinforce people's
general disempowering.

Readers must develop the ability to read through and around
literary self-inflation, scaling it down to size. Similarly, readers must

be able to resist reading or viewing non-inflated literary work in jaded ways. By now, most of us are simply too fatigued by the sheer volume of duplicative work to be able to scrutinize writing carefully for its real quality. And sometimes "good" work filters through the screens of power, either deliberately published by gutsy houses or simply misread by editors who imagine it to be more of the same. Clearly, certain books have mattered in world history, the Bible, Koran, *Capital*. Although it is much less likely that singular writings can have the same impact today, given the inherently self-eroding nature of writing meant to be read quickly and then tossed away, one can never be sure that one's writing will not matter. And whether books have a transformative impact depends as much on readers as on writers; reading can turn into a new version itself where readers respond creatively to what they have read. As well, reading can take life as social practice where books counsel the alteration of certain social arrangements. Marx did not compose *Capital* merely to advance economic theory; he wanted "reading" to become a new world.

Readers reproduce their own subordinate relationships to power where they remain subordinate to the words and images they consume passively. Deconstructive literary theory usefully suggests a distinction between strong and weak readings; the former engage dialogically with texts and thus remake them and the world to which they are an address, where the latter merely mouth words mentally, thus freezing books into fate. Strong reading is most likely to become writing, hence political practice, where the readers are writers themselves (and where writers read). The two practices are inseparable: one's writing is always silent dialogue, where one's reading intends to start and extend dialogues, thus forming community. Literary political economy, as we know it today, divides readers and writers into two distinct strata, the one lower than the other. Reading (like viewing) is an occupation of mass society, where writing is an elite activity by its very nature; after all, few who scribble get published.

This is the crux of a critical postmodernism, inspired by Derrida's revaluation of the relationship between original writing and criticism, philosophy and literature, speech and writing: modernity is characterized by overdetermined, overlapping, mutually reinforcing hierarchies, here *the hierarchy of writers over readers* (as well as editors over writers and publishers over editors). Postmodernism would destroy this hierarchy not by reversing it in the fashion of Hegel's master-slave relationship whereby the slave secretly becomes master because he or she alone grants recognition to the master, whose identity rests on the whim of the enslaved. Readers as such are not writers, as Derrideans would posit. But they can *become* writers by seizing the day – dialogue chances, communicative competence, editorial decision-making, all the constitutive functions of the polity. That is the real postmodern aim: *readers would write*, hence attaining both publicity and democracy. By the same token, writers would read, no longer being just sources of literary labor power. Their writing would echo in dialogue, the ceaseless conversations of humanity (Oakeshott, 1962; O'Neill 1974).

It is facile to recommend writing courses for the person-in-the-street. Yet self-help can become a political notion where it empowers people to appropriate power, here the power to read strongly, thus to write. Austin (1962) was right to view language as a speech *act*; indeed, even reading inserts itself into an embryonic community with the writer. The political question is whether readers and writers share power equally: today they do not, anymore than other social and economic relationships are formed in equality. Becoming a writer can be nucleically political where it represents, and leads to, empowering in other realms. And the ability to read (and thus rewrite) strongly decodes the elite argots that people typically take to be gospel, whether dispensed by priests, politicians or professionals.

In any case, readers have a responsibility for recreating the literary public sphere. They can treat literary work distantly, either as works of inspired genius or as ephemera of entertainment, or they can engage with textuality as a real political problem. There is no simple or singular political agenda for readers; it is folly to imagine disgruntled readers petitioning publishers for "better" books. Yet in our literary culture the printed word has a divinity undue it; most of the world's many are stupefied in face of what they read and view, failing to recognize the artifice-like nature of writing and hence of reading. Words do not fall from the sky or drift off in gusts of wind. They are crafted in the here-and-now by writers who are no different from you and me. They repose precariously on the page or on celluloid; they could have been written differently. Therefore, they must be written differently: that is the post-postmodern reader's manifesto.

Refusing Discipline, Mainstreaming Marginality

It is one thing to be singularly heroic, imagining that "good work" will see us through. Unfortunately, that usually fails simply because the literary market is hostile to serious writing. It is quite another thing to engage in struggle against marketplace criteria of intellectual worthiness. If we do not struggle against the assumption that ideas, like people, can be bought and sold, we only redouble discipline – the external and self-imposed constraints on intellectual and political freedom. The *Zeitgeist* is not fixed; it can be reshaped, but only if we resist taken-for-granted definitions of what constitutes "good" work. In literary capitalism, "good" is equivalent to what sells, the standard equation of utility and exchange value. Not only must we fight to create a viable public space; we must also refuse our relegation to the margins. We must not allow the marketplace, mediated by publishers, producers, editors, colleagues, readers, to dictate our own value to us.

Of course, value today *is* exchange value – how much we and our work are "worth". Ignoring this invites destitution; moral redemption for heroic literary figures happens only in an afterlife, if even then. Although we must make a living, we must resist all attempts to define us in terms of the value at which our work trades in the marketplace. The writer who writes a blockbuster is not "better" than the poor soul unable to find a publisher. He or she is very likely worse according to the standard of imaginative public discourse. In any case, an important mode of literary resistance is to *argue* these standards, refusing to allow the market to dictate our value to us. "Success", circularly derived from what is successful in the marketplace, is not to be prized; nor should it become an objective standard against which to degrade those who do not measure up, either because they refuse to play the game or because, when they play, they discover that the game is rigged.

After all, literary political economy is *not* an open marketplace: there are all kinds of collusion, price-setting, insider trading, networking. Even if one suspects these things, it is tempting to believe (to *want* to believe) that merit really matters in the literary outcomes accruing to one. Thus, to fail, as most of us do, is often internalized; one ends up blaming oneself for rejection, bad reception, the ignominy of literary lonesomeness. Standards, even if debunked as arbitrary, insinuate themselves into the substratum of our consciousness. We tend to adopt them even when we do not believe in them, or refuse to believe they are applied fairly. The left prattles on about "merit" and "excellence" just as much as the mainstream. This disables our attempt to overthrow these standards as illegitimate. It also disempowers those, like us, who refuse to play the game.

This is especially prevalent in the academic world, where scholarship is supposedly evaluated objectively. Although many academics recognize that tenure and promotion are slanted in favor of mainstream scholars who lead mainstream, unthreatening lives, we surround ourselves with the illusions of academic objectivity. Otherwise, we fear standardlessness; in addition, those who have "made it" want to believe they earned it fair and square. One can see subtle changes in academics who are tenured or receive other professional blessings: overnight, they seem to believe they deserve whatever good fortunes came their way, thus adding value to the "rules of the game" imposed on all of us. Discipline in the university works as much from the inside out as the other way around: faculty members valorize academic objectivity even where most of them recognize that academic evaluation is capricious.

Post-postmodern writers must view marketplace standards as only that: They are literary laws of supply and demand, and imperfect ones at that. Post-mod literary figures who proclaim the death of the absolute fall back on the market itself as an adjudicator of competing cultural claims. Judgments about value are encoded in words like "hot" and "happening", not "good" and "true". Not only works are hot, but people themselves. They cluster together in chic dining spots in Los Angeles; they frequent galleries in Manhattan; in between, in the great wasteland of middle America, they clamor to "get to" New York, Los Angeles and Boston. Making it is equivalent to geographic mobility, winning one proximity to certain cultural epicenters and the people who control them.

The academic equivalent of this is attendance at academic professional association meetings, where "big" people expose themselves to the hoipolloi, including less erudite faculty and even graduate students. One hopes that a modicum of stardom will "rub off", giving one crucial markers that can be exchanged in the academic marketplace. The level of intensity at such conferences is extraordinary. Ego is transacted as the functional equivalent of currency. Self-promotion probably explains as much about academic promotions as anything else (Lewis, 1975). This not to say that individuals are solely to be held responsible for their own eventual success; after all, most people cannot catch the eye or ear of those with power, notably the power to annoint.

Everyone wants to join the "mainstream", which is determined entirely by what sells most briskly. A publishing representative recently told one of my colleagues that a certain textbook is best because it sells the most; she expressed an unreflected faith in the ability of the marketplace to make qualitative judgments. Being mainstream is prized for its own sake, even if the objective rewards for being mainstream are few. This is the logic of conformity, deriving standards of appropriate behavior from the behavior in which people regularly engage. The logic of the market produces conformity; people who want to succeed must imitate those who have succeeded before. Eventually, even in the absence of market rewards, cultural conformity is valued for its own sake, even by radicals.

It does not take clinical skills to note that many outsiders simply want to be inside. This does not disqualify radical politics or cultural counterhegemony out of hand but only acknowledges the enormous power of a system leading most of us to define our worth in terms of others' appraisal of it. Even when we know that obsessive other-direction destroys our literary work, we crave "positive feedback". Indeed, those on the outside unaccustomed to praise crave it all the more. I know numerous left-wing academics who fondly dream about gaining acceptance into the power circles of their discipline's mainstream, both attaining elective office in their respective professional associations and achieving publication in the major outlets. Typically, they rationalize these desires in terms of political strategy: their mainstreaming will make it that much easier for their colleagues to gain equivalent access. And this may be true. Yet what is at issue is the way in which the drive to "make it" both distorts one's own work, domesticating it, and redoubles the value of mainstream standards in the first place.

We value playing by the rules yet fail to recognize that the game is rigged. Or, even if we recognize the inequities of the literary marketplace, we explain our own drive for upward mobility in terms of the precedent this will create for others like us. Literary workers must reject the mainstream both for the way it arrogates power to itself (and denies power to others) and because the mainstream marketplace logic is the wrong one with which to evaluate literary work. Sheer sales, unalloyed popularity, are not signs of merit; indeed, they may well indicate its absence. After all, why should "the public" be correct in its cultural and political tastes where taste is a thoroughgoing product of manipulation?

Saying this invites the charge of elitism. But elitism is the assumption that the people can never be correct. Elitists like Bloom prescribe a definitive set of values with which to uplift homely popular taste. But recognizing that people are manipulated to "want" bad books, movies, television, political candidates does not deny them the capacity to make informed choices, even to become cultural producers themselves. On the contrary, demonstrating the management of popular culture empowers people to acute self-consciousness about the ways in which they succumb to the blandishments and banalities of the quotidian. Elitists, dressed up as liberals, charge radicals with elitism in order to veil their own will to power. Of course, some radicals are elitist, too, assuming that the rabble can only be guided "from without", in Lenin's telling phrase. Yet this is not a defect of radicalism as much as a flaw in radicals themselves, indeed an understandable one given their status as outsiders.

Discipline crushes down on all of us – readers, writers, editors. Once we recognize our common plight, we can better move to transform it. It is not enough to change editors or start new journals or presses; that only circulates literary elites but does not overthrow elitism. We resist the erosion of discipline for we fear the vacuum of authority, whether literary or political, inviting either tyranny or anarchy. But readers who gain competence as writers, and writers who read and thus open themselves to dialogue, can change the world; indeed, the world is changed in no other way but through communicative media, mediating the conditioning forces of economy, polity and technology. The history of social change movements shows unequivocally that writers and readers played very central roles, whether those who crucified apostates or those who took Che literally as a harbinger of revolution.

But these are portentous examples. For most of us, reading and writing have to do with the potboilers adorning supermarket check-out lines or the mundane journal articles submitted by academics in their specialized fields. Literary work seems remote from politics. But politics is a thoroughly literary practice, whether in the way positivist writing reproduces the world it only seems to reflect or in the way that political campaigns are scripted, and hence decided, by advertising agencies. The literariness of the world increases the less textuality seems to be political; culture and politics by appearing separate are that much more closely entangled. Public discourse is simply the way people talk to each other, changing each other and arriving at collective decisions. If politics is understood that way, then we can view our literary work, whether reading or writing, differently. Texts matter not least because they are matter, encoding various messages about the nature of the world (Agger, 1989a). The more texts are controlled by a few, notably those who write them and those who pay for their dissemination, the less access people have to the public sphere. The decline of discourse is a political problem where it both reflects and reproduces a general disempowering in late capitalist society.

McLuhan's (1968) "global village", tethered through world-wide electronic media, seems to bring people closer together. Yet for our ability to beam Moscow or the moon into our living rooms, we have lost the capacity to understand each other and especially to make our views known to the powerful. Power protects, and thus reproduces, itself through media; differential access to communication outlets both parallels and reinforces differential access to wealth and political power. By now, in a televisionized polity, these facts are unsurprising. Yet much political sophistry bemoaning the collapse of "traditional" public and personal values seems to disregard them: it is ludicrous to argue for "great books" when people cannot and do not read any books – when textuality, for them, is techno-political imagery screened in the Americanized global village.

My own quite typical undergraduates are frustrated by reading textbooks, let alone great books. Their parents read *People*, not Plato. They all watch television, and participate in a televisionized polity vicariously. The world is a chimera, reflected through the screens of power (Luke, 1989) presenting the world as an inanimate, if often irrational, given. Culture, like everything else, is something that comes from somewhere else; although many literary workers write feverishly for popular culture and academia, they are a tiny minority: most Americans are not cultural producers but merely cultural consumers. In this context, it makes sense to begin sweeping social change in the interstices of people's "everyday" lives, transvaluing their relationships to the abstract institutions otherwise experienced, and thus reproduced, as intractable. In turn, this transvalues the everydayness of everyday life into something extraordinary, open to world-making transcendental projects. For culture to become tangible, for it be something strongly read and thus potentially rewritten, is a first step toward overall political, economic and social transformation.

This calls upon themes in cultural politics from surrealism, expressionism and the counter-culture. Marcuse, like other members of the original Frankfurt School, has devoted considerable effort to theorizing the political nature of cultural activity. This all too quickly leads to the one-dimensional aestheticization of politics (Schoolman, 1980; Agger, 1988); politics is still about power, not only paintbrushes or pens. Yet culture is a crucial factor in oppression; through culture we learn to mute ourselves. A peculiarly horrible version of the world is routinized through the established texts and screens of power. Positivist culture, in particular, teaches us to accept the given as well as to ameliorate our unhappiness through insubstantial diversions. What Horkheimer and Adorno (1972, pp. 120-167) called the "culture industry" refers to the role culture plays in prolonging advanced capitalism, equally as important as the welfare state, which intervenes in the economic system in order to smooth out its irrationalities. Culture addresses psychic crisis, the grinding sense of meaninglessness experienced by people locked into jobs, families, cities and classrooms. It palliates these crises by diverting people from their real source, a world hierarchized into those who produce and those who consume.

The Postmodern Response to Cultural Crisis

The problem with postmodernism is that it celebrates meaninglessness as the flattening of history into an anesthetized, embourgeoisified eternal present. But ideology need not transmogrify into the boredom of jaded cosmopolites. Social life is still desperate for nearly everyone on the planet. Derrida and his ilk do not trace boredom to underlying material misery but rather to a civilization that has falsely set itself on the course of progress. Although the Frankfurt theorists and many postmodernists reject the Enlightenment's vision of the abolition of scarcity through technology as a ruse, Lyotard's postmodernism splits politics and culture into antagonistic terms. The Frankfurt thinkers, like Marcuse, Adorno and Horkheimer, attempted to establish the political contributions of "culture industry" to overall political and economic domination, implicitly premising a mode of cultural politics and hence cultural studies both resisting domination and auguring a new world.

Culture both keeps us down and dumb and also helps us develop visions of a better world. This is the tellingly double nature of art: by representing the miserable present it bespeaks a redeemed order of things (Adorno, 1984; Marcuse, 1978). Culture debunks, delights and builds community. One cannot ignore culture, as many orthodox Marxists do, because culture is less salient than economics. It is not; ideology deepens the domination done to people: it is domination people do to themselves, if unaware of what is going on. This is not to freight culture, whether books, journalism, television or movies, with too much political responsibility. Rather, it is a way of understanding the role of culture both as oppressor and, potentially, as critique. Reading and viewing can spark the electric moment when people realize they have nothing to lose but their chains.

The postmodern world is nearly devoid of vision in this sense. Whether we ought to describe this world as modern or postmodern is irrelevant. Yet the word "postmodern" has been developed by cultural critics who argue for the abandonment of teleological notions of historical change; instead, they argue, history is essentially patternless, having completed itself in an internationalized, televisionized capitalism. As a result, they continue, we ought to draw our personal and political inspirations from an eclectic melange of styles, values and practices. These are to be drawn horizontally from diverse cultures and vertically from diverse historical eras. But cultural and historical diversity are manufactured by the American culture industry: they are intellectual versions of ethnic cooking proffered as proof of urban heterogeneity. Like American Chinese food or Tex-Mex, they are tailored to middle-brow American consumers who only desire America's version of difference, not difference itself. The postmodern response to cultural and political crisis confuses description with diagnosis: it is true that history literally is going nowhere; teleologies force facts into the rigid mold of preconceived historical motion. Yet this does not mean that we should abandon reason, the project of positing certain desirable political possibilities in the historical contexts framing them. Cosmic meaninglessness does not warrant its celebration; indeed, for us on the left, it provokes new efforts to theorize history anew.

Postmodern thinkers, like cultural conservatives, reject Marxism for its untoward certainties about history's vector. Marx himself added to the confusion where he seemingly guaranteed socialism as a dialectical outcome of failed capitalism. But another version of Marx reveals his skepticism about either first or final historical causes; he merely posits socialism as one among a number of possible outcomes of self-contradictory economic tendencies. Marxist determinism is both empirically and ontologically false. No more than Enlightenment optimism, it fails to capture the essential indeterminacy of history. Existentialists like Sartre and Merleau-Ponty attempted to recast Marxism within this indeterminate perspective on history; as Merleau-Ponty (1964a, pp. 81-82) once wrote, "the date of the revolution is written on no wall nor inscribed in any metaphysical heaven". History is open, thus essentially meaningless.

Yet, as Sartre (1966) showed so forcefully in his *Being and Nothingness*, we *give* history, and thus ourselves, meaning in our "projects", the activities with which we fill and sustain life. Although Sartre's own finished version of Marxism was to await his (1976) book, *Critique of Dialectical Reason*, he, like Merleau-Ponty somewhat differently, anticipates the postmodernist response to cultural and political crisis. Unlike his existentialist kin, Albert Camus, Sartre recognizes that mortality does not obviate the search for values, if not absolute ones. Although Camus (1956) rightly traces the postulate of absolute values to tyranny, he unnecessarily forsakes history-making projects such as social change. This is reflected in the quite different political trajectories of Camus' and Sartre's careers; where Camus philosophized and essayed, Sartre developed a politics of literary engagement that led him to the barricades as well as onto stage.

I am not insisting that Sartre's version of reason is the correct one, or even one that has much relevance today. I favor Merleau-Ponty for temperamental reasons. Yet both, and Beauvoir, too, address a history devoid of intrinsic meaning, the existential void, with reason – the plenitude of "projects" filling our time and social space (Poster, 1975). Left existentialism anticipates the postmodern problematic: how are we to confront the meaninglessness, even the dread, of history? Of course, Nietzsche initiated this discussion where he interrogated both Enlightenment and theological absolutisms. The Paris existentialists, unlike postmodernists today, respond to history's void not with the fashionable relativism dismissing socialist ontologies out of hand. Instead, Sartre and his comrades argue that, in his terms, reason is "dialectical", perpetually alternating between personal subject and societal object. Although this truncates political existentialism far too much, it is clear that Sartre, Merleau-Ponty and Beauvoir share Nietzsche's sense of cosmic absence yet reject the post-mod attempt to dismiss all subjectivity – struggle, hope, practice – as ridiculously old-wave.

I do not canonize the Paris existentialists but simply indicate the relative insularity of postmodernisms, especially French ones, that somehow bypass these intellectual figures. For the most part, Sartre goes unknown or ignored in France because he is easy to caricature as an enfeebled Maoist; indeed, there is no denying the instructive discontinuities in Sartre's own thought among his fiction and plays, philosophy and political practice. Yet Sartre and Merleau-Ponty demonstrate an alternative version of post-Nietzschean thought, one that retains a political moment and rejects the ephemera of cultural and political style.

Toward the Post-Postmodern

To conclude a book such as this, documenting the absence of real books, with some simple nostrums or a new worldview is to invite the wrath of the affirmative postmodernism I criticize so unsparingly. I agree that the cultural and political wasteland is barren of real thought and writing; yet I want to understand these things less as philosophical or personal failures than as institutional outcomes. This does not mean that subjectivity – people – cannot make a difference but only to interrogate the notion of difference as *the* central problematic of political and cultural theory today. We will solve little unless we conceptualize the problem clearly: writers, intellectuals, artists cannot ply their trades, and thus change the world, without succumbing to the logic of cultural capital and thus literary hegemony. Writers today, whether they work for television or universities, write "for" everyone but the public, thus diluting and distorting the force of their critical imagination. Trade fiction writers who compose formulaic blockbusters, no less than academics who write journal articles read by hundreds, not hundreds of thousands, contribute to the decline of public discourse. But these are the ways writers live today; they are institutional outcomes of a commodified and hegemonized literary world.

In a dualist world, it is difficult to avoid the simple choices placing the blame on (or ascribing the transformative responsibility to) "either" cowardly writers "or" overweening editors, publishers and producers. These either/ors are undialectical; that is, they simplify a complex reality in which we all bear some responsibility for what happens. Saying that, though, risks dispensing blame or responsibility so freely that critique loses its sharp edge. After all, who would disagree that people should be more "loving" or "caring"? Or better writers and readers? Although writers too often make expedient choices, they do so because literary political economy constrains the opportunities available to cultural workers. Although power is structural, power is mediated through, and around, individuals. True, Gulf + Western owns fossil fuel, publishing houses and Madison Square Garden. But Gulf + Western is run by people and employs people. As such, there is hope, however meager.

Lyotard's postmodernism is hopeless; or better its prayers have all been answered in the eternal present of late capitalism. Thus postmodernism responds to the dismal present with a cynicism no less absolute, hence arbitrary, than millennial optimism. In the meantime, the post-mod literary lifestyle is just that – a way to avoid real work and struggle. Where modernism clearly separated image from reality in order to sharpen insight and heighten perception (e.g., Brecht's "estrangement effect"), postmodernism blurs this line so much that the world becomes a text – in Derrida's terms, "with no outside". Although Derrida is properly a poststructuralist and not a postmodernist (a theorist of knowledge and not of culture), poststructuralism and postmodernism are connected by their common interest in the constitutive powers of language. They both proclaim the "subject" dead where they recognize the enormously determinative power of culture; it tends to use us, rather than we it.

In the absence of positive hope, anything goes, or, at least, anything is worth trying once. Relativism avoids absolutism, hence authoritarianism, only to become another absolute in its own right. We simply cannot be sure that the future holds more of the same, whether in political or cultural terms. Postmodernists are fatigued by looking forward, thus preferring to plumb the past as well as other cultures for both insight and gratification. Indeed, it seems old-wave, whether modernist or Marxist, to locate utopia in the time ahead. Of course, postmodernists equally reject the cultural-conservative notion that utopia lies behind us, either. They scrap the concept of a better world altogether and instead attempt to deal with the world "as it is", that is, uncritically.

My own college students view the '60s as a weirdly energized period, too warm by the present standard of cool. Hair, marches, music, politics seem to have no cultural significance for them; instead, they relate to these things *for what they are*, that is, what they appear to be. Although it is risky to inflate music or dress into a *Zeitgeist*, the absence of political hope is both reflected and reproduced in the lack of critical significance attached to these personal styles. Style does not *stand for something else*, notably a better world, as it did for both romanticism and modernism before it. Of course, my students scarcely understand that the cultural alternatives arrayed before them do not come out of thin air but are determinate outcomes of literary political economy. Taste is as much manufactured as it is reflected in cultural commodities, an insight basic to cultural Marxists for over half a century.

Postmodernism rejects Marxism and feminism. These are seen to be passe, heavy, just irrelevant. Yet post-postmodernism, or better postmodernism as critical theory, has to engage the politics of culture as well as the culture of politics; ideology can be no more wished away today than in the '50s, when Daniel Bell (1960) declared it dead. Why Americans and Europeans reject Marxism is another discussion, necessarily making reference to Marxism-Leninism, the Soviet Union, economic determinism, parliamentarism, even the middle-class. It is unconvincing simply to name the post-postmodern "Marxist" and "feminist", or even "Marxist-feminist". Yet that is nearly unavoidable if we want our cultural expression to create the very world embryonically, notably between writers and readers, that we want politically.

This is Marcuse's (1969, pp. 31-54) notion of the "new sensibility", as he outlined it in 1969 (Agger, 1976a). It is impossible to separate revolutionary process and product, culture and politics here.

Slogans will never end slogans. Post-postmodern does no more work than its predecessors, whether romanticism, expressionism, modernism, Marxism, feminism; the decline of discourse robs words of meaning. Thus, it is especially difficult to conceptualize an alternative cultural politics – concretely, lives that writers can lead – where we are all so exhausted by political failures, hermeneutic theoretical work, authoritarian study groups, all the things we do to ourselves and others needlessly. Yet – the single spark of hope – writers write through it all. This is a book, even if it is unlikely to make a difference. Indeed, my topic has been why writing rarely makes a difference in a commodified literary world. I wish it were different. I know that others do, too.

Let me offer some particular ways in which writers can modify their own literary consciousnesses and practices in a post-postmodern mode. This begs dismissal as yet another self-help guide or simply as irrelevant to the political-economic forces bearing down on writers today. It is precisely my point in this book that writers are more or less at the mercy of institutions paying their way and thus dictating their literary output. Yet individuals and institutions never completely merge: there is always a non-identity, non-overlap, between the writers who write writing and their paymasters; revolt is sparked by recognizing this (Adorno, 1973b). At the very least, in the absence of cheerfully positive nostrums, there are definitely some pitfalls that the politically and intellectually aware writer can avoid. Postmodernism is a trap into which we fall when we fail to examine our literary and cultural practices from the outside. If we get caught up in the hype, whether Nielson ratings games or the academic prestige ladder, and thus allow our writing to be dictated by someone else, we are bound to lose our voices. As a result, public discourse will continue to decline. Sometimes knowing what not to do is more important than knowing exactly what to do; avoiding mistakes is a positive political agenda in these dismal times.

1. The Postmodern Hustle

Recognizing that heroic writing is largely a thing of the past, both failing to put bread on the table and change the world, many scribes for the networks and academic journals cynically embrace the transformation of literary work into networking. They thus rob themselves of valuable working time, seeking publishers, producers and notoriety; as well, they reinforce literary networking as a norm, requiring other writers to do it, too. One can turn one's back on this mode of literary entrepreneurship without moving to Walden Pond, giving up caffeine or otherwise removing oneself from the mainstream in a suicidal way. Not that caffeine is necessary for the literary life! Yet the refusal to kowtow not only signals one's independence, a valuable edge when dealing with cut-throat literary producers, but it also slightly diverts the mainstream, even if imperceptibly. If enough writers refused to "play the game", knuckling under to editors, agents, publishers and producers, the literary world could be turned on its head.

I doubt very much that enough writers will find alternatives to the literary main street or harmless pastoral retreat to shake the system profoundly. Even if such efforts fail, refusing the postmodern *Zeitgeist* is essential for one to do one's own work relatively unburdened by the extraordinary demands of the literary hurlyburly. Chic chews up crucial writing time and, perhaps more important, imaginative energy. Of course, no amount of "good" work will ensure publication; that is my basic point. One must always scrap to find a literary outlet. But finding that outlet is useless if one has not spent enough time perfecting one's craft and maturing one's imagination. Some high-powered academics are adept at finding publishers and editors willing to air their work simply on the basis of their names; yet many of the "names" in our own disciplines not only rest on their laurels but, scandalously, never deserved to be there in the first place. Through a combination of good fortune, breeding, conferencing and genuflecting they have managed to crack the codes affording them access to elite publication outlets. Typically, though, as in the popular literary world, those who "make it" lose their minds; their work is derivative and insubstantial.

2. Meritocracy

"Meritocracy" (Young 1958) describes the distribution of scarce resources according to talent – merit. Capitalism is supposed to be such a system, yet even conservative economists recognize that the game is fixed to some extent if only in the fact that parents can pass along their wealth to their children, thus giving them a significant head start in the merit chase. We are taught that capitalism is a meritocracy in order to justify the privilege of those at the top of the ladder and motivate those nearer the bottom. Perhaps even more than in capitalism, though, the literary world is dominated by the assumption that "good" writing will eventually find its place in the sun. Whether trade fiction or academic scholarship, this belief runs deep; John Stuart Mill's "marketplace of ideas" is a seductive concept in its appeal to those who are born without privilege and want to believe that their own honest effort will be rewarded.

To say that meritocracy is a myth is not news. Numerous studies have documented the deep-seated inequalities of class, race and gender pervading American society. People come to believe that they can ascend the various vertical ladders of success simply through hard and good writing. Instead of networking, they work. On the one hand, this is better than the postmodern hustle in that people actually devote themselves to their literary craft. On the other hand, though, literary meritocracy is largely a ruse, disappointing those who "fail" to make good simply by dint of their own literary excellence. Failure, then, is interpreted as personal failure, where in fact it is an institutional outcome: differential success is a result of differential access to the means and control of literary production. And "success" is interpreted as proof of one's, and the system's, worth.

The critique of postmodernism frequently takes a meritocratic form. The hustle and hype of self-promotion are eschewed in favor of a certain literary purity. Just writing good books is thought to be sufficient to make a living and even achieve positive notoriety. Although one must, by definition, write good books for good books to be published, the ideology of meritocracy punishes "losers" and rewards "winners"; personal effort counts for much less than connections, accidents of birth, good timing, luck. Members of the literary world, especially academics, desperately want to believe that "merit matters". That way, they explain their own success and blame those without success. And, in these cynical, glitzy times, the belief in meritocracy seems an effective antidote to the self-serving postmodern *Zeitgeist*. But that is an illusion: literary political economy grinds us all down; only the fortunate survive unscathed. The unlucky not only lose; they are losers.

For writers to believe that good work matters is one thing; I am trying to explain the structural impediments to doing and publishing good work. But for writers to believe that good work is willy-nilly rewarded is quite another thing. Good work is usually turned back on grounds of dubious profitability or, in academia, lack of conformity to mainstream disciplinary standards. Writers should write good work in order to establish standards of quality as well as democratic community in which many readers write, too. Yet for writers to suppose that "the system works", that their scribbling will find sympathetic ears in far-off Manhattan and Hollywood *simply because it is "good"*, is folly. That illusion shields literary political economy from critical eyes. Merit not only does not matter; it is inimical to the profit and discipline requirements of popular culture and academia, respectively.

Although statements like this can and should be qualified, thus nurturing the rare work that falls through the cracks in spite of itself, even a cursory inspection of the literary landscape will bear them out. Does good work get published or produced? Can persistent writers break down the barriers keeping most of us on the outside? These are empirical questions. But for most defenders of meritocracy, they are matters of faith: good work "should" matter; therefore, it is erroneously concluded, it does matter. But 'ought' cannot derive from 'is'. Whether talent is rewarded is decided by the large institutional forces bearing down on writers who write to live.

3. Writing to be Read

Advocating clarity is tantamount to urging capitulation: Today clarity stands for conformity, even stupidity, especially where clarity is decided in terms of what the market – readers – will bear. Pedestrian writing reproduces pedestrian readers, thus only compounding the problem. The advocacy of commonsense standards of knowledge and language fails to address the social manufacture of ignorance; today, commonsense stands for the absence of intelligence. Yet, in this light, we are tempted to reject clarity – communication itself – altogether as a literary goal. Derrida and other poststructuralists fatally write *for themselves*, thus blunting their otherwise provocative message. Form and content are neither identical nor completely sundered; the valorization of dialogical openness is enhanced by dialogically open writing.

This is not to suggest that writing must be terse or use short words; such writing often obfuscates more than complex and allusive prose. But writing must address readers and other writers. Only in this way can writing form the sort of dialogical community inimical to literary commodification and gigantism. Readers must at least *be considered*, factored into one's writing as the counterpoint or counterpart voice provoking writing in the first place. Not to consider one's reception is no better than to be obsessive about it; either way, authorial voice fails to contribute to good literary, hence political, community. This is the sense of Jacoby's call for public books written by people able to engage with large issues of the time. Jacoby opposes positivist strictures about clarity, and yet he also refuses the Derridean wordplay indulging only itself.

Jacoby shows concern for his readers, as does Bloom in his way. Other literary workers also write and compose publicly, even if they are the rare exceptions in literary capitalism. Showing such concern need not domesticate one's argument or expression especially where one intends to be read by serious readers. Although serious readers are few and far between, made ever scarcer by the absence of serious writing, the possibility of serious reading should not be dismissed out of hand. All sorts of isolated yet inquisitive individuals work hard to read, and even to write, challenging books. People who reduce cultural and intellectual criticism to the broad brush-strokes of one *Zeitgeist* or another, whether postmod or post-postmod, oversimplify; indeed, it is a lazy habit, and one typical of our culture, to reduce complex issues to slogans – "the" mind-set, "the" worldview.

Precisely because these people, and others, write and compose publicly, even if they are accorded little public reception, there is cause for cautious hope. At least, it is cause *for writing*, refusing to still one's pen or paintbrush simply because the managers of the culture industry as well as reading public tend to disqualify serious intellectual expression. And writers must write *as if* readers exist, thus helping educate readers to their own constitutional responsibilities and opportunities. Readers have been beaten down, too; they are capable of reading and even writing at a higher level, and they must be addressed as intelligent, intelligible interlocutors. Only this way can lonely writers make connections with a public hospitable to them, if not the whole public comprising the world's billions. Writing and reading constitute an embryonic social relationship, prefiguring a whole host of social relationships extending far beyond textuality per se. It is not only irresponsible intellectually to write only for oneself, whatever that might mean; it is also irresponsible politically: today's challenged readers might be tomorrow's writers and then next week's public citizens.

In the last analysis, the post-postmodern ends what Marx called prehistory, the long reign of domination. It is not a specifiable set of cultural texts apart from the literary and political practices opening cultural creation, and thus political and economic power, to the disempowered. The post-postmodern literary world can be decommodified; ideas will not be bought and sold. Of course, for this to happen all commodification – capitalism – will have to be undone, again presenting us with a revolutionary chicken-egg problem. Although self-announced dialectical thinkers refuse to pin down how, or where, social change must begin, insisting that it must occur both globally and locally, my discussion of literary commodification indicates that this should give writers no comfort. The long odds against total change should not inhibit the local attempts of people to shift the huge preponderance of oppression, both increasing their own room to move and at once creating viable examples of a decent polity. What sociologists call "publics" can begin in classrooms, workplaces, households, between two people; indeed, bureaucratic, corporate and national gigantism makes it extremely unlikely that social change will start with mass movements, political parties or palpable shifts in the *Zeitgeist*.

Literary workers confront their own political and economic dilemmas: they try to make a living as well as a difference but confront the exigencies of cultural commodification. Making a living is hard enough; making a difference, recreating the public sphere through the example and substance of one's own work, is even more difficult. But, occasionally, these things happen. And, in any event, writers write. Some of them write unbidden to corporate or academic imperative. Then we call their work culture, intellectual creation. The world, while preponderant, is not seamless; cracks around the edges indicate the instability of the whole. It is up to us to find them and then to exploit them. Succumbing to literary political economy is not the best way; playing by the system's own rules destines a bad outcome. Yet literary heroism is heroic only from the point of view of the starving artist; it does not move the world forward or in a different direction.

The worst temptation for postmodern writers is to suspect that one's work makes a significant difference; it is always possible to garner praise and thus succumb to self-elevation. What is euphemistically called "good critical notice" may be no more correct than the bad critical notices routinely fielded by people outside the mainstream. Success is just that – a market judgment. There is no reason for the marketplace to adjudicate truth claims accurately. Today, there is every reason for the market to be wrong, whether consumers of trade fiction and mainstream cinema or academic journal and book referees. A good reception may amount to nothing more than the banality of one's work; it sometimes adds up to fame and fortune.

Of course, capitalism evaluates people in terms of their wealth and stature, literary workers no less than everyone else.

The basic problem with Lyotard's influential postmodernism is that it offers no critical social theory, no critique of capitalism, domination, mindlessness (Kellner, 1988). It pretends to be a cultural, but not a political, movement. In this pretense, it is all the more political. Avoiding power only reinforces it. Posturing aesthetic detachment only detaches the artist from real social processes, increasing his or her vulnerability to corporate manipulation. I have attempted to think about the social, economic and cultural roles of writers in terms of larger institutional tendencies in advanced capitalism. Writing is not everything, but neither is it nothing. Writers write in order to create a world in their own image; even if writing appears to lack this hortatory tone, description recommends. Writers are utopians in that they want to be read, and then to provoke response, in a way prefiguring a decent, gentle community. There are enormous forces arrayed against writers who write with these motives; literary political economy causes discourse to decline. Yet even to think the problem this way – how can writers live in order to write? – offers some respite. Literary resistance to the numbing mindlessness prevailing today may not change the world in itself. But, at least, it is better than literary acquiescence; after all, if writers capitulate, they may as well seek employment in the professions or in business.

A business civilization lowers the rate of intelligence; only intelligence can raise its own level. This is the irony confronting all of us, not least writers. Acknowledging the irony does not resolve it. But in our society we too frequently assume that problems have easy solutions or, as with postmodernism, no solutions at all. Complexity can educate if, indeed, the world from which it arises is complexly structured. Writers ought not to shoulder the blame for the commodification of the literary world. Yet, by the same token, they ought not to assume that, "because" they did not create capitalism, they are somehow immune to it. Intelligence must persistently address the social arrangements frustrating it. Cynicism, whether postmodern or some other kind, is not a viable political posture.

Chapter 9

. . . Or the Decline of Theoretical Discourse?

Theory as Public Speech

I now return to my opening chapter, where I laid out a theoretical framework of sorts within which to house my subsequent empirical argument about the decline of discourse. This will help me conclude, tying together the theoretical, descriptive and diagnostic phrasings that threaten to split apart this book schizophrenically. Another way to read this last chapter is in terms of my opening concern about whether theory itself contributes to the decline of discourse, albeit unwittingly. *At stake is the public sphere, the polity.* The decline of discourse matters because discourse connects us to an authentic realm of political discussion and practice otherwise controlled by elites. Unwittingly, people who theorize about politics, especially leftists, often contribute to the specialization and professionalization of public language by composing themselves in ways accessible to a few hundred, not a few hundred million. The left critique of declining discourse ironically only compounds the problem.

Part of this is inevitable: analyses of what is going wrong with our literary political economy cannot proceed without some reliance on abstract and technical concepts, whether words like "commodification" or "hegemony". Of course, these terms can be defined and hence democratized; they must be, if we are to create the populist polity in which what Habermas calls dialogue chances (McCarthy, 1978, pp. 306-310) are democratically distributed. But this book demonstrates that social analysis and diagnosis can proceed without involuted technical categories only deepening the problem they originally intended to address. The Frankfurt School (e.g., Marcuse, 1969) has called this prefiguration – the inescapable fact that what we do and say in the present helps create a certain future in its image. For example, oppressing our colleagues and comrades out of alleged revolutionary exigency only entrenches authoritarianism, albeit flying different flags. By the same token, writing as if people could understand it and join one's discourse dialogically helps create that very polity, albeit in halting, accumulating steps.

It is unlikely that any book will have the same sweeping impact as Marx's oeuvre. Books are too readily co-opted by the culture industry for all that, either defused as the ravings of lunatics or sold profitably as evidence of the system's alleged openness (precisely what happens when academic presses publish left-leaning work). Yet as I have said above *books matter* if only because they are matter; they are what Wittgenstein (1953) called "language games" with their own interpretive and dialogical rules. Textual politics is not all politics, yet it is undeniably political, especially in light of a theory of ideology that attunes itself to the way popular discourse helps maintain the status quo. Thus, people who theorize discourse must attend to their own political stance, their own complicity in worsening the very problem they bemoan – here, the erosion of a genuinely public language with which to create a new polity and hence a whole new world.

British analytic philosophers continually lament the inability or refusal of European social theorists to write clearly. They read obscurantism as incorrigible elitism and infantilism. It is not as simple as that if only because the complex world requires a good deal of conceptual and empirical complexity in order to be understood. International capitalism demands training in sophisticated economic theory, just as cultural criticism forces one to study labyrinthine interpretive theories. But that does not mean that critical theorists ought to ignore the prefigurative implications of their own writing for the very polity they so desperately desire. C. Wright Mills, a self-styled "plain Marxist" (1962), argued eloquently against academic obscurantism (1959), showing in the example of his own work an admirable ability to write clearly about broad-gauged issues of social criticism.

Russell Jacoby (1987) is correct to lament the absence of the accessible public book typified by those of Mills. Of course, as he well knows, this is largely conditioned by literary political economy itself: commercial publishers want blockbusters and hence they avoid controversy. Academic publishers demand intellectual conformity plus the rarefied, stultified methodological apparatus of "scholarship". And, as I said before, Mills' own house, Oxford University Press, has become largely a trade publisher concerned to make money. But Jacoby correctly holds writers, especially left-wing ones, responsible for blithely complying with these external imperatives, even endorsing them. Left academics are frequently no less obscurantist than centrist and right-wing ones; their commitment to elitist academese outweighs their political commitment to a democratic world. The example of Habermas is prominent here: he writes about the importance of "universal speech situations" and democratized "dialogue chances" in a code that is virtually impossible to crack without years of training in European philosophy and social theory. He justifies this literary strategy as an attempt to legitimate critical theory in the bourgeois university. But that is a meager benefit when balanced against the loss of his public voice. Where C. Wright Mills influenced and energized the New Left, particularly the Port Huron Statement of the original Students for a Democratic Society (SDS), Habermas' comments about the "colonization of the lifeworld" by oppressive "systems" provokes little but ennui. His architectonic Parsonian Marxism produces footnotes but not political passion. One has to dig deep beneath the surface of his text to find the secret heartbeat at the core of every act of literary artifice.

Neoconservatives valorize plain language simply to restrict public access to elite codes of power (Freire, 1970; Bernstein, 1971; O'Neill, 1976). In no way should the left take all the blame for the gaping distance between elites and masses today. But the left cannot ignore its own victimization by academic discourse that reproduces hierarchy and conformity. Left critics must write straight ahead through the thickets of confusion and complexity confronting any responsible social analyst; this confusion and complexity *can be simplified*, even if one must acknowledge that simplification always threatens to recede deconstructively into the murky soup out of which clarification initially arises in a bold stroke. That nothing is simple today is all the more reason for theorists to write simply and forcefully.

We must avoid the methodologization of this notion of public discourse, however, whereby we try to translate difficulty into simplicity directly. There are no one-for-one principles of translation or semiotization according to which we can replace a complex concept with a simpler, terser one. The responsibility for writing public discourse is more a matter of temperament and style than a methodological injunction to craft brief sentences. As Adorno shows in much of his most powerful and penetrating prose, dialectical allusion is often clearer than the linearity pretending to grasp complexity in monosyllables. The principle of public speech involves a commitment to *political education*, the systematic consciousness raising that allows the disempowered to learn and use complex languages and thus to challenge power.

Today, especially in North America, political education smacks of agitprop. Then call it consciousness raising, a concept concocted by the women's movement in response to the male supremacy of the New Left. Or simply call it public discourse. It matters little what pedigree we give our commitment to creating a new polity in which dialogue chances are more or less equal. This commitment has been called many things: socialism, feminism, democracy etc. Whatever words we use to talk about the restoration of the public sphere, we must recognize that our analytic and diagnostic language itself bears responsibility for the world we would create: intellectuals are political actors; hence we must address the politics of intellectuality, as I have tried to do in this book.

The Politics of Textuality/Intellectuality

Textual politics are politics, although not all politics. Literary political economy, as I have called it, helps us understand what happens to writing and writers when they become merely white-collar employees (Mills 1951), losing both autonomy and vision. Literary political economy, which I derive from a version of postmodernism emphasizing its liberatory possibilities, has both economic and ideological features. On the one hand, the commodification of literary activity turns writing into yet another exchange value and writers into wage and salary slaves. On the other hand, literary political economy involves hegemony, a dominant culture of ideas and values reproduced by these literary underworkers. It is still true (viz. *German Ideology* (Marx and Engels, 1947)) that the ruling ideas are the ideas of the ruling class, propagated through what Horkheimer and Adorno (1972, pp. 120-167) called the culture industry. Original Marxism was long on economic analysis of commodification but short on ideological and cultural critique showing the interconnection between profit motive and political/ideational/cultural hegemony. Marx's model of ideology was simplistic; he characterized ideology as a "camera obscura" through which people are coaxed to view the world upside down.

Gramsci's (1971) notion of hegemony renders the discussion of ideology more sophisticated. One cannot trace hegemony to an original conspiracy of editors, publishers and producers any more than one can reduce each and every cultural expression to the profit motive per se. There are all sorts of dissonance around the edges of the late-capitalist totality, notably including postmodernism itself which, in significant respects, veers away from traditional bourgeois concepts of modernity, the subject, reason, values etc. Although the affirmative version of postmodernism that I rejected in my opening chapter is affiliated to the project of capitalist modernization (e.g., for all practical purposes Bell Lyotard), postmodernism addresses and legitimates a much more complex late capitalism (Jameson, 1984b, following Mandel, 1975) in which "difference" (Derrida, 1976) is supposedly the best post-modern, post-capitalist, post-rationalist principle of integration. Of course, this is fraudulent; difference, once deconstructed, can be traced to all the usual centers and samenesses of capital, gender, race. Postmodernity is no more pluralist than modernity; in fact, to the extent to which postmodernism functions as an occluding ideology duping people about the prevalence of real difference, postmodernity regresses *behind* earlier stages and versions of modernity that ambivalently contained both the project of general enlightenment and liberation (viz. Habermas' (1981b, 1987a, 1987b) valorization of enlightenment) on the one hand and co-optation/coercion/discipline on the other.

In this sense, then, modernity and modernism are somehow more dialectical than postmodernity and postmodernism, which flatten bourgeois civilization into a Nietzschean tableau of eternal presentness – unproblematic gratification. Marcuse (1955) already carefully explained late capitalism's need for "repressive desublimation", loosening discipline's hold on people lest they chafe too much against early-Protestant superego restraints. Postmodernism in its neoconservative Lyotard variant theorizes and legitimizes this repressive desublimation, outfitting the world in Gucci clothes, feeding them with American fast-food as well as Americanized "foreign" food, entertaining them with the "pastiches" and "collages" (Jameson, 1984b) of cultural expression drawn from diverse historical and global sources, and housing them in a postmodern cityscape apparently adding some soul and depth to the usual modernist skyscrapers, offices and factories. Indeed, I have serious doubts that Jameson's own (1984b, p. 92; 1988) strategy of "cognitive mapping" can help overcome the very "multinational capitalism" he decries. But I do not pretend to have a better strategy.

As such, postmodernism is both an economic and cultural phenomenon, what Jameson (1984b) correctly called the "cultural logic of late capitalism". In my opening chapter I tried to suggest a version of postmodernism much more closely affiliated to the culture-critical project of western Marxism, especially the Frankfurt School.

I derived an empirical and dialectical sociology of culture from it, notably a theory of literary political economy allowing me to address the decline of discourse in concrete terms: what writers write and how they live are largely dictated by the forces of literary commodification. As such, literary liberation must address the culture industry squarely and neither lament the passing of a golden age that never existed (e.g., freelancing) nor burden heroic, solitary writers with the weight of the world: writers can only do so much to change things around, although it is undeniable that they must involve themselves in overall social change – the politics of textuality/intellectuality. At the very least, this will help transform the culture industry and thus dominant ideology in general.

Unfortunately, textual politics have a decidedly ambiguous status in American higher education and American letters generally, especially on the left. This relates to larger questions about the role of critical intellectuals, which I want to address in this closing chapter. First, here, I discuss the false duality of materialist and idealist perspectives on the politics of intellectuality and then I conclude with a discussion of the postmodern intellectual and postmodern intellectual life (although I should properly call it post-postmodern if we are talking about postmodernism as affirmative ideology and not as critical theory).

The ambiguous status of textual and cultural politics on the left has very much to do with the classical problem of economism in Marxism. Although Horkheimer (1972b) definitively laid to rest the notion that Marx was economistic or reductionist in his method, thus suggesting a critical theory that closely linked economic with cultural and ideological processes, the Frankfurt School's perspective on cultural politics is far from universally accepted on the left. More orthodox Marxists reject what they take to be the untoward focus on culture on the part of western Marxists and others heavily involved in literary theory and cultural criticism. Although I believe that they are wrong not to recognize the imbeddedness of literary political economy in political economy generally, an imbeddedness I have tried to demonstrate in this book by looking at the literary world concretely, culture critics tend to fetishize textuality to the exclusion of almost everything else.

This fetishism ignores the political economy of textuality and intellectuality. Poststructuralists and postmodernists fond of Derrida's notion that the text has no outside only continue a line of argument embraced earlier by the New Criticism (Ransom, 1941; for a critique, see Fekete, 1978). This is ironic in that poststructuralist and postmodernist literary criticism formulated itself in opposition to the textual objectivism of New Criticism, where each text is treated critically on its own terms. As I read it, this is only a family difference. Derrida, and later those Americans who have methodologized poststructuralism into deconstruction (e.g., the Yale School), also close off textuality from a kind of social reading, although deconstruction expands the notion of the text from literature per se – the actual pages on which it is inscribed – to all manner of social and cultural expressions. Poststructuralist sociologists even write books called *Society as Text* (Brown, 1987), reflecting this tendency to extrapolate the notion of textuality from the authorial product per se into a veritable ensemble of interpersonal and cultural expressions. The poststructural and postmodern fetishes of textuality (Agger, 1989a, Chapter 6) miss the dynamic, non-identical relationship between (material) text and (material) world, ignoring literary political economy altogether.

But textuality *is* a political battleground and must be addressed materially, albeit in a way that recognizes that the "texts" of ideology are powerfully constitutive in their own right. Ignoring postmodern textual politics is tantamount to ignoring ideology which, as Marx, Lukacs and the Frankfurt theorists knew, is a crucial political factor in its own right. Indeed, Horkheimer's (1972b) original 1937 article on "Traditional and Critical Theory" argues that political economy includes both economic and ideological elements *that are virtually impossible to separate*. Regrettably, though, once one enters into the thicket of conceptual, interpretive and empirical problems surrounding the radical sociology of culture, notably the close examination of the culture industry, one is almost inevitably trapped on the sticky fly-paper of literary and cultural theory oblivious to the material nature of textuality. Deconstruction, fetishized in American departments of English and Comparative Literature, is one result: it is apolitical, precious and pretentious. In claiming the world for textuality (Derrida: the text has no outside), this textualism loses the world. Stanley Fish's influential book *Is There a Text in this Class?* (1980) needs to be reformulated materially. Indeed, John O'Neill has done so (1991). He asks: is there a class in this text? Not frequently enough, in the work of the deconstructors.

Stanley Aronowitz remarked that some postmodernists invest themselves so deeply in literature and the literary that their soi-disant Marxism loses its political co-ordinates. Aronowitz lamented the degeneration of critical literary theory into aestheticism. He said that he can write of Dickens and still ground his argument in empirical political theory – what for the left are the bread-and-butter issues of the theory/practice merger. Here, Adorno's later considerations of aesthetic theory (e.g., 1984) suggest the impasse of Frankfurt critical theory, later occasioning the Kantian and Parsonian Marxism of Habermas (1984, 1987b). Adorno's *Negative Dialectics* (1973b) suggests an ideology-critical agenda for critical theory that by 1984 (*Aesthetic Theory*) he had largely foresworn in favor of a critical theory ensconced in aesthetic interpretation and opposition. Although there is much that is attractive about the various Frankfurt perspectives on aesthetic politics (Agger, 1976a), Adorno's 1984 book and Marcuse's own 1978 book, *The Aesthetic Dimension*, retreat to aesthetic expression as adequate (or the only available) modes of political resistance, the fateful trajectory of Marcuse's (1964, p. 257) Great Refusal. Interestingly, the trajectory of Jameson's own work (from *Marxism and Form* (1971) to *The Political Unconscious* (1981) has been similar, threatening to lose touch with the political moment of aesthetic theory in favor of a highly self-referential theory of interpretation.

Empirically, Adorno, Marcuse and Jameson are correct: late capitalism swallows virtually every resistance and opposition, requiring dissent to find unconventional, even nondiscursive, forms. This is the essential message of the theory of the culture industry, and one that is central to this book. I accept Frankfurt aesthetic theory as far as it goes. But aesthetic theory, especially in the frames of poststructuralism and postmodernism, almost inevitably becomes aestheticism, an approach to cultural studies long on interpretation and short on politics. Of course, we can and must redefine the region of the political. But culture is not a world apart from political economy and thus our criticism must address culture in thoroughly material terms, asking phenomenologically how, where, why, when and what real flesh-and-blood writers can write in order to avoid the implosive tendencies of aesthetic commodification.

The Frankfurt School's aesthetic theory, especially pre-*Aesthetic Theory*, kept this firmly in mind. Some of Adorno's discussions of television (1954), radio (1945) and journalism (1974b) are unparalleled examples of materialist cultural criticism that avoids its own empty methodologization. Tellingly, Adorno's WWII exodus to the U.S., when he collaborated first with Paul Laszarsfeld, one of the doyens of sophisticated social-science empirical research methodology, and then with the California social psychologists on *The Authoritarian Personality* (Adorno et al., 1950), was among his most productive in terms of this nuanced cultural criticism and media studies (Adorno,

1969). After he and Horkheimer returned to West Germany Adorno reverted to earlier, more apocalyptic and philosophically abstract modes of theorizing (Jay, 1984). The politically promising sociology of culture that Adorno and some of his other Frankfurt colleagues like Marcuse had begun during the 1940s gave way to the world-historical musings of *Minima Moralia* and *Aesthetic Theory*.

It is important to note that the issue here is not simply political pessimism or the lack of it (Slater, 1977; Agger, 1983). Orthodox Marxists who ground optimism in a socialist dialectic of nature mislead themselves as much as do postmodernists who disdain political discourse as shabby and out-of-date. Pessimism and optimism are temperamental categories, nothing more. Political predictions are empirical, nothing less. Adorno's lack of hopefulness during the post-WWII reconstruction period, when capitalism repaired itself back together on a global scale, thus integrating aspects of fascism (Foucault's disciplinary society), was largely justified on the evidence. Yet his ventures in aesthetic theory closed off some very real political possibilities. Of course, were he alive today, he might well recant some of strictures on the impossibility of political resistance. Adorno was much less a metaphysician than met the untutored eye. As Jay (1984) and Ryan (1982) have pointed out, there are some important continuities between Adorno's critical theory and both poststructuralism and postmodernism. The postmodern problematic only emerged in somewhat clearer light since Adorno's death, making predictions about whether he would have approved of a left version of postmodernism impossible. Perhaps an engagement with the problematic of modernity and postmodernity (e.g., Habermas, 1981b) would have softened Adorno's commitment to purely aesthetic resistance, or led him to reformulate that resistance in a more political-economic direction, like the work here. *The Decline of Discourse* is scarcely imaginable without Adorno's concept of negative dialectics (1973b), indeed without the example of his whole oeuvre.

But the tone of this discussion is precisely the problem with theory today. People's search for pedigree becomes all-consuming; we forget the empirical and political issues of the day in favor of scholarship, the career capital of academics. Then again, intellectuals almost inevitably become academics in late capitalism. The intellectual as a social category is archaic. To talk about the politics of intellectuality is really to talk about the relationship among academics, university, state and culture. *The Decline of Discourse* is a contribution to that discussion, although I need to extend that discussion into a fuller consideration of intellectuality and intellectual life today. Who/what is the postmodern intellectual?

The Postmodern Intellectual

Above all, the postmodern intellectual is a writer; that is my theme. Whether writers today are intellectuals is another question. My answer has been largely negative. Writers do everything but think, indentured to producers, publishers, studios, editors, department heads, promotion-and-tenure committees. I include myself in this, of course. Obscurantism is a virtually unavoidable outcome of academic discourse in the late-capitalist university. People like Jacoby (1987) who rail against academization are voices in the wilderness. But I decided to compose this book in a more pedestrian discourse than my earlier work and certainly than my intellectual heroes like Adorno. We must write *as if* there were an intelligent public capable not only of understanding what we are saying but joining us in community-building dialogue.

This is to say that we must take Habermas' (1979) *ideal speech situation* seriously as a radical goal. In doing so, we must not exempt ourselves as intellectuals and writers from the requirement of public discourse; indeed, as I said in my opening chapter, we prefigure the world we want in what we do today, including how we treat our intimates and how we talk about our larger political aims. Habermas is a stunning example of a radical intellectual who contradictorily preaches communicative democracy but thwarts it at every turn, falling back on academicism and its technical argot. One can argue that Habermas is merely doing what any rigorous intellectual would in expecting his readers to master the various civilizational oeuvres constituting our intellectual culture. It is impossible to understand our own political and cultural formation without having tackled Plato, Kant, Hegel, Marx, Freud, Habermas. But Habermas is a critical theorist who wants dialogue chances and thus power to be democratized. Therefore his own discourse bears examination as a prefigurative medium: he only invites scorn by those who hold him out as an example of yet another phony radical who cannot bring himself to talk to the people in a language they can understand.

Above all, the postmodern intellectual will accept some responsibility for creating the ideal speech situation and hence the democratic polity. Interestingly, American feminists have been more sensitive to the constitutive nature of their own discourse than have most male leftists. This might reflect only the fact that Marxism derives canonically from the hallowed oeuvre of Marx and his epigones; feminism is only as old as yesterday and thus it poses fewer interpretive and devotional problematics (quickly being remedied by the involution of the French poststructuralist feminists!). But I suspect it reflects something deeper: American feminists may be more democratic than American and European male leftists, an issue addressed by those who trace the origins of feminism in the male-dominated New Left (e.g., Evans, 1980).

Now the parallel between western Marxism, and particularly critical theory feminism, has been noted before (Marshall, 1988; Agger 1990). But critical theorists, with few notable exceptions, have been unable or unwilling to jettison their own elite symbolic codes for more accessible ones; they have never overrated the agitational possibilities of critical theory. And American feminists, although more discursively democratic, have been short on theory, frequently failing to articulate their own critique of male supremacy in terms of a larger theory of class, gender and race interrelations. This has slowly begun to change, especially where critical theorists and feminist theorists are starting to recognize not only their own possible political mutuality but the extraordinary fact that their critiques of sexist capitalism are very similar at root (e.g., Marshall, 1988).

The postmodern intellectual is post-specialist and post-elitist, even if his or her theoretical discourse is sometimes fine-grained and complex. Where the world's difficulty provokes analytical difficulty, the postmodern intellectual must work as hard as possible to prevent difficult language from sedimenting itself into a code so impossibly restricted that public comprehension and hence consensus formation – political mobilization – are thwarted. That is the nub of the issue: intellectuals today fail to engage the public because they have either neglected or forgotten the practical and political role of intellectual activity. Habermas, other critical theorists, left feminist theorists, poststructuralists and postmodernists want to restore a decent, democratic public sphere. But that is all the more reason why they must prevent the decline of their own discourse lest they merely reproduce hierarchies in their own lives. In the next section, I will discuss more concretely the nature of public voice. Here I want to consider just where intellectuals have failed to attend to the politically constitutive nature of their own discourse as a way of suggesting some remedies, below.

I want to contrast archetypes of the modernist and postmodernist intellectual. The modernist intellectual is typified by Marx, Beckett,

Adorno, Benjamin, Beauvoir, Sartre, Habermas. The modernist intellectual feverishly wants things to change, to improve, and thus devotes his or her intellectual energy to dissecting and diagnosing the dismal present. Marx's engagement remains exemplary for this intellectual archetype. Where Marx in the *Manifesto* called working people to arms, suggesting to them their own world-historical opportunity for ending class society, in *Capital* he analyzed the functioning of capitalism in rigorously detailed terms, authoring Marxism as a dialectical science of society. Unfortunately, at least among Marxists and Marxologists, the second book has received much more interpretive attention than the first. After all, it is longer, denser, more susceptible to close hermeneutic work. And it purports to lay the foundation for Marxism as a systematic theory or science. Similarly, Adorno's essays (e.g., 1967) blaze the way for his philosophical (1973b) and aesthetic-theoretic (1984) magnum opuses. They are thus read as preparatory, even if Adorno intended them as self-sufficient in their own right.

Modernist left scholarship almost inevitably intends itself as a dialogue with others who speak in restricted symbolic codes. Most fail to examine or counteract the irony that these very leftists argue for the democratization of dialogue chances and the ideal speech situation, in Habermas' terms. Modernist intellectuals fail to descend from the rarefied heights of scholarship, interpretation and historiography to the terra firma of public discourse. Indeed, many of us on the critical left have become adept at defending our aloofness in terms of the very empirical theories of late capitalism that explain the co-optation of intellectual work in convincing terms (e.g., Marcuse's 1964 *One-Dimensional Man*). Although this defense is credible it is also self-serving. Better, it fails to move beyond itself toward a theoretical practice – public discourse – that empowers non-specialists to join the debates.

At one level, then, the postmodern intellectual must deal with the disproportion, the hierarchy, between intellectuals and the masses in much the way Marx and Gramsci first formulated the problem. Marx prophesied an all-around individual capable of shifting from one role to another without taking on their life-long imprints (Marx and Engels, 1947); Gramsci suggested an organic intellectual devoted to a "philosophy of praxis" that explicates the necessity of democratizing intellectuality. These modernists took seriously their own responsibility for transcending the very world making them intellectuals and others laborers. That is why both Marx and Gramsci took pains to elaborate the political role of radical intellectuals.

Although the Frankfurt theorists were also committed to a demo-cratic public sphere (e.g, Habermas, 1975; Keane, 1984), they were less convinced than Marx and Gramsci that modernity could be rearranged in significant ways. If Marx was an early modernist, Adorno was a high or late modernist, if not sufficiently postmodern in the way he theorized the relation between intellectuals and public life. And if Adorno was a late modernist, Habermas is a late-late modernist, given the circumlocutions of his highly byzantine critical theory. Irony abounds here for Habermas (1981b) was among the first to take Lyotard's postmodernism to task for betraying the project of the Enlightenment and hence of modernity. Perhaps he realizes that his commitment to ideal speech and his inability to engage in it are clearly contradictory! I fully agree with his condemnation of Lyotard-postmodernism as neoconservative in its thoroughgoing anti-Marxism.

A genuinely postmodern intellectual would not have to recant the radical theories and perspectives of earlier modernists, notably Marx and Marxists. In fact, I believe that one cannot inhabit the contem-porary world and hope to improve it without being powerfully energized by the modernist impulse, dating all the way back to the Enlightenment. Nietzsche's critique of the Enlightenment only goes so far. At a certain point, his negation must be negated and we must salvage what we can from the *philosophes'* vision of a new world, albeit refusing Comte's imagery of a benevolent reign of technocrats. But modernism fails precisely where it is elitist: modernists in one way or another endorse vanguardism – the notion that societies will only change where small groups of leaders enforce discipline (including intellectual discipline) on the masses, leading them out of the wilderness. In this sense, modernism inhibits democracy.

The issue is not whether the masses need leadership, education, enlightenment. That is certainly not arguable in the era of the culture industry and authoritarian state (Horkheimer, 1973). But modern-ist intellectuals embrace their own vanguard roles too cavalierly, unself-consciously lapsing into esoteric language that only perpetu-ates itself "after" the revolution, in spite of Marx's, Gramsci's and Freire's warnings to the contrary. Indeed, for Marxist intellectuals to warn themselves and others against vanguardism is thoroughly ironic for it was Marxism itself that gave birth to the notion of ideology-critique, if also to the notion of educating the educator, ever the left-modernist dilemma. We can read Marx in a host of different ways. I choose to read Marx as humble before the task of political education. I think he understood how precarious it was for intellectuals and tacticians to take license with the communicative and intellectual incompetence of the masses, especially on the part of those who genuinely wanted the elitist state to wither away after capitalism.

But, after Marx, we have Marxists, feminists, critical theorists, poststructuralists and postmodernists who do not heed the warning of Marx. We assume that educating-the-educator is no longer problematic since we all sport doctoral degrees from the finest institutions of higher education, have healthy curriculum vitae full of erudite publications, and possess the gift of professional gab which we refine at professional meetings and in the classroom. *Theory talk is inevitably rarefied these days, only compounding the problem of political education.* This is the legacy of modernism to which a genuinely radical postmodernism must be a response. Modernist theorizing is so Apollonian, so elevated, that virtually no one can climb these mighty peaks without years of acclimation, not just trusty road-maps. Unavoidably, this entombs theoretical conversation in the university, ensuring that theory itself will not help revivify the public sphere – ever our most important political agenda.

Even to utter these thoughts will earn the disrespect of my left colleagues who have worked so hard to learn Kant, Hegel, Marx, Freud, Frankfurt, deconstruction, feminism. I am not pulling rank, although I have spent my share of time sweating through this arduous apprenticeship. But there is something profoundly unreflexive about theory that forgets its own connection to the body politic (O'Neill, 1972), even hastening the dissolution of this connection. Modernity is permeated by expert cultures that disempower those on the outside. The most constitutive expert culture is called capitalism, as Marx recognized. But there are others, too. One of the aims of an interdisciplinary critical theory is precisely to weave together a narrative about how these expert cultures fit together and, together, sustain themselves. We use a variety of terms like capitalism, sexism and racism to do this job. But we must also attend to critical theory itself as an expert culture that inhibits its own democratization, hence democracy in general.

This is less a doctrinal question than one of temperament. My left comrades are committed to democracy as a radical endpoint. But too few of them are genuinely democratic in their mood; hence they ignore the contribution their own argot makes to hierarchy, empowering only those who speak in the arcane phrases of European high theory. Theory has become an academic specialty, not a mode of address to the political world. How many theorists address the flesh-and-blood individuals who could not care less about Kristeva and Habermas but seek desperately to make the world be a less hellish place? Too few. Theory is a modern project in that it does not doubt the legitimacy of its own epistemological privilege. Left theorists ironically would end capitalist modernity by professionalizing and specializing their discourse even further. They call this postmodernism. But this only further marginalizes critical theory as well as entrenches expertise.

Postmodern intellectuals must question the contribution of intellectual and political modernism to the very world we all profess to oppose. At the same time, we must not recant the liberating modernism of the Enlightenment, Marxism, feminism etc. The alternative to capitalist modernity, with its self-perpetuating expert cultures, is not counter-modernity – a left Luddism. The only suitable alternative is a rethinking of the modern in a way that makes theory responsible for its own agitational and rhetorical stance toward the masses. Whether this means we should simply democratize our language is a question I take up shortly, in this chapter's concluding section. I suspect it is not as simple as that for theory must overcome the tendency of all intellectuality since the Greeks to seal itself off hermetically from the ebb-and-flow of everyday life, the body politic. Even Marxists have not learned enough from Marx about how to engage theory with the non-expert cultures occupied by most of the world's billions in order to change the very value of intellectuality, making it "committed" in Sartre's (1965) terms.

The postmodern intellectual must address his or her public role politically; this inevitably requires some degree of de-academization, of distancing from the lifeworld of professional journals, books, conferences, classrooms. I am not suggesting that intellectuals deny their intellectuality, embracing whatever excrescence of so-called popular culture is most current or most profitable. American survey research knows nearly everything there is to know about public opinion. Instead, postmodern intellectuals must find a way to offer their discourse as a rule of societal reconstruction, neither shrinking from analytical difficulty and abstraction nor ignoring the tendency of theory itself to become a hierarchical language game – just another expert culture to which access is granted through credentialing processes. Postmodern intellectuality must invent itself, and thus a whole new world, without renouncing the liberating tendency of genuine modernism. But we must be clear about this: the modernist intellectual, whether Adorno or bourgeois social scientists, contributes to bad modernity where he or she not only ignores but increases the social distance between the lifeworlds of theory and popular experience.

An Agenda of Radical Cultural Studies

This immediately suggests a postmodern research agenda to be formulated in a democratizing rhetoric that I call *the public voice*. Let me describe this agenda and then conclude with a few comments about the public voice. Of course, these two things are inseparable: I am not distancing the topics of radical writing from the writing itself. Methodology will not win the day, especially where methodology has itself become a suffocating expert culture. Programmatism must already write in the voice it recommends: that is one of the key postmodern insights. Writing is already a social practice; it creates a new public world through the prefigurative and constitutive example of its very word. Of course, although writing is not all of politics, textual politics is definitely an arena and vehicle of the political, especially in a fast capitalism in which images, concepts, advertising dominate our public discourse. Ignoring cultural politics is suicidal for those who would both understand and transform the public sphere.

In this sense, theorists must cease their exhaustive and exhausting exegetical work (haven't we learned enough already about the classics of high theory?) and instead turn their attention to critiques of the culture industry – political education, critique of ideology or consciousness raising. Names matter less than the deconstructive practice of opening seemingly deauthored cultural texts to the reality of their own artifice, thus inviting new texts; I have done this with regard to positivist social science (Agger, 1989b, 1989c). One of the central claims of a radical postmodernism is that cultural discourses do not just fall from the sky but can traced backward to authorial gestures that could have been made differently. In this sense, postmodernism explodes the distinction between high and low culture, or at least renders that distinction inherently dialectical at a time when it is difficult to draw a clear line between them. The culture industry mobilizes all sorts of texts against the threat of utopian imagination – popular culture more than high culture, in fact. For this reason, a radical cultural studies must address these entwining texts as political practices, refusing to ignore them simply because they are pedestrian. Their pedestrian character is precisely their efficacy when it comes to shutting down political imagination.

Deconstruction can become a vital critical methodology once liberated from its fetishism in English departments as yet another interpretive perspective on the literary canon. Derrida meant for deconstruction to undo the hidden contradictions and ironies of texts that are otherwise smoothly integrated into the world as the truths they purport to contain (Culler, 1982). Deconstruction lets authorial artifice shine through, revealing, for example, network television to be a corrigible, deliberate product of busy scribes and not the intractable piece of nature it often appears to be, as close to hand as the remote-control channel changers. As such, by "reading" television (e.g., Miller, 1988) through the deconstructive lens of radical cultural studies we can not only undo its hold on us but even *rewrite* it, or at least formulate a possible television appropriate to a socialist-feminist-postmodernist society.

Cultural studies, like poststructuralist deconstruction, tends to fetishize itself, missing the materialist foundation of commodified discourses. For this reason, I have formulated my version of cultural studies as literary political economy, thus stressing the connection between the study of literary commodification on the one hand and literary hegemony on the other. These things are fundamentally inseparable: television's thirst for profit is reflected in, and reproduces, the way in which television is a screen of power (Luke, 1989) basically vitiating critical intelligence and utopian imagination. My study of textual politics here demonstrates the possible relevance of literary political economy to a larger discussion of the future of the public sphere especially as I focus on the nature and status of the postmodern intellectual.

The Public Voice

Let me return to the role of postmodern intellectuals, having suggested that our primary political work will fall under the rubric of radical cultural studies (once armed with literary political economy). As I said, to programmatize a postmodern research agenda is absolutely inseparable from a discussion of (and in) the postmodern critical voice – the language game of postmodernity, one might say. I have already lamented the tendency for modernist intellectuals to deny their own imbeddedness in a self-reproducing expert culture, suggesting by implication a postmodern intellectuality opposed to the cult of its own expertise. But there is a difference between expertise and the cult of expertise: At some level, we must admit that intellectuals are still occupants of a a rare and privileged social stratum and thus have a peculiar political opportunity unavailable to almost everyone else. Political education assumes that some need education more than others; my point here is that political educators – postmodern intellectuals – must never forget that their discourse itself, notably its attitude toward its own monologic tendencies, has extraordinarily powerful implications for the "content" of that education to be imparted. It is one thing to preach democracy; it is quite another to preach democracy democratically, as if one is really willing and ready to generalize one's communicative competence over a whole body politic.

Can we meaningfully talk of intellectuals as a distinct social stratum when everyone is capable of engaging in creative intellectual discourse or simply public speech? I think not, although we are very far from that day. How many radical intellectuals are willing to relinquish their own privilege? How many really embrace lifeworld-grounded ideal speech – real democracy – in Habermas' terms? Fewer than one would expect if one focuses on radicals' unwillingness to open up their self-perpetuating rhetoric. The left abounds with what Habermas calls "left fascism". This is to understand left obscurantism as a purposeful strategy and not just an occupational hazard: political vanguardism plays out on rhetorical and epistemological levels.

Postmodern intellectual discourse is just discourse itself – public speech spoken in an accessibly public voice. In this sense, discourse is an antidote to left fascism. Let me define that public voice, recognizing that any definition of that voice must already speak in it. *By public voice I am referring to the way postmodern discourse is non-technical but nonetheless can understand, and even use, technical language where necessary: public voice expertly subverts its own expert culture*, broadening communicative competence as well as utopian imagination far beyond its own academic ranks.

It is a mistake to confuse public voice with ordinary language; ordinary language is riddled with unconsciousness, acquiescence, lapses and contradictions where public voice comprehends the deformation of discourse in thoroughly political terms. British analytic philosophers who mute the esoteric tones of high theory do so not in order to create the ideal speech situation but simply to undercut radical insight delivered complexly. Public voice does not shrink from difficulty or abstraction but labors hard to make these maximally accessible, in the process educating itself about its own unreflected reliance on categories and catechism. Too many theorists use their technical conceptual apparatus without really thinking about the utility of their neologisms. Theory deconstructs itself where it tries to break its own dependence on a theoretical apparatus that essentially robs thought of vitality: we must try to remember what sharp concepts meant before they became dulled by their ceaseless repetition. Words like domination, oppression, freedom, liberation can be restored to meaningfulness if we work hard to counteract their tendency to become cliches, used whenever we cannot solve intellectual and political problems in their own terms.

Public voice abhors the decline of discourse into cliches, although it does not dispense with all technical language, as intellectual Luddites might. As Freire (1970) has amply demonstrated, the process of "conscientization" requires a political pedagogy empowering the disempowered to understand and use languages heretofore reserved for elites. Expert culture in defending its own privilege gives expertise a bad name, as much on the left as in the mainstream. There is simply no excuse for theorists to invest so much in their own rhetoric that they forget how to think beyond the received wisdom of their particular language games. I could repeat terms like "decline of discourse" or "literary political economy" a million times without getting them to solve intellectual problems in a genuine way. As a result, much of this book has been written in a way that invites the non-expert reader to develop a facility with the occasional theoretical digressions required to raise my writing from mere description to analysis and diagnosis. After all, against Lyotard's postmodernism, the world's totality cannot be grasped without the aid of totalizing categories like exploitation, domination, hegemony and patriarchy.

This is a delicate balance: On the one hand, we must use abstract concepts to understand the mammoth structuring forces invading and constituting our lives. On the other hand, we must avoid the ritualization of these categories lest they cease to do any useful analytical work. Most important, we must *democratize expert cultures of all sorts*, including the culture of theory. This democratization does not just flatten theory into prosaic terms of everyday discourse; that would only rob critical categories of their diagnostic ability. It trades on theoretical insights without turning theory itself into a new force of mystification and elite self-justification. Democratizing expert language reinvents language, overcoming the distinction between quotidian discourse and a more rarefied code heretofore monopolized by jealous professionals, including the left.

This reinvention of language is easier said than done. I fully intend *Decline of Discourse* to contribute toward that reinvention, moving back and forth between theory and a lower-level discourse unashamed of its popular nature. The decline of discourse will be reversed only if we transform popular culture so that it incorporates heretofore recondite elements of expert language, *transvaluing the very distinction between lay and expert rationalities*. This is a profoundly political project today given the enormous power of the culture industry and its textual politics. It takes little rigorous research to show that television, journalism, science have constitutive roles in shaping the body politic and thus in perpetuating an unequal distribution of wealth and power. Writers write discourse commodified and displaced into the "texts" of popular and academic culture. As such, they could reinvent these texts as well as the whole world to which they are addresses.

I am not simply saying that writers comprise a new vanguard, for that whole military metaphor of tactics and conquest is inappropriate to radical democracy. Yet writers matter because writing matters; we who compose are firmly ensconced in literary political economy, which is part of a larger political economy generally. Our words are converted into economic, cultural and career capital. They have enormous political impact if what we write is sucked into the vortex of the culture industry both as a mode of production and reproduction. A playful deconstructor might say that our words constitute a cultural *vortext*. In any case, writers, including academics, constitute an important class and cultural fraction. Ideology is written through us and thus it could be written differently. Of course, in Chapters 7 and 8 I also said that solitary literary heroism will have little impact on the machine of cultural production. It is precisely for that reason that I call for critical writers to develop a public voice with which to enter into dialogue with those convinced that the present social order is inherently intractable or, as some say, postmodern.

Ultimately, the problem with postmodernism as a discourse is that it pretends too clean a rupture between the fluid period of industrializing modernity and the present period of hardened postmodernity. One cannot date or periodize the shift between the two any more than one can specify the transition between feudalism and modernity. Certainly postmodernity did not dawn on the morning after the French publication of Lyotard's *The Postmodern Condition: A Report of Knowledge*. Existentialism reminds us that history is open; there are no certainties, either about the eternity of social perfection or the inevitability of decline. Instead, history is indeterminate, as such susceptible to transformations. Dialecticians – better, call us ironists – recognize that in transforming the world we are ourselves transformed. Or, more aptly, we cannot change things without working to change ourselves in the process. Otherwise, change is chimerical: things stay the same, albeit under different flags, different regimes.

I would prefer to see modernity and postmodernity as a continuum, a perpetual set of possibilities. We will never escape modernity unless we fry and chill ourselves into nuclear winter, the only conceivable end-of-history. Short of that, we will face a future somehow continuous with the past and present and yet also open to being radically rerouted. Writing as public speech is a way of inserting ourselves into history, a way of making a difference. In any case, capitalism requires writing in order to script the products, lifestyles and imagination appropriate to it. Commodities must be textualized just as texts become commodities themselves. Otherwise, they will fail to traffic in the marketplace, appearing to be the false needs (Marcuse, 1964; Heller, 1976; Leiss, 1976, 1978) they really are. And without a restless, frenetic consumerism, capitalism grinds to a halt, just as Marx perspicaciously foresaw. At root, literary political economy exists to prime the general economy (in which texts, too, acquire exchange value or status value).

It is tempting to end by methodologizing my notion of public voice, offering a set of inflexible criteria by which we can judge talk as public or not. But that is foreign to the dialogical, dialectical project of genuine discourse, which responds to the world and to other interlocutors in a comprehensible, comprehending sense making. We must work hard to be understood, just as we want to raise the level of understanding. A nation that watches *Miami Vice* and *White Christmas*, reads *People* and tabloids, and votes for Reagan(twice) and then Bush-Quayle must be addressed in its own pedestrian terms, although without forgetting that the point of public discourse is to remake the polity by democratizing expert culture (hence blurring the boundary between lay and expert rationalities).

This is political education in the best sense of the word. But that is not to endorse didacticism any more than it is to eschew polemic and passion. These are conditional qualities of discourse and not axiomatic. One of the left's historic problems has been its inflexibility with regard to what is now tellingly called political correctness. Apart from some general commitments to life, liberty and social justice, public life necessarily defies the institutional ritualism that all too quickly leads to a combination of tyranny and mass apathy. There are no singular or simple answers to what ails us apart from some general observations about the colonizing imperatives of capital, patriarchy, racism and the domination of nature (e.g., Habermas, 1984, 1987b). The most pressing political work ahead is the critique of ideology, revealing the aporias of literary claims about the rationality of reality. We literary workers must deconstruct cultural claims made on behalf of the given order of things as a way of reauthoring the world.

We must recognize that we are being used as conduits of ideology and ontology. It seems that books (scripts, advertisements, journal articles etc.) write authors, not the other way around. Literary political economy pierces this illusion; in fact, writers write the texts of ideology further diminishing our public competence to think, speak, write and act in ways that answer to our fundamental human needs. No matter how impenetrable the dense web of capitalist textual politics, no matter how disempowered the solitary author, *ideology does not fall from the sky: it is composed by people working in the service of ideology, the busy wage slaves of the culture industry*. Even to recognize this is a step in the right direction, toward a public literary culture. Of course, recognizing it is not enough. We must reauthor the whole public world, not just theorize about what is going wrong.

In this sense, writers who attain public voice must narrate the world anew, suggesting heretofore suppressed social possibilities in believable, convincing terms. Marxism and to a lesser extent feminism make little headway in North America because their scant imageries of a different world are too remote from North American experience. The working-class white people and minorities who voted for Reagan are not addressed by political education relying heavily on European left theory; no matter how comprehensible, *The Communist Manifesto* does not play in Peoria. It never will. American leftism (Agger, 1979a; Kann, 1982) must speak American: that is, we on the left must pay attention to the thematic issues of our time, as well as to the current (low) level of political consciousness, and not hope to transmit the recondite truths of high European social theory by injection or hypnotism. Although we have learned from Marx, Lukacs, Frankfurt, Gramsci, feminism, we must cease an exegetical mode of political education. Even if ordinary working-class and middle-class Americans would sit still for courses in the Basic Texts of Modern Marxism, the point is not to impart book knowledge of these canonical writers and texts but to help average Americans apply notions like domination, hegemony and alienation to their own daily lives and then to reinvent their sense of what is possible.

Ultimately, our political education will be a dismal failure if we do not empower these dulled readers to become writers – public figures – themselves. Everyone can learn the public voice, at least to the extent to which people begin to resist elite culture on the local level. If this sounds like a Tocqueville version of American Marxism and feminism, so be it. The New England town meeting is our own equivalent of the Paris Commune and we must respect this difference lest we doom ourselves to irrelevance. This does not mean that we theorists and writers should recant the analytical and diagnostic apparatus of Marxism-feminism but only that we must generalize the liberatory insights of this tradition to a generic public practice; here, I call it public voice, although, obviously, we could name it differently.

The notion that everyone can and must become writers – public speakers – is genuinely radicalizing at a time when virtually everyone capitulates to the imperatives imposed on them by experts. Critical theorists (e.g., Mueller, 1973; Wellmer, 1976; Habermas, 1979, 1984, 1987b) have made communication thematic precisely because the monopoly of wealth and power is reinforced, and reinforces, the monopoly of information, expertise and dialogue chances. The culture industry both creates false needs and diverts us from true needs. To the extent to which culture could be scripted differently, the notion that everyone can produce culture is potentially powerful. A radical version of cultural studies represents what I think is most enduring about the long legacy of critical theory since Marx. But it is imperative that cultural studies resist its own academization; books about culture written by and for other specialists only compound the problem. For this reason, critical theorists must carefully examine their own unreflected reliance on elite discourse. Critical theory can and must be written in a new voice; I have called this the public voice, suggesting the political relevance of critical theory at a time when both criticism and theory are only academic projects. Reversing the decline of discourse begins at home.

Bibliography

Adorno, T. (1945) 'A Social Critique of Radio Music', *Kenyon Review*, 8, 2, pp. 208–217.
- (1954) 'How to Look at Television', *Quarterly of Film, Radio and Television*, 3, pp. 213–235.
- (1967) *Prisms*, London, Neville Spearman.
- (1969) 'Scientific Experiences of a European Scholar in America', in Fleming, D. and Bailyn, B. (Eds) *The Intellectual Migration*, Cambridge, Mass., Harvard University Press.
- (1973a) *The Jargon of Authenticity*, Evanston, Ill., Northwestern University Press.
- (1973b) *Negative Dialectics*, New York, Seabury.
- (1974a) *Minima Moralia*, London, New Left Books.
- (1974b) 'The Stars Down to Earth: The Los Angeles Times Astrology Column: A Study in Secondary Superstition', *Telos*, 19, pp. 13–90.
- (1978a) 'Commitment', in Arato, A. and Gebhardt, E. (Eds) *The Essential Frankfurt School Reader*, New York, Urizen, pp. 300–318.
- (1978b) 'Subject and Object', in Arato, A. and Gebhardt, E. (Eds) *The Essential Frankfurt School Reader*, New York, Urizen, pp. 497–511.
- (1984) *Aesthetic Theory*, London, RKP.
Adorno, T. W., Frenkel-Brunswik, E., Levinson, D. and Sanford, R. N. (1950) *The Authoritarian Personality*, New York, Harper and Row.
Agger, B. (1976a) 'On Happiness and the Damaged Life', in O'Neill, J. (Ed) *On Critical Theory*, New York, Seabury, pp. 12–33.
- (1976b) 'Marcuse and Habermas on New Science', *Polity*, 9, 2, pp. 151–181.
- (1979a) *Western Marxism: An Introduction*, Santa Monica, Ca., Goodyear.
- (1979b) 'Work and Authority in Marcuse and Habermas', *Human Studies*, 2, pp. 191–208.
- (1982) 'Marcuse's Freudian Marxism', *Dialectical Anthropology*, 6, 4, pp. 319–336.
- (1983) 'Marxism 'or' the Frankfurt School?', *Philosophy of the Social Sciences*, 13, 3, pp. 347–365.
- (1985) 'The Dialectic of Deindustrialization: An Essay on Advanced Capitalism', in Forester, J. (Ed) *Critical Theory and Public Life*, Cambridge, Mass., MIT Press, pp. 3–21.

(1988) 'Marcuse's Aesthetic Politics: Ideology-Critique and Socialist Ontology', *Dialectical Anthropology*, 12, pp. 329–341.

(1989a) *Fast Capitalism: A Critical Theory of Significance*, Urbana, Ill., University of Illinois Press.

(1989b) *Reading Science: A Literary, Political and Sociological Analysis*, Dix Hills, NY., General Hall.

(1989c) *Socio(onto)logy: A Disciplinary Reading*, Urbana, Ill., University of Illinois Press.

(1990) 'Critical Theory, Poststructuralism and Postmodernism', *Annual Review of Sociology*.

Althusser, L. (1969) *For Marx*, London, Allen Lane.

Appelbaum, J. and Evans, N. (1978) *How to Get Happily Published: A Complete and Candid Guide*, New York, Harper and Row.

Arac, J. (1986) (Ed) *Postmodernism and Politics*, Minneapolis, University of Minnesota Press.

Arendt, H. (1958) *The Human Condition*, Chicago, University of Chicago Press.

Armer, A. (1988) *Writing the Screenplay: Television and Film*, Belmont, Ca., Wadsworth.

Aronowitz, S. (1981) *The Crisis in Historical Materialism*, New York, Praeger.

(1988) *Science as Power: Discourse and Ideology in Modern Society*, Minneapolis, University of Minnesota Press.

(1990) *The Crisis in Historical Materialism*, 2nd ed., Minneapolis, University of Minnesota Press.

Austin, J. L. (1962) *How to Do Things with Words*, Cambridge, Mass., Harvard University Press.

Balkin, R. (1977) *A Writer's Guide to Book Publishing*, New York, Hawthorn Books.

Banfield, E. (1970) *The Unheavenly City: The Nature and Future of Our Urban Crisis*, Boston, Little, Brown.

Barthes, R. (1970) *Writing Degree Zero*, Boston, Beacon Press.

(1974) *S/Z*, New York, Hill and Wang.

(1975) *The Pleasure of the Text*, New York, Hill and Wang.

Baudrillard, J. (1981) *For a Critique of the Political Economy of the Sign*, St. Louis, Telos Press.

(1983) *Simulations*, New York, Semiotext.

Becker, H. (1986) *Writing for Social Scientists*, Chicago, University of Chicago Press.

Bell, D. (1960) *The End of Ideology*, Glencoe, Ill., Free Press.

(1973) *The Coming of Post-Industrial Society*, New York, Basic Books.

(1976) *The Cultural Contradictions of Capitalism*, New York, Basic Books.

Bendix, R. (1974) *Work and Authority in Industry*, Berkeley, University of California Press.

Benhabib, S. (1984) 'Epistemologies of Postmodernism', *New German Critique*, 33, pp. 103–126.

Benjamin, W. (1978) 'The Author as Producer', in Arato, A. and Gebhardt, E. (Eds) *The Essential Frankfurt School Reader*, New York, Urizen, pp. 254–269.

Berger, P., Berger, B., and Kellner, H. (1974) *The Homeless Mind: Modernization and Consciousness*, New York, Vintage.

Berman, A. (1988) *From the New Criticism to Deconstruction: The Reception of Structuralism and Post-structuralism*, Urbana, Ill., University of Illinois Press.

Berman, M. (1982) *All that is Solid Melts into Air*, New York, Simon and Schuster.

Bernstein, B. (1971) *Class, Codes and Control*, London, RKP.

Best, S. (1989) 'The Commodification of Reality and the Reality of Commodification: Jean Baudrillard and Post-Modernism', *Current Perspectives in Social Theory*, 9, pp. 23–51.

Best, S. and Kellner, D. (1988a) '(Re)Watching Television: Notes Toward a Political Criticism', *Diacritics*, 17, 2, pp. 97–113.

(1988b) 'Watching Television: The Limits of Postmodernism', *Science as Culture*, 4, pp. 44–70.

Blacker, I. (1986) *The Elements of Screenwriting: A Guide for Film and Television Writers*, New York, Macmillan.

Blackburn, R., Behymer, C. E. and Hall, D. E. (1966) 'Correlates of Faculty Publication', *Sociology of Education*, 59, pp. 381–390.

Bloom, A. (1987) *The Closing of the American Mind*, New York, Simon and Schuster.

Bluestone G. (1957) *Novels into Film*, Baltimore, Johns Hopkins University Press.

Blum, R. (1980) *Television Writing: Formats, Techniques and Marketplaces*, New York, Hastings House.

Bourdieu, P. (1977) *Outline of a Theory of Practice*, Cambridge, Cambridge University Press.

(1984) *Distinction: A Social Critique of the Judgment of Taste*, Cambridge, Mass., Harvard University Press.

Brady, B. and Lee L. (1988) *The Understructure of Writing for Film and Television*, Austin, University of Texas Press.

Brady, J. and Fredette, J. (Eds) (1981) *Fiction Writer's Market*, Cincinnati, Writer's Digest Books.

Braverman, H. (1974) *Labor and Monopoly Capital*, New York, Monthly Review Press.

Breines, P. (1985) 'Redeeming Redemption', *Telos*, 65, pp. 152–158.

Brenkman, J. (1987) *Culture and Domination*, Ithaca, NY, Cornell University Press.

Brodkey, L. (1987) *Academic Writing as Social Practice*, Philadelphia, Temple University Press.

Bronfeld, S. (1981) *Writing for Film and Television*, Englewood Cliffs, N.J., Prentice-Hall.

Brown, R. (1987) *Society as Text*, Chicago, University of Chicago Press.

Bureau of Competition, Federal Trade Commission (1978) 'Concentration and Conglomeration in Book Publishing', *Proceedings of the Symposium on Media Concentration*, vol. 2, pp. 549–648.

Burns, A. and Sugnet, C. (Eds) (1981) *The Imagination on Trial: British and American Writers Discuss Their Working Methods*, London, Allison and Busby.

Bystryn, M. (1978) 'Art Galleries as Gatekeepers: The Case of the Abstract Expressionists', *Social Research*, 45, 2, pp. 392–408.

Callinicos, A. (1985) 'Postmodernism, Post-structuralism and Post-Marxism?', *Theory, Culture and Society*, 2, 3, pp. 85–101.

Camus, A. (1956) *The Rebel*, New York, Vintage.

Caplow, T. and McGee, R. (1958) *The Academic Marketplace*, New York, Basic Books.

Castells, M. (1977) *The Urban Question: A Marxist Approach*, Cambridge, Mass., MIT Press.

   (1983) *The City and the Grassroots*, Berkeley, University of California Press.

Chancellor, J. (1983) *The News Business*, New York, Harper and Row.

Chomsky, N. (1966) *Syntactic Structures*, The Hague, Mouton.

Clark, R. (1987) *Free to Write: A Journalist Teaches Young Writers*, Portsmouth, N.H., Heinemann.

Clemente, F. (1973) 'Early Career Determinants of Research Productivity', *American Journal of Sociology*, 79, pp. 409–419.

Compaine, B. (1978) *The Book Industry in Transition: An Economic Analysis of Book Distribution and Marketing*, White Plains, NY, Knowledge Industry Publications.

Coser, L., Kadushin, C. and Powell, W. (1982) *Books: The Culture and Commerce of Publishing*, New York, Basic Books.

Crane, D. (1965) 'Scientists at Major and Minor Universities: A Study of Productivity and Recognition', *American Sociological Review*, 30, pp. 699–714.

Crider, A. (1982) *Mass Market Publishing in America*, Boston, G. K. Hall.

Culler, J. (1982) *On Deconstruction: Theory and Criticism after Structuralism*, Ithaca, NY, Cornell University Press.

Commins, D. (1978) *What is an Editor? Saxe Commins at Work*, Chicago, University of Chicago Press.

Curran, J. (1979) 'Capitalism and Control of the Press, 1800–1975', in Curran, J., Gurevitch M. and Woollacott, J. (Eds) *Mass Communication and Society*, Beverly Hills, Sage.

Curtis, R. (1989) *Beyond the Bestseller: A Literary Agent Takes You Inside the Book Business*, New York, New American Library.

Curwen, P. (1986) *The World Book Industry*, London, Euromonitor.

Dahlin, R. (1980) 'Bantam and its Film Development Subsidiary Find Box Office in Book-Movie Projects' in *Publishers Weekly*, 4 April, pp. 38–39.

D'Amico, R. (1978) 'Desire and the Commodity Form', *Telos*, 35, pp. 88–127.

Debord, G. (1983) *Society of the Spectacle*, Detroit, Red and Black.

de Certeau, M. (1986) *Heterologies: Discourse on the Other*, Minneapolis, University of Minnesota Press.

Demers, D. and Nichols, S. (1987) *Precision Journalism: A Practical Guide*, Newbury Park, Ca., Sage.

Denzin, N. (1991) 'Empiricists: Cultural Studies in America: A Deconstructive Reading', *Current Perspectives in Social Theory*, 11.

Derrida, J. (1976) *Of Grammatology*, Baltimore, Johns Hopkins University

Press.

(1978) *Writing and Difference*, Chicago, University of Chicago Press.

(1987) *Glas*, Lincoln, University of Nebraska Press.

Dews, P. (1984) 'Power and Subjectivity in Foucault', *New Left Review*, 144, pp. 72–95.

(1987) *Logics of Disintegration: Post-Structuralist Thought and the Claims of Critical Theory*, London, Verso.

Dillard, A. (1982) *Living by Fiction*, New York, Harper and Row.

Donovan, J. (1985) *Feminist Theory*, New York, Ungar.

Eagleton, T. (1983) *Literary Theory: An Introduction*, Minneapolis, University of Minnesota Press.

(1985) 'Marxism, Structuralism, and Poststructuralism', *Diacritics*, 15, 4, pp. 2–56.

Eliasoph, N. (1987) 'Politeness, Power, and Women's Language: Rethinking Study in Language and Gender', *Berkeley Journal of Sociology*, 32, pp. 79–103.

Engebretson, H. and Gillespie, J. (1974) *Getting Started. . .in Journalism: A Mini Course*, Blackwood, N.J., Educational Impact.

Evans, S. (1980) *Personal Politics: The Roots of Women's Liberation in the Civil Rights Movement and the New Left*, New York, Vintage.

Ewen, S. (1974) 'Advertising as Social Product', in Reid, H. (Ed) *Up the Mainstream*, New York, David McKay.

(1976) *Captains of Consciousness: Advertising and the Social Roots of the Consumer Culture*, New York, McGraw-Hill.

Faigley, L. and Miller, T. (1982) 'What We Learn from Writing on the Job', *College English*, 44, 6, pp. 557–569.

Fanon, F. (1966) *The Wretched of the Earth*, New York, Grove Press.

Feagin, J. (1989) 'The Future of Blacks in America: Race and Class in American Cities', lecture, Albert A. Levin Lecture Series, Cleveland State University, May 18.

Fein, H. (1979), 'Is Sociology Aware of Genocide?: Recognition of Genocide in Introductory Sociology Texts in the United States, 1947–1977', *Humanities in Society*, 3, 3, pp. 177–193.

Fekete, J. (1978) *The Critical Twilight: Explorations in the Ideology of Anglo-American Literary Theory from Eliot to McLuhan*, London, RKP.

Feyerabend, P. (1975) *Against Method*, London, New Left Books.

Finkelstein, M. (1984) *The American Academic Profession*, Columbus, Ohio State University Press.

Fischer, M. (1985) *Does Deconstruction Make Any Difference?*, Bloomington, Indiana University Press.

Fish, S. (1980) *Is There a Text in this Class?: The Authority of Interpretive Communities*, Cambridge, Mass., Harvard University Press.

Foster, H. (1984) '(Post)Modern Polemics', *New German Critique*, 30, pp. 155–177.

Foucault, M. (1970) *The Order of Things*, New York, Pantheon.

(1977) *Discipline and Punish*, New York, Pantheon.

(1978) *The History of Sexuality*, Vol. 1, New York, Pantheon.

(1980) *Power/Knowledge*, New York, Pantheon.

Fraser, N. (1984) 'The French Derrideans: Politicizing Deconstruction or Deconstructing the Political?', *New German Critique*, 33, pp. 127–154.

(1990) *Unruly Practices: Power, Discourse and Gender in Contemporary Social Theory*, Minneapolis, University of Minnesota Press.

Freire, P. (1970) *Pedagogy of the Oppressed*, New York, Seabury.

Friedan, B. (1963) *The Feminine Mystique*, New York, Norton.

Gadamer, H. G., (1975), *Truth and Method*, New York, Seabury.

Gans, H. (1979) *Deciding What's News: A Study of CBS Evening News, NBC Nightly News, Newsweek and Time*, New York, Pantheon.

Gardner, J. (1983) *On Becoming a Novelist*, New York, Harper and Row.

Gellner, E. (1959) *Words and Things*, London, Gollancz.

Gerth, H. and Mills, C. W. (1953) *Character and Social Structure*, New York, Harcourt, Brace.

Gilder, G. (1981) *Wealth and Poverty*, New York, Basic Books.

Gilligan, C. (1982) *In a Different Voice*, Cambridge, Mass., Harvard University Press.

Gilroy, A. (1980) 'An Economic Analysis of the U.S. Domestic Book Publishing Industry: 1972–Present', Congressional Research Service Report no. 80–79E.

Gitlin, T. (1979) 'News as Ideology and Contested Area: Towards a Theory of Hegemony, Crisis and Opposition', *Socialist Review*, 9, pp. 11–54.

(1987) *The Sixties: Years of Hope, Days of Rage*, New York, Bantam.

(1988a) 'Hip-Deep in Postmodernism', in *The New York Times Book Review*, 6 November, pp. 1, 35–36.

(1988b) review symposium on Gitlin's *The Sixties*, *Contemporary Sociology*, 17, 6, pp. 729–739.

Gomme, I. (1985) 'First Light, a Review of Five Introductory Sociology Texts', *Canadian Review of Sociology and Anthropology*, 22, 1, pp. 146–153.

Gottlieb, Annie (1987) *Do You Believe in Magic? Bringing the '60s Back Home*, New York, Simon and Schuster.

Gouldner, A. (1979) *The Future of the Intellectuals and the Rise of the New Class*, New York, Seabury.

Gramsci, A. (1971) *Selections from the Prison Notebooks*, London, Lawrence and Wishart.

Grossberg, L. (1986) 'Teaching the Popular', in Nelson, C. (Ed) *Theory in the Classroom*, Urbana, Ill., University of Illinois Press, pp. 177–200.

Habermas, J. (1970a) 'Technology and Science as 'Ideology'', in Habermas, J., *Toward a Rational Society*, Boston, Beacon Press.

(1970b) *Toward a Rational Society*, Boston, Beacon Press.

(1971) *Knowledge and Human Interests*, Boston, Beacon Press.

(1975) *Legitimation Crisis*, Boston, Beacon Press.

(1979) *Communication and the Evolution of Society*, Boston, Beacon Press.

(1981a) 'The Dialectics of Rationalization: An Interview with Jurgen Habermas', *Telos*, 49, pp. 5–31.

(1981b) 'Modernity versus Postmodernity', *New German Critique*, 22, pp. 3–14.

(1981c) 'New Social Movements', *Telos*, 49, pp. 33–37.

(1984) *The Theory of Communicative Action*, Vol. 1, Boston, Beacon Press.

(1987a) *The Philosophical Discourse of Modernity*, Cambridge, Mass., MIT Press.

(1987b) *The Theory of Communicative Action*, Vol. 2, Boston, Beacon Press.

Hallin, D. (1985) 'The American News Media: A Critical Theory Perspective', in Forester, J. (Ed) *Critical Theory and Public Life*, Cambridge, Mass., MIT Press, pp. 121–146.

Hansen, K. (1987) 'Feminist Conceptions of Public and Private: A Critical Analysis', *Berkeley Journal of Sociology*, 32, pp. 105–128.

Hardin, N. (1975) 'For Paperback Houses, There's No Business Like Show Tie-in Business' in *Publishers Weekly*, 17 February, pp. 46–51.

Harmetz, A. (1979) 'Courtship of Hollywood and Novelists Moves Closer to Marriage' in *The New York Times*, 26 November, p. 15.

Harrington, M. (1962) *The Other America*, New York, Macmillan.

Harvey, D. (1973) *Social Justice and the City*, London, Arnold.

(1985a) *Consciousness and the Urban Experience*, Oxford, Basil Blackwell.

(1985b) *The Urbanization of Capital*, Oxford, Basil Blackwell.

Hassan, I. (1987) *The Postmodern Turn: Essays in Postmodern Theory and Culture*, Columbus, Ohio State University Press.

Hauser, A. (1982) *Sociology of Art*, London, RKP.

Hayden, T. (1988) *Reunion: A Memoir*, New York, Random House.

Heller, A. (1976) *The Theory of Need in Marx*, New York, St. Martin's.

Herrick, R. (1980) 'Nineteen Pictures of a Discipline: A Review of Recent Introductory Sociology Textbooks', *Contemporary Sociology*, 9, 5, pp. 617–626.

Hirsch, E. D. (1987) *Cultural Literacy*, Boston, Houghton, Mifflin.

Holt, P. (1979) 'Turning Best Sellers into Movies' in *Publishers Weekly*, 22 October, pp. 36–40.

Horkheimer, M. (1972a) *Critical Theory*, New York, Herder and Herder.

(1972b) 'Traditional and Critical Theory', in Horkheimer, M. *Critical Theory*, New York, Herder and Herder, pp. 188–243.

(1973) 'The Authoritarian State', *Telos*, 15, pp. 3–20.

(1974) *Eclipse of Reason*, New York, Seabury

Horkheimer, M. and Adorno, T. W. (1972) *Dialectic of Enlightenment*, New York, Herder and Herder.

Horowitz, I. L. (1986) *Communicating Ideas: The Crisis of Publishing in a Post-Industrial Society*, New York, Oxford University Press.

Howe, I. (1982) *The Margin of Hope*, San Diego, Harcourt, Brace, Jovanovich.

Husserl, E. (1965) *Phenomenology and the Crisis of Philosophy*, New York, Harper and Row.

Huyssen, A. (1984) 'Mapping the Postmodern', *New German Critique*, 33, pp. 5–52.

(1986) *After the Great Divide: Modernism, Mass Culture, Postmodernism*, Bloomington, Indiana University Press.

Hymes, Dell (1974) *Foundations in Sociolinguistics: An Ethnographic Approach*, Philadelphia, University of Pennsylvania Press.

Illich, I. (1977) *Disabling Professions*, New York, Calder and Boyars.

(1978) *The Right to Useful Employment*, London, Calder and Boyars.

(1981) *Shadow Work*, Boston, Marion Boyars.

Irigaray, L. (1985) *This Sex Which is Not One*, Ithaca, NY, Cornell University Press.

Iser, W. (1974) *The Implied Reader: Patterns of Communication in Prose Fiction from Bunyan to Beckett*, Baltimore, Johns Hopkins University Press.

(1978) *The Act of Reading: A Theory of Aesthetic Response*, Baltimore, Johns Hopkins University Press.

Jacoby, R. (1975) *Social Amnesia*, Boston, Beacon Press.

(1976) 'A Falling Rate of Intelligence?' *Telos*, 27, pp. 141–146.

(1981) *Dialectic of Defeat*, New York, Cambridge University Press.

(1983) *The Repression of Psychoanalysis*, New York, Basic Books.

(1987) *The Last Intellectuals: American Culture in the Age of Academe*, New York, Basic.

Jaggar, A. (1983) *Feminist Politics and Human Nature*, Totowa, NJ, Roman and Allenheld.

Jameson, F. (1971) *Marxism and Form*, Princeton, Princeton University Press.

(1981) *The Political Unconscious: Narrative as a Socially Symbolic Act*, Ithaca, NY, Cornell University Press.

(1984a) 'The Politics of Theory: Ideological Positions in the Postmodernism Debate', *New German Critique*, 33, pp. 53–65.

(1984b) 'Postmodernism, or the Cultural Logic of Late Capitalism', *New Left Review*, 146, pp. 53–93.

(1988) 'Cognitive Mapping' in Nelson, C. and Grossberg, L. (Eds) *Marxism and the Interpretation of Culture*, Urbana, Ill., pp. 347–357.

Jay, M. (1973) *The Dialectical Imagination*, Boston, Little, Brown.

(1984) *Adorno*, Cambridge, Mass., Harvard University Press.

Jencks, C. (1987) *Post-Modernism: The New Classicism in Art and Architecture*, New York, Rizzoli.

Jensen, M. (1984) *Love's $weet Return: The Harlequin Story*, Bowling Green, Oh., Popular Press of Bowling Green State University.

Johnson, Paul (1988) *Intellectuals*, New York, Harper and Row.

Johnstone, J., Slawski, E. and Bowman, W. (1976) *The News People*, Urbana, Ill., University of Illinois Press.

Kamenka, E. (1962) *The Ethical Foundations of Marxism*, New York, Praeger.

Kaminsky, S. (1988) *Writing for Television*, New York, Dell.

Kann, M. (1982) *The American Left*, New York, Praeger.

(1986) *Middle Class Radicalism in Santa Monica*, Philadelphia, Temple University Press.

Katz, J. (1984) *The Ad Game: A Complete Guide to Careers in Advertising, Marketing and Related Areas*, New York, Barnes and Noble.

Keane, J. (1984) *Public Life and Late Capitalism*, Cambridge, Cambridge University Press.

Kellner, D. (1981) 'Network Television and American Society: Introduction to a Critical Theory of Television', *Theory and Society*, 10, pp. 31–62.

(1984–1985) 'Critical Theory and the Culture Industries: A Reassessment', *Telos*, 62, pp. 196–206.

(1988) 'Postmodernism as Social Theory: Some Challenges and Problems', *Theory, Culture and Society*, 5, 2/3, pp. 239–269.

(1989a) 'Boundaries and Borderlines: Reflections on Jean Baudrillard and Critical Theory', *Current Perspectives in Social Theory*, 9, pp. 5–22.

(1989b) *Critical Theory, Marxism and Modernity*, Cambridge, Polity Press.

(1989c) *Jean Baudrillard: From Marxism to Postmodernism and Beyond*, Cambridge, Polity Press.

Kingston, P. and Cole, J. (1981) 'Summary of Findings of the Columbia University Economic Survey of American Authors', *Art and the Law*, 6, 4, pp. 83–95.

Kirkpatrick, F. (1982) *How to Get the Right Job in Advertising*, Chicago, Contemporary Books.

Kline, S. and Leiss, W. (1978) 'Advertising, Needs and 'Commodity Fetishism'', *Canadian Journal of Political and Social Theory*, 2, 1, pp. 5–32.

Klinkowitz, J. (1988) *Rosenberg/Barthes/Hassan: The Postmodern Habit of Thought*, Athens, GA, University of Georgia Press.

Knorr-Cetina, K. (1981) *The Manufacture of Knowledge: An Essay on the Constructivist and Contextual Nature of Science*, New York, Pergamon.

Kostelanetz, R. (1974) *The End of Intelligent Writing: Literary Politics in America*, New York, Sheed and Ward.

Kovel, J. (1970) *White Racism*, New York, Pantheon.

Kowinski, W. (1985) *The Malling of America*, New York, William Morrow.

Kristeva, J. (1980) *Desire in Language*, New York, Columbia University Press.

Kroker, A. and Cook, D. (1986) *The Postmodern Scene*, New York, St. Martin's.

Kuhn, T. (1970) *The Structure of Scientific Revolutions*, 2nd ed., Chicago, University of Chicago Press.

Kuklick, H. (1979) 'Sociology's Past and Future: Prescriptive Implications of Historical Self-Consciousness in the School of Social Sciences', *Research in Sociology of Knowledge, Sciences and Art*, 2, pp. 73–85.

Laclau, E. and Mouffe, C. (1985) *Hegemony and Socialist Strategy*, London, Verso.

Lamont, M. and Larreau, A. (1988) 'Cultural Capital: Allusions, Maps and Glissandos in Recent Theoretical Developments', *Sociological Theory*, 6, 2, pp. 153–168.

Lasch, C. (1977) *Haven in a Heartless World: The Family Besieged*, New York, Basic Books.

(1984) *The Minimal Self*, New York, Norton.

Laskin, D. (1986) *Getting into Advertising*, New York, Ballantine.

Leavis, F. R. (1973) *The Great Tradition*, New York, New York University Press.

Leiss, W. (1976) *The Limits to Satisfaction: An Essay on the Problem of Needs and Commodities*, Toronto, University of Toronto Press.

(1978) 'Needs, Exchanges and the Fetishism of Objects', *Canadian Journal of Political and Social Theory*, 2, 3, pp. 27–48.

Leiss, W., Kline S. and Jhally, S. (1986) *Social Communication in Advertising: Persons, Products and Images of Well-Being*, Toronto, Methuen.

Lenhardt, C. (1976) 'The Wanderings of Enlightenment', in O'Neill, J. (Ed) *On Critical Theory*, New York, Seabury, pp. 34–57.

Levi-Strauss, C. (1963) *Totemism*, Boston, Beacon Press.

(1966) *The Savage Mind*, Chicago, University of Chicago Press.

Lewis, L. S. (1975) *Scaling the Ivory Tower: Merit and its Limits in Academic Careers*, Baltimore, Johns Hopkins University Press.

Lichtheim, G. (1971) *From Marx to Hegel*, New York, Herder and Herder.

Lightfield, T. (1971) 'Output and Recognition of Sociologists', *American Sociologist*, 6, pp. 128–133.

Lobkowicz, N. (1967) *Theory and Practice*, Notre Dame, Notre Dame University Press.

Lukacs, G. (1971) *History and Class Consciousness*, London, Merlin.

Luke, T. (1989) *Screens of Power: Ideology, Domination and Resistance in Informational Society*, Urbana, Ill., University of Illinois Press.

(1991) 'The Discourse of Development', *Current Perspectives in Social Theory*, 11.

Lyotard, J-F. (1984) *The Postmodern Condition: A Report of Knowledge*, Minneapolis, University of Minnesota Press.

Maccoby, M. (1976) *The Gamesman: The New Corporate Leaders*, New York, Simon and Schuster.

MacIntyre, A. (1970) *Herbert Marcuse*, New York, Viking.

Macpherson, C. B. (1962) *The Political Theory of Possessive Individualism*, Oxford, Oxford University Press.

Madison, C. (1966) *Book Publishing in America*, New York, McGraw-Hill.

(1974) *Irving to Irving: Author-Publisher Relations 1800–1974*, New York, R. R. Bowker.

Malley, L. (1989) personal correspondence.

Mandel, E. (1968) *Marxist Economic Theory*, New York, Monthly Review Press.

(1975) *Late Capitalism*, London, New Left Books.

Mandell, R. (1977) *The Professor Game*, Garden City, Doubleday.

Marcuse, H. (1955) *Eros and Civilization*, New York, Vintage.

(1958) *Soviet Marxism*, New York, Columbia University Press.

(1960) *Reason and Revolution: Hegel and the Rise of Social Theory*, Boston, Beacon Press.

(1964) *One-Dimensional Man*, Boston, Beacon Press.

(1969) *An Essay on Liberation*, Boston, Beacon Press.

(1978) *The Aesthetic Dimension*, Boston, Beacon Press.

Marshall, Barbara (1988) 'Feminist Theory and Critical Theory', *Canadian Review of Sociology and Anthropology*, 25, 2, pp. 208–230.

(1991) 'Reproducing the Gendered Subject', *Current Perspectives in Social Theory*, 11.

Marx, K. (1961) *Economic and Philosophic Manuscripts of 1844*, Moscow, Foreign Languages Publishing House.

(n.d.) *Capital*, Vol. 1, Moscow, Progress Publishers.

Marx, K. and Engels, F. (1947) *The German Ideology*, New York, International Publishers.

(1964) *The Communist Manifesto*, New York, Washington Square Press.

Maryles, D. (1978) 'Harlequin to Launch Mystery Books via Tested Market Strategies' in *Publishers Weekly*, 28 August, pp. 375–376.

Maslow, W. (1981) 'Academic Sociology as a 'Classist' Discipline: An Empirical Inquiry into the Treatment of Marx in the Textbooks of North American Sociology, 1890–1965', *Humanity and Society*, 5, 3, pp. 256–275.

McCarthy, E. D. and Das, R. (1985) 'American Sociology's Idea of Itself: A Review of the Textbook Literature from the Turn of the Century to the Present', *The History of Sociology*, 5, 2, pp. 21–43.

McCarthy, T. (1978) *The Critical Theory of Jurgen Habermas*, Cambridge, Mass., MIT Press.

McPherson, M. and Winston, G. (1988) 'The Economics of Academic Tenure: A Relational Perspective', in Breneman, D. and Youn, T. (Eds) *Academic Labor Markets and Careers*, Lewes/Philadelphia, Falmer Press, pp. 174–199.

McInerney, J. (1989) 'The Writers of Wrong', in *Esquire*, July, pp. 104–114.

McLuhan, M. (1964) *Understanding Media: The Extensions of Man*, New York, Signet.

(1968) *War and Peace in the Global Village*, New York, McGraw-Hill.

Menaker, D. (1981) 'Unsolicited, Unloved MSS.' in *The New York Times Book Review*, March 1, pp. 3, 22.

Meredith, S. (1974) *Writing to Sell*, New York, Harper and Row.

Merleau-Ponty, M. (1964a) *Sense and Non-Sense*, Evanston, Ill., Northwestern University Press.

(1964b) *Signs*, Evanston, Ill., Northwestern University Press.

Merton, R. (1957) *Social Theory and Social Structure*, Glencoe, Ill., Free Press.

Miller, M. C. (1988) *Boxed In: The Culture of T. V.*, Evanston, Ill., Northwestern University Press.

Mills, C. W. (1951) *White Collar*, New York, Oxford University Press.

(1959) *The Sociological Imagination*, New York, Oxford University Press.

(1962) *The Marxists*, New York, Dell.

Mohanty, S. P. (1986) 'Radical Teaching, Radical Theory: The Ambiguous Politics of Meaning', in Nelson, C. and Grossberg, L. (Eds) *Theory in the Classroom*, Urbana, Ill., University of Illinois Press, pp. 149–176.

Morgan, J. G. (1983) 'Courses and Texts in Sociology', *The History of Sociology*, 5, 1, pp. 42–65.

Morrissette, B. (1985) *Novel and Film: Essays in Two Genres*, Chicago, University of Chicago Press.

Moynihan, D. P. (1969) *Maximum Feasible Misunderstanding*, New York, Free Press.

Mueller, C. (1973) *The Politics of Communication*, New York, Oxford University Press.

Mulkay, M. (1984) *Opening Pandora's Box: A Sociological Analysis of Scientists' Discourse*, Cambridge, Cambridge University Press.

Newman, C. (1985) *The Postmodern Aura: The Act of Fiction in an Age of*

Inflation, Evanston, Ill., Northwestern University Press.

Nietzsche, F. (1955) *Beyond Good and Evil*, Chicago, Henry Regnery.

(1956) *The Birth of Tragedy and the Genealogy of Morals*, Garden City, Doubleday.

Nozick, R. (1974) *Anarchy, State and Utopia*, New York, Basic Books.

Oakeshott, M. (1962) *Rationalism in Politics and Other Essays*, London, Methuen.

Offe, C. (1984) *Contradictions of the Welfare State*, Cambridge, Mass., MIT Press.

(1985) *Disorganized Capitalism*, Cambridge, Mass., MIT Press.

Okrent, D. and Wulf, S. (1989) *Baseball Anecdotes*, New York, Oxford University Press.

O'Neill, J. (1972) 'Public and Private Space', in O'Neill, *Sociology as a Skin Trade*, New York, Harper and Row, pp. 20–37.

(1974) *Making Sense Together: An Introduction to Wild Sociology*, New York, Harper and Row.

(1976) 'Critique and Remembrance', in O'Neill, J. (Ed) *On Critical Theory*, New York, Seabury, pp. 1–11.

(1985) 'Decolonization and the Ideal Speech Community: Some Issues in the Theory and Practice of Communicative Competence', in Forester, J. (Ed) *Critical Theory and Public Life*, Cambridge, Mass., MIT Press, pp. 57–76.

(1986) 'The Disciplinary Society: From Weber to Foucault', *British Journal of Sociology*, 37, 1, pp. 42–60.

(1991) 'Is There a Class in this Text?', manuscript.

Paci, E. (1972) *The Function of the Sciences and the Meaning of Man*, Evanston, Ill., Northwestern University Press.

Papp, W. (1981) 'The Concept of Power: Treatment in 50 Introductory Sociology Textbooks', *Teaching Sociology*, 9, 1, pp. 57–68.

Parini, J. (1989) 'The Courage of Intellectuals Has Dwindled in the Age of Academe' in *The Chronicle of Higher Education*, July 12, pp. 82–83.

Parsons, T. (1951) *The Social System*, Glencoe, Ill., Free Press.

Perrucci, R. (1980) 'Sociology and the Introductory Textbooks', *The American Sociologist*, 15, 1, pp. 39–49.

Phillips, D. (1971) *Knowledge From What?*, Chicago, Rand McNally.

Piccone, P. (1971) 'Phenomenological Marxism', *Telos*, 9, pp. 3–31.

Porter, J. (1981–1982) 'Radical Sociology Textbooks: A Review Essay', *Humboldt Journal of Social Relations*, 9, 1, pp. 198–206.

Portoghesi, P. (1983) *Postmodern, The Architecture of the Postindustrial Society*, New York, Rizzoli.

Poster, M. (1975) *Existential Marxism in Postwar France*, Princeton, Princeton University Press.

Powell, W. (1979) 'The Blockbuster Decade: The Media as Big Business', *Working Papers*, July–August, pp. 26–36.

(1980) 'Competition versus Concentration in the Book Trade', *Journal of Communication*, Spring, pp. 89–97.

(1985) *Getting into Print: The Decision-Making Process in Scholarly Publishing*, Chicago, University of Chicago Press.

Rachlin, A. (1988) *News as Hegemonic Reality*, New York, Praeger.

Ransom, J. C. (1941) *The New Criticism*, Norfolk, Conn., New Directions.

Raulet, G. (1984) 'From Modernity as One-Way Street to Postmodernity as Dead End', *New German Critique*, 30, pp. 155–177.

Reskin, B. (1977) 'Scientific Productivity and the Reward Structure of Science', *American Sociological Review*, 42, pp. 491–504.

Reuter, M. (1980) 'The Trade Market: How Bad is it? How Bad is it Going to Be?' in *Publishers Weekly*, 2 May.

Reynolds, P. (1980) *The Writing and Selling of Fiction*, New York, Morrow.

Robinson, M. and Olszewski, R. (1978) 'The Economics of Book Publishing', Federal Trade Commission Symposium on Media Concentration, Vol. 2, pp. 604–644.

Rosen, S. (1969) *Nihilism: A Philosophical Essay*, New Haven, Yale University Press.

Ross, A. (1988) 'The New Sentence and the Commodity Form: Recent American Writing', in Nelson, C. and Grossberg, L. (Eds) *Marxism and the Interpretation of Culture*, Urbana, Ill., University of Illinois Press, pp. 361–380.

Rousseau, J-J. (1973) *The Social Contract and Discourses*, London, Dent.

Rubin, B. (1985) (Ed) *When Information Counts: Grading the Media*, Lexington, Mass., Heath.

Ryan, M. (1982) *Marxism and Deconstruction*, Baltimore, Johns Hopkins University Press.

(1989) *Politics and Culture*, Baltimore, Johns Hopkins University Press.

Sartre, J-P. (1963) *Search for a Method*, New York, Vintage.

(1965) *What is Literature?*, New York, Harper and Row.

(1966) *Being and Nothingness*, New York, Washington Square Press.

(1976) *Critique of Dialectical Reason*, London, New Left Books.

Sarup, M. (1989) *An Introductory Guide to Post-Structuralism and Postmodernism*, Athens, Ga., University of Georgia Press.

Schiller, D. (1981) *Objectivity and the News*, Philadelphia, University of Pennsylvania Press.

Schoolman, M. (1980) *The Imaginary Witness: The Critical Theory of Herbert Marcuse*, New York, Free Press.

Sennett, R. (1978) *The Fall of Public Man*, New York, Vintage.

Shatzkin, L. (1982) *In Cold Type: Overcoming the Book Crisis*, Boston, Houghton Mifflin.

Sheehan, D. (1952) *This Was Publishing: A Chronicle of the Book Trade in the Gilded Age*, Bloomington, Indiana University Press.

Shell, M. (1982) *Money, Language, and Thought: Literary and Philosophical Economies from the Medieval to the Modern Era*, Berkeley, University of California Press.

Sica, A. (1988) *Weber, Irrationality and Social Order*, Berkeley, University of California Press.

Siegfried, J. and White, K. (1973) 'Teaching and Publishing as Determinants of Academic Salaries', *Journal of Economic Education*, 5, pp. 90–99.

Silverman, H. and Welton, D. (1988) (Eds) *Postmodernism and Continental Philosophy*, Albany, SUNY Press.

Simmel, G. (1978) *Philosophy of Money*, London, RKP.

Slater, P. (1977) *Origin and Significance of the Frankfurt School*, London, RKP.

Sloane, W. (1983) *The Craft of Writing*, New York, Norton.

Smart, B. (1983) *Foucault, Marxism and Critique*, London, RKP.

Spivak, G. C. (1988) 'Can the Subaltern Speak?' in Nelson, C. and Grossberg, L. (Eds) *Marxism and the Interpretation of Culture*, Urbana, Ill., University of Illinois Press, pp. 271–313.

Trachtenberg, S. (1985) (Ed) *The Postmodern Moment: A Handbook of Contemporary Innovation in the Arts*, Westport, Conn., Greenwood.

Ueland, B. (1987) *If You Want to Write*, St. Paul, Graywolf.

U.S. Department of Commerce (1980) 'Book Publishing', in *U.S. Industrial Outlook*, Washington, D.C.

Villemez, W. (1980) 'Explaining Inequality: A Survey of Perspectives Represented in Introductory Sociology Textbooks', *Contemporary Sociology*, 9, 1, pp. 35–39.

Weaver, D. and Wilhoit, G. (1986) *The American Journalist*, Bloomington, Indiana University Press.

Weber, M. (1968) *The Methodology of the Social Sciences*, New York, Free Press.

Weedon, C. (1987) *Feminist Practice and Poststructuralist Theory*, Oxford, Basil Blackwell.

Wellmer, A. (1976) 'Communications and Emancipation: Reflections on the Linguistic Turn in Critical Theory', in O'Neill, J. (Ed), *On Critical Theory*, New York, Seabury, pp. 231–263.

Wells, A. (1979) 'Conflict Theory and Functionalism: Introductory Sociology Textbooks, 1928–1976', *Teaching Sociology*, 6, 4, pp. 429–437.

Wells, S. (1986) 'Jurgen Habermas, Communicative Competence, and the Teaching of Technical Discourse' in Nelson, C. (Ed) *Theory in the Classroom*, Urbana, Ill., University of Illinois Press, pp. 245–269.

Wernick, A. (1983) 'Advertising and Ideology: An Interpretive Framework', *Theory, Culture and Society*, 2, 1, pp. 16–33.

Wexler, P. (1982) *Critical Social Psychology*, London, RKP.

(1991) 'Citizenship in the Semiotic Society', *Current Perspectives in Social Theory*, 11.

Whiteside, T. (1981) *The Blockbuster Complex: Conglomerates, Show Business and Book Publishing*, Middletown, Conn., Wesleyan University Press.

Whyte, Jr., W. (1957) *The Organization Man*, Garden City, Doubleday.

Williams, R. (1975) *Television: Technology and Cultural Form*, New York, Schocken.

Williamson, J. (1978) *Decoding Advertisements*, London, Marion Boyars.

Wittgenstein, L. (1953) *Philosophical Investigations*, Oxford, Basil Blackwell.

Wolfe, A. (1989) *Whose Keeper?: Social Science and Moral Obligation*, Berkeley, University of California Press.

Wolin, R. (1984) 'Modernism versus Postmodernism', *Telos*, 62, pp. 9–30.

Young, M. (1958) *The Rise of the Meritocracy*, London, Thames and Hudson.

Zukin, S. (1982) *Loft Living: Culture and Capital in Urban Change*, Baltimore, Johns Hopkins University Press.

Index